In planning the *Rougon-Macquart* cycle Zola was concerned to provide a panoramic survey of society and consequently a detailed consideration of the world of the bourgeoisie.

Brian Nelson here sets out to illuminate an aspect of Zola's work which, although of obvious importance, has not previously received specific and systematic attention. He describes and analyses Zola's depiction of the bourgeoisie and identifies the value-structures which emerge, calling into question some of the assumptions often made by those who have written about Zola. Is Zola's posture towards the bourgeoisie systematically hostile, for example? Does his anti-bourgeois satire imply a global condemnation of the bourgeoisie as a class and, if not, what redeeming qualities does he see in the class? What becomes of the bourgeoisie in the socialistic utopian society outlined in the later fiction? Is there any evolution in Zola's conception of the bourgeoisie?

The first part of the book looks at Zola's work as a whole and examines the basic configurations of his bourgeois world. The second part is devoted to the interpretation and elucidation of four representative works: *La Curée*, *Une Page d'amour*, *Pot-Bouille* and *L'Argent*.

Zola and the Bourgeoisie represents a general reappraisal of Zola's social attitudes and the chapters on the individual novels constitute the most perceptive and substantial readings of these works yet published. Perhaps its greatest contribution, however, is in bringing out the paradox that the nineteenth-century writer who aroused the greatest hostility and fear among bourgeois readers and critics had a more complex and less negative attitude towards the bourgeoisie than is generally assumed.

ZOLA AND THE BOURGEOISIE

Zola and the Bourgeoisie

A Study of Themes and Techniques in
Les Rougon-Macquart

Brian Nelson

Barnes & Noble Books
Totowa, New Jersey

First published in the USA 1983 by
BARNES & NOBLE BOOKS
81, Adams Drive
Totowa, New Jersey 07512

ISBN 0–389–20110–3

Printed in Hong Kong

Library of Congress Cataloging in Publication Data

Nelson, Brian, 1946–
    Zola and the bourgeoisie.

    Bibliography: p.
    Includes index.
    1. Zola, Émile, 1840–1902—Political and social views.
2. Middle classes in literature.   I. Title.
PQ2541.M53N4   1982   843'.8   81–10954
ISBN 0–389–20110–3   AACR2

To Evi

Contents

Acknowledgements

Many people have helped me in the preparation of this book. I should particularly like to thank here Dr Merlin Thomas, who supervised my D.Phil. thesis (of which this book is a modified version) and provided me with constant and invigorating support; Professor Ian McFarlane and Professor Richard Griffiths, who offered much valuable criticism and advice; and Rhiannon Goldthorpe, who read parts of the draft and made a number of helpful suggestions. My thanks are also due to the British Academy and the University College of Wales, Aberystwyth, for research grants which enabled me to visit the Bibliothèque Nationale in Paris, and to Roland Desné for his most generous hospitality.

Parts of this book originally appeared in the form of articles in *Australian Journal of French Studies*, *Essays in French Literature*, *Nottingham French Studies*, *Orbis Litterarum* and *Romance Notes*. I am grateful to the respective editors for permission to reprint those articles here.

The publishers and I are grateful to Paul Elek Ltd for permission to quote from Jean Stewart's translation of *Une Page d'amour* (*A Love Affair*, London: Paul Elek, 1957). I have also used A. Teixera de Mattos's translation of *La Curée* (*The Kill*, first published by the Lutetian Society [London] in 1895 and republished in England by Weidenfeld & Nicolson [1954], Paul Elek [1958] and Arrow Books [1967]. All other translations are my own.

Parler de la bourgeoisie, c'est faire l'acte d'accusation le plus violent qu'on puisse lancer contre la société française.

Zola, Notes de travail, B.N. MS. *Nouv. acq. fr.* 10321, folio 1

Si l'on savait combien le buveur de sang, le romancier féroce, est un digne bourgeois. . .

Zola, preface to *L'Assommoir*

Note on references and translations

All references to *Les Rougon-Macquart* are to the Pléiade edition, edited by Henri Mitterand, 5 vols (Paris: Gallimard, Bibliothèque de la Pléiade, 1960–7); volume and page numbers appear in parentheses in the text.

All quotations are given both in the original and in English translation. Shorter translations are included in the text immediately after quotations; longer translations have been placed in the notes.

Introduction

Zola's unsentimental but sympathetic portrayal of the working class in *L'Assommoir* and *Germinal* largely constitutes his literary status. Few readers of *Les Rougon-Macquart* would disagree with Angus Wilson's comment that 'no nineteenth-century novelist, perhaps, succeeded so well in depicting the courage and honesty of the individual, aspiring workman of the century'.[1] But the very conception of the Rougon-Macquart cycle, as well as Zola's belief, as a social realist, that the modern novel should embrace the whole of contemporary reality, clearly implies a panoramic survey of society and, consequently, a detailed consideration of the world of the bourgeoisie. In his initial plan for the cycle, Zola wrote:

> La famille dont je conterai l'histoire, représentera le vaste soulèvement démocratique de notre temps; partie du peuple, elle montera aux classes cultivées, aux premiers postes de l'Etat, à l'infamie comme au talent. Cet assaut des hauteurs de la société par ceux qu'on appelait au siècle dernier les gens de rien, est une des grandes révolutions de notre âge. L'oeuvre offrira par là même une étude de la bourgeoisie contemporaine.[2]

It is thus not surprising to find E.J. Hobsbawm recommending *Les Rougon-Macquart* as the best guide to the bourgeoisie in the third quarter of the nineteenth century.[3] I hope that the present study will illuminate an aspect of Zola's work which, although of obvious importance, has not previously received specific and systematic attention.

There are immediate problems of definition attached to the amorphous but much-used term 'bourgeoisie', for interpretations of class and class structure vary considerably. Class dif-

1

ferentiations are more blurred in the twentieth than in the
nineteenth century because of the pluralistic nature of modern
industrial societies, the greater degree of social mobility in the
twentieth century, the extension of social and educational opportunities, and the improved economic position – and consequent
embourgeoisement – of the working classes. The problem of definition is less difficult in the nineteenth century, which was, after
all, the classical age of the bourgeoisie: during the nineteenth
century the bourgeoisie progressively displaced the aristocracy
(which figures only marginally in *Les Rougon-Macquart*) as con-
troller of most of France's wealth and provider of the bulk of the
nation's political élite. Hobsbawm, asking what we mean by the
bourgeoisie as a class in the third quarter of the nineteenth
century, comments that 'its economic, political and social defini-
tions differed somewhat, but were still sufficiently close to each
other to cause relatively little difficulty'.[4] Marx conceived of the
social hierarchy of nineteenth-century capitalist society primarily in terms of economic interest, and Hobsbawm writes that:

> . . . economically, the quintessential bourgeois was a 'capital-
> ist' (i.e. either the possessor of capital, or the receiver of an
> income derived from such a source, or a profit-making entre-
> preneur, or all of these things). And, in fact, the characteristic
> 'bourgeois' or member of the middle class in our period
> included few people who did not fit into one or other of these
> pigeon-holes.[5]

A typology of Zola's bourgeois, while revealing the extremely
disparate composition of the class, confirms this statement. The
spectrum includes the *grande bourgeoisie*, big financiers, industrial
managers, politicians, the liberal professions, *rentiers*, small
shopkeepers and artisans. Max Weber showed that factors of
status and power also determine the division of society into
strata, and that the criteria of class, status and power, although
closely interrelated, are not synonymous. Hobsbawm writes:

> . . . the main characteristic of the bourgeoisie as a class was
> that it was a body of persons of power and influence, indepen-
> dent of the power and influence of traditional birth and status.
> To belong to it a man had to be 'someone'; a person who

counted *as an individual*, because of his wealth, his capacity to command other men, or otherwise to influence them.[6]

He asserts that, more than anything else, to be a bourgeois meant superiority:

> The bourgeois was not merely independent, a man to whom no one (save the state or God) gave orders, but one who gave orders himself. He was not merely an employer, entrepreneur or capitalist but socially a 'master', a 'lord' (*Fabrikherr*), a '*patron*' or '*chef*'. The monopoly of command – in his house, in his business, in his factory – was crucial to his self-definition . . .[7]

Zola is certainly concerned with the exercise of authority, and this study will examine the role of the bourgeoisie in the context of the theme of social leadership.

Although common denominators are difficult to find, there is general agreement on the ideology and values most commonly associated with particular types of nineteenth-century bourgeois: a materialist preoccupation with money and commerce, a concern with appearances and respectability, greed, cupidity, egoism, social pretentiousness, hypocrisy (especially in matters of sex), a narrow puritanism of morals and religion, competitive energy, individual enterprise and self-help, an ideal of moderation, worship of property, thrift and hard work. This study will examine the patterns and emphases which emerge from Zola's treatment of bourgeois values rather than describe his depiction of the bourgeoisie against the background of the actual social and historical developments of the nineteenth century. In other words, the approach adopted is largely structural. I am not concerned with the representational value of Zola's novels, or with their documentary sources, but with the coherence and structure of his social vision and with some of the ways in which it is articulated.

My aims are thus, first, to describe and analyse the salient features of Zola's depiction of the bourgeoisie and to identify the value structures which emerge from this picture; secondly, to relate his conception of the bourgeoisie to the general context of his social vision as a whole and to the development of that vision; and thirdly, to examine closely the specifically literary qualities of the novels chosen for extended analysis, not least because some of Zola's 'bourgeois' novels (most notably *Une Page d'amour* and *Pot-Bouille*) have been unjustifiably neglected. These novels are of greater literary value than has generally been recognised. A systematic examination of Zola's treatment of the bourgeoisie, and an attempt to determine whether a coherent pattern of values emerges from his delineation of the bourgeois world, will clearly involve a reappraisal of Zola's social attitudes. Given that there is a major element of social criticism in Zola's work, what are the principal terms of that criticism and what part does the bourgeoisie play in it?

It is well known that no nineteenth-century writer was so consistently vilified in the bourgeois press as Zola. He incurred the particular displeasure of the *bien-pensant* bourgeoisie because of the new sexual candour his novels embodied. The increased erotic verisimilitude of his fiction, which reflected the Naturalistic belief in total integrity of representation, offended bourgeois susceptibilities. Victorian society even went so far as to imprison Henry Vizetelly for the publication of obscenity as a result of his son Ernest's translation of *La Terre* in 1888. But Zola was never regarded with affection by conservative opinion for reasons other than purely moralistic ones. His reputation as an 'anti-establishment progressive'[8] rests largely on the humanitarian eloquence of his celebrated proletarian novels, which vividly describe the horrors of urban industrial existence and the abuses of capitalism; on his aggressive, radicalist critique of the Second Empire, particularly in the earlier volumes of the *Rougon-Macquart*; on the ferocity of his attacks on insalubrious aspects of bourgeois life in such novels as *Pot-Bouille*; and on his defence of Dreyfus and the vigorous anticlericalism of his later works. Indeed, it has been plausibly suggested[9] that essentially political motives lie behind the strident attacks made on Zola by hostile bourgeois critics like Brunetière and Faguet[10] for his crude materialism, narrowness of vision, lack of psychological penetration, stylistic ineptitude and persistent obscenity. These attacks may well mask bourgeois fear of the politically seditious nature of Zola's fiction. Although Marxists from Engels to the present day have criticised Zola for his undialectical and 'detached' conception of society, he is still popularly regarded as a writer of the Left because of his deep feeling for social justice and his life-long struggle against bourgeois reaction, cant, convention and hypocrisy.

Although Zola's sympathy for the poor is beyond question, is his posture towards the bourgeoisie systematically hostile? Does his anti-bourgeois satire and his reputation as a *bête noire* of the bourgeoisie imply a global condemnation of the bourgeoisie as a class? Is it correct to describe him, as one critic has done, as 'one of the most anti-bourgeois novelists in history'?[11] If the bourgeoisie is not treated in an exclusively satirical vein in *Les Rougon-Macquart*, what redeeming qualities does Zola see in the class? If he expresses a degree of approval of the bourgeoisie, then the brand of socialism he advocates in his final works will require careful examination. What becomes of the bourgeoisie in the socialistic utopian society outlined in the later fiction? If Zola discerns some redeeming features in the bourgeoisie, what is the precise relationship between these features and the social optimism that emerges from his later works? Is there any evolution in Zola's conception of the bourgeoisie? If the bourgeoisie is heterogeneous, what kinds of oppositions, contrasts and conflicts exist within its ranks? Is Zola's treatment of the bourgeoisie primarily expressive of a political *parti pris* or of basically moralistic concerns? How does Zola view the relationship between the bourgeoisie and the Church? Does his satire of bourgeois mismanagement and degeneracy signify faith in the political self-help of the workers and approval of working-class militants? If not, what is the nature of the ideal social and political leadership Zola appears to envisage in *Les Rougon-Macquart*? And what kinds of solutions does he propose to the problem of social corruption and decay portrayed in the bourgeois novels?

Part I of this book, divided into what I consider the most useful analytic categories, examines systematically the basic configurations of Zola's bourgeois world, while Part II concentrates on the interpretation and elucidation of four individual works. The separation of categories like 'Waste and Parasitism', 'Leadership', etc., enables us to circumscribe those areas which constitute the salient features of bourgeois life and values as seen by Zola, although in focusing on any one of these perspectives on the bourgeoisie we are unavoidably dealing with the other categories as well. The criteria of selection regarding the novels chosen for special analysis were, in the first instance, that the bourgeoisie should be in the forefront and that these novels should contain a significant element of social comment. This immediately excluded *La Faute de l'abbé Mouret, L'Assommoir, La*

Joie de vivre, Germinal, L'Oeuvre, La Terre, Le Rêve, La Bête humaine, La Débâcle and *Le Docteur Pascal*. *La Faute de l'abbé Mouret* and *Le Rêve* may be described as personal fantasies. *La Joie de vivre* is autobiographical rather than 'social'. *L'Oeuvre* is both autobiographical and a *roman à clefs*. *Le Docteur Pascal* also reflects personal preoccupations and acts as a sort of summarising conclusion to the cycle. *Germinal* clearly remains an important novel in the context of this study and will be discussed in Part I. Of the novels which preceded *L'Assommoir* I felt that *La Curée* was the richest and most representative, although *Le Ventre de Paris* will receive special comment in the section on 'Waste and Parasitism'. A further criterion of selection was the desirability of illustrating the time-span of Zola's career. *L'Argent* (1891) was thus chosen in preference to *Au Bonheur des Dames* (1883), which immediately follows *Pot-Bouille*; *L'Argent* is also highly pertinent to the theme of leadership and gives a clearer reflection than *Au Bonheur des Dames* of the ways in which Zola's thought moves towards the utopianism of the later novels.

It may be noted that there is no one-to-one relationship between Part I and Part II in the sense that no single novel in Part II embodies in an exclusive manner any of the analytic categories of Part I. There is considerable overlap, although certain themes obviously figure more prominently in one novel than in another. *La Curée* is a good example of the arguments postulated in Part I concerning the theme of waste. *L'Argent*, as I have already indicated, focuses on the problematics of leadership that inform Zola's treatment of the bourgeoisie. *Pot-Bouille* chooses itself for separate analysis in that it constitutes Zola's most comprehensive and savage indictment of bourgeois life – with a strong emphasis on sexuality. A differing view of bourgeois sexual attitudes is offered by the more muted *Une Page d'amour*, whose selection for special discussion may seem surprising. Although the main focus of this novel is (like *Pot-Bouille*) on the theme of sexuality, it does manage to convey a sharp critique of bourgeois values while (unlike *Pot-Bouille*) deliberately eliminating a satirical tone and suggesting an innocuous surface. *Une Page d'amour* is an excellent example both of the heterogeneity of Zola's bourgeois world and of the bourgeois world of appearances already explored in *La Curée*. Finally, although this study concentrates on the Rougon-Macquart cycle, detailed reference is made in Part I to *Travail* (1901), which confirms and completes the analyses of *Les Rougon-Macquart*.

Part I

THE BOURGEOIS WORLD

Waste and Parasitism

Zola's critique of the bourgeoisie in *Les Rougon-Macquart* is largely defined by the interrelated themes of waste and parasitism. On the one hand, his satirical portrayal of 'la bousculade des ambitions et des appétits' ('the jostle of ambitions and appetites')[1] is rooted in his horror at the waste of human energies; on the other hand, he sharply attacks the sterile egoism of unregenerate parasites like the Quenu family in *Le Ventre de Paris*. The final sentence of *Le Ventre de Paris* ('Quels gredins que les honnêtes gens!') ('What swine decent people really are!) (I, 895) sums up his approach to the bourgeoisie in the early novels of the series. The aggressive anti-Imperial polemic in *Les Rougon-Macquart*, which is expressed most directly in the novels that preceded *Pot-Bouille* (1882), is as much moralistic as ideological. The objects of this polemic are the corruption, frivolity and greed of Second Empire society. *La Fortune des Rougon* (1871) describes the brutal beginnings of the régime as reflected in the founding of the family's fortune. *La Curée* (1872) is a powerful picture of the large-scale financial corruption which accompanied the *haussmannisation* of Paris. The action of *Le Ventre de Paris* (1873) centres on the ensnarement of a revolutionary deportee, Florent Quenu, who represents a menace of disruption to the prosperous existence of his sister-in-law, Lisa, who embodies in caricatural form the social mentality of the complacent *petite bourgeoisie*. *La Conquête de Plassans* (1874) shows the Bonapartist régime, through the agency of the Abbé Faujas, establishing its hold over the provinces. *Son Excellence Eugène Rougon* (1876) focuses on the cynicism and savagery of political life under the Second Empire. *Nana* (1880) describes the rampant moral corruption of Imperial high society.

    La Fortune des Rougon is a novel of political violence, murder and treachery. It depicts the stealthy seizure of power by the

bourgeois Rougons through their exploitation of the conflicting
factions in the provincial town of Plassans, and it describes the
massacre of republican insurgents which enables them to
triumph. Pierre Rougon, who has become a member of the
lower bourgeoisie through marriage and acquisition of his
mother's property, climbs up into the upper bourgeoisie by
being rewarded for his services on behalf of Louis Bonaparte
with the lucrative post of tax-collector. The tonality and dominant themes of the novel are expressed in images of blood and
redness.[2] A key passage, describing Félicité and Pierre in bed
after Félicité has explained her plan of campaign to her husband,
brings together the motifs of blood, dream and money:

> Ils s'embrassèrent encore, ils s'endormirent. Et, au plafond, la
> tache de lumière [of the night-lamp] s'arrondissait comme un
> oeil terrifié, ouvert et fixé longuement sur le sommeil de ces
> bourgeois blêmes, suant le crime dans les draps, et qui voy-
> aient en rêve tomber dans leur chambre une pluie de sang,
> dont les gouttes larges se changeaient en pièces d'or sur le
> carreau. (I, 270)[3]

The Rougons' 'fortune' is paid for in blood; their 'crime' signifies
guilt and depends on the sordid bargain struck with Macquart;
and the blood turning into gold coins looks forward to the real
gold pieces handed over to Macquart after the Rougons' success is assured. After the ambush at the Hôtel-de-Ville, the corpses and the pools of blood become the visible evidence of Pierre's
heroism. Throughout the morning the whole town gathers on the
square and inspects the mutilated bodies: 'Ce fut ainsi que ce
grotesque, ce bourgeois ventru, mou et blême, devint, en une
nuit, un terrible monsieur dont personne n'osa plus rire. Il avait
mis un pied dans le sang' (I, 289).[4] With the Rougons' triumph,
Tante Dide, the foundress of the family, goes mad. As Rougon
hands over the gold to Macquart in Dide's hovel, she has a
strange, cataleptic vision, composed of a series of disconnected
images of murder, treachery, gold and blood. Silvère becomes
confused with old Macquart, and the gendarme killed by old
Macquart becomes confused with Rengade, the vengeful gendarme who executes Silvère; and Pascal, with his naturalist's
eye, seems to glimpse the family's future: 'Il crut entrevoir un
instant, comme au milieu d'un éclair, l'avenir des Rougon-

Macquart, une meute d'appétits lâchés et assouvis, dans un flamboiement d'or et de sang' (I, 301).[5]

The central social theme of the early Rougon-Macquart novels is, then, the rush for the spoils which followed Louis-Napoleon's *coup d'état* of 2 December. The motif of 'la curée' dominates these novels, which describe the acquisitive brutality of Second Empire society. The title of *La Curée*, which becomes a central symbolic image, suggests why it may be regarded as the richest and most representative of the novels which preceded *L'Assommoir*. *La Curée* focuses on the rebuilding of Paris by Haussmann, which attracted to the capital large numbers of unscrupulous speculators and fortune-hunters who wished to exploit the economic possibilities offered by the new Imperial régime. In his preparatory notes, Zola wrote: '*Déchaînement des appétits* . . . Aristide appétit d'argent; Sidonie appétit de bien-être; Renée appétit de luxe et de volupté; Maxime appétit naissant et sans frein moral.'[6] The word 'appétits' focuses Zola's intentions in embarking on *Les Rougon-Macquart*. It figures prominently in the preface to *La Fortune des Rougon*, which contains an important statement by Zola of his theories and aims. The cycle, he writes, is to have two main themes, physiological and historical; the demonstration of the laws of heredity is to be paralleled by the portrayal of a certain social age, whose characteristics are exemplified by the Rougon-Macquart family: 'Les Rougon-Macquart. . .[ont] pour caractéristique le débordement des appétits, le large soulèvement de notre âge, qui se rue aux jouissances' ('The characteristic of the Rougon-Macquart is the upsurge of appetites, the great upheaval of our age, with its mad pursuit of pleasure') (I, 3). The family covers the whole social spectrum and the movement is upwards. The cycle itself is to be 'le tableau . . . d'une étrange époque de folie et de honte' (the portrayal . . . of a strange epoch of madness and shame') (I, 4). It is an age of frenzied desire, brutal sensuality, wild excess, social and moral corruption, decadence and cynicism. The Empire is thus pictured as a ceaseless carnival. The night Florent was deported from Paris in *Le Ventre de Paris* was a carnival night, with the lighted windows of the boulevard restaurants, and masked, bare-shouldered ladies affecting disgust towards the passing convicts. When Florent returns to Paris, he finds that the carnival continues. The Emperor's reception at Compiègne in *Son Excellence Eugène Rougon* is an extended image of sumptuous luxury: 'C'était ... une arrivée gourmande dans un milieu de luxe, de lumière et de tiédeur, comme un bain sensuel où les odeurs musquées des toilettes se mêlaient à un léger fumet de gibier, relevé d'un filet de citron' (II, 160).[7]

Zola's characters are defined and circumscribed by appetites and instincts which are reinforced by certain atavistic or hereditary predispositions. At the centre of *La Fortune des Rougon* is the theme of cupidity, the bourgeois greed and ambition of the Rougons: 'Au fond, tous les membres de cette famille avaient la même rage d'appétits brutaux' ('In reality, all the members of this family had the same brutal, frenzied appetites') (I, 130). The action of many of the Rougon-Macquart novels is largely shaped by the fulfilment or frustration of these appetites. Savage appetites and the violent tonality of Zola's world correspond to pervasive images of animality.[8] Zola persistently translates psychological characteristics into physiological detail. In *La Fortune des Rougon* Félicité, with her cunning and her quick, nervous gestures, is compared to a cicada, a stonemarten and a cat. The sly Aristide inherits his mother's weasel-like features, while the brutish Eugène inherits his father's bull-like appearance. In *Le Ventre de Paris* the complacent Lisa Quenu basks like an overfed cat at her doorway. The hapless Mouret is reduced by the end of *La Conquête de Plassans* to an animal state, while the villainous Trouches are compared to 'des loups à l'affût' ('wolves lying in wait') (I, 1012). A central image of *Nana*, evoking the novel's main theme, is that of a bitch followed by a pack of dogs. The animal analogies are sometimes inconsistent and confused, but the motif of 'la curée' tends to dominate Zola's bestiary; the *Rougon-Macquart* is as much a world of predators and victims as Balzac's *Comédie humaine*: 'Selon l'opinion commune, les Rougon-Macquart chassaient de race en se dévorant entre eux; la galerie, au lieu de les séparer, les aurait plutôt excités à se mordre' (*La Fortune des Rougon*, I, 115).[9] In her cataleptic vision Tante Dide stammers: 'je n'ai fait que des loups ... toute une famille, toute une portée de loups ... Chacun a donné son coup de dent; ils ont encore du sang plein les lèvres' (*La Fortune des Rougon*, I, 300–1).[10] Silvère, Miette, Florent, Mouret and Renée are all victims in a society governed by a dog-eat-dog mentality.

The speculators and fortune-hunters evoked in *La Curée* are thus seen as savage predatory animals. Larsonneau, Saccard's ruthless henchman, is described as 'un terrible monsieur qui

aurait poursuivi le paiement d'un billet jusqu'au suicide du sig-
nataire, sans rien perdre de son amabilité' ('a terrible gentleman, who would have insisted on the payment of a note of hand
until he had driven the acceptor to suicide, and this without
losing a grain of amiability') (I, 468). Saccard himself is an
arch-predator whose arrival in Paris is described as a *prise de
possession*: 'Artistide Rougon s'abattit sur Paris, au lendemain du
2 Décembre, avec ce flair des oiseaux de proie qui sentent de loin
les champs de bataille' ('Aristide Rougon swept down upon
Paris on the morrow of the 2nd December, like a carrion bird that
scents the field of battle from afar') (I, 359). There is a luminous
passage in which Saccard, looking down over the entire city from
the heights of Montmartre with his first wife, Angèle, sees Paris
as an unsuspecting prey. His dramatic gestures as he details his
schemes for the plunder of the city to his gaping wife are compared with savage sword-thrusts, while the new boulevards he
describes are seen as so many wounds inflicted on a helpless
giant: 'La petitesse de cette main, s'acharnant sur une proie
géante, finissait par inquiéter; et, tandis qu'elle déchirait sans
effort les entrailles de l'énorme ville, on eût dit qu'elle prenait un
étrange reflect d'acier, dans le crépuscule bleuâtre' (I, 389).[11] The
metaphor of 'la curée' informs all aspects of the novel's themes
and language: Renée becomes the helpless victim of Saccard,
caught in the trammels of his financial schemes; the herma-
phroditic Maxime becomes Renée's prey, the object of her
extravagant sexual desires; Saccard, in an extraordinary image,
is seen as 'mâchant ses pièces d'or en courant' ('munching his
gold pieces while he ran') (I, 574).

The avid appetites of Zola's characters correspond to the
motifs of food and eating: 'Le coup d'Etat les a aidés [i.e. Pierre
and Félicité] à satisfaire un rêve de jouissances qui les torturait
depuis quarante ans. Aussi quelle gloutonnerie, quelle indigestion of bonnes choses!' (*La Conquête de Plassans*, I, 951).[12] The
incest in *La Curée* is preceded by ravenous eating, while the *bal
travesti* is accompanied by extreme gluttony. In *La Fortune des
Rougon* Antoine Macquart eats a whole roast chicken before leading the assault on the Hôtel-de-Ville, and the Rougons' final
success is celebrated by a Lucullan feast. In *Le Ventre de Paris*
Zola attempts to create the impression of a social class obsessed
with food by establishing a symbolic equation between mountains of food and bourgeois complacency. The whole novel may

be read as an amplification of the thematic image which gives it its title. The core of Zola's vision lies in the colossal symbolic configurations of Les Halles, and a network of alimentary and organic imagery governs the structure and texture of the novel, shapes its dramatic action and defines its moral and political significance. *Le Ventre de Paris* complements *La Curée* in its social criticism; the large-scale financial swindles of Saccard are balanced by the smug, placid *honnêteté* of Lisa Quenu: '[*Le Ventre de Paris*] complète *La Curée*, elle est la curée des classes moyennes, le rut à la nourriture grasse et à la belle digestion tranquille . . . Au fond, même avachissement, même décomposition morale et sociale.'[13]

La Ventre de Paris embodies more graphically than any of his other novels Zola's general conception of the novel: 'Balzac dit qu'il veut peindre les hommes, les femmes et les choses. Moi, . . . je soumets les hommes et les femmes aux choses' ('Balzac says that he wants to portray men, women and things. My aim is to subject men and women to things').[14] Fear of enclosure and fear of suffocation are closely related motifs in the imaginative complex of claustrophobia created in *Les Rougon-Macquart*. Nausea and delirium, and the nightmarish menace of the dissolution of the personality, lie at the centre of *Le Ventre de Paris*. When he arrives in Les Halles, Florent is plunged into a world of greasy matter. Although the painter, Claude Lantier, sees in Les Halles a magnificent incarnation of the 'poetry of modern life', food and the asphyxiating profusion of matter are also invested with corrupt and hostile qualities. The novel constantly transcends the mere inventory of objects to attain a hallucinatory pitch. The first chapter, which describes Florent's nocturnal arrival in Paris on the back of a cart, builds up into a sustained nightmare vision. Having escaped from exile in Cayenne, he rediscovers Paris overflowing with prosperity. The structure of the descriptions, as of the novel itself, is based on counterpoint. The central opposition of the novel is that between *les gras* and *les maigres*, between prosperous fatness and the constantly reiterated fact of Florent's wasted thinness. His hunger and misery are set against endless images of plenitude and complacent well-being. The pervasive emphasis on glutted excess corresponds to proliferating descriptive detail. The invasion of the consciousness by the amorphous profusion of matter ends in blind terror and the frenetic desire to escape: 'Aveuglé, noyé, les oreilles sonnantes, l'estomac écrasé par tout ce qu'il avait vu, devinant de nouvelles et incessantes profondeurs de nourriture, il demanda grâce, et une douleur folle le prit, de mourir ainsi de faim, dans Paris gorgé, dans ce réveil fulgurant des Halles' (I, 633–4).[15] The re-establishment of his passion for politics is clinched, later on, by one of the novel's recurring global descriptions of Les Halles, in which the social symbolism is quite explicit:

> Les Halles géantes, les nourritures, débordantes et fortes, avaient hâté la crise. Elles lui semblaient la bête satisfaite et digérant, Paris entripaillé, cuvant sa graisse, appuyant sourdement l'Empire. Elles mettaient autour de lui des gorges énormes, des reins monstrueux, des faces rondes, comme de continuels arguments contre sa maigreur de martyr, son visage jaune de mécontent. C'était le ventre boutiquier, le ventre de l'honnêteté moyenne, se ballonnant, heureux, luisant au soleil, trouvant que tout allait pour le mieux, que jamais les gens de moeurs paisibles n'avaient engraissé si bellement. (I, 733)[16]

While Florent fears (Flaubertian/Sartrian) invasion by matter, Lisa represents a complacent world of fat and fatness, which suppresses any disturbance, even sexual, in its need to maintain stability and order. Her submission to things is opposed to Florent's revolt, his *nervosité* is opposed to her bovine tranquillity. Lisa and her shop, 'cette chapelle du ventre' ('this cathedral of the stomach') (I, 637), triumphantly symbolise the material prosperity of the age: 'C'était un monde de bonnes choses, de choses fondantes, de choses grasses' ('This was a world of good things, things that melted in the mouth, things of great succulence') (I, 636). Watched behind her counter by the mutely adoring Marjolin, she is transfigured, magnified, and as if dehumanised, by her multiple reflections in the mirrors of the shop: 'C'était toute une foule de Lisa, montrant la largeur des épaules, l'emmanchement puissant des bras, la poitrine arrondie, si muette et si tendue, qu'elle n'éveillait aucune pensée charnelle et qu'elle ressemblait à un ventre' (I, 667).[17] We have the impression that she is drained of feelings and humanity, having been absorbed by her natural surroundings: 'le profil de Lisa, avec sa forte encolure, ses lignes rondes, sa gorge qui avançait, mettait une effigie de reine empâtée, au milieu de ce lard et de ces chairs crues' (ibid.).[18] Rather than characters with independent physical and psychological existences, the *gras* are extensions or appendages of their milieu, seem to resemble animals, or assume the features of the foodstuffs they sell. Lisa, who has been described as 'the supreme example of the bourgeoise',[19] embodies the selfishness of her social class. Complacency and conformism are the keynotes of her 'politique des honnêtes gens':

> Je suis reconnaissante au gouvernement, quand mon commerce va bien, quand je mange ma soupe tranquille, et que je dors sans être réveillée par des coups de fusil... C'était du propre, n'est-ce pas, en 48? L'oncle Gradelle, un digne homme, nous a montré ses livres de ce temps-là. Il a perdu plus de six mille francs... Maintenant que nous avons l'Empire, tout marche, tout se vend...
>
> Certainement que je profite du bon moment et que je soutiens le gouvernement qui fait aller le commerce. S'il commet de vilaines choses, je ne veux pas le savoir. Moi, je sais que je n'en commets pas... (I,757–8)[20]

The Empire maintains order and thus creates prosperity, while revolutionaries represent disorder. Lisa's view of religion is determined by her social philosophy. Although not a practising Catholic, she sees religion as a necessary 'police morale', an essential bulwark of society against subversion. Naturally, Florent is not to be trusted, and he is eventually denounced to the police. Lisa's social and political attitudes, reflected in the concept of the eternal struggle between *Les gras* and *les maigres*, are rooted in an explicit belief in the survival of the fittest. The bourgeoisie, in other words, justifies itself in terms of an implacable Darwinism.

The Quenus are the first of a series of 'respectable' bourgeois families found elsewhere in Zola. Their counterparts are the Campardons (*Pot-Bouille*), the Grégoires (*Germinal*), the Charles (*La Terre*) and the Mazelles (*Travail*). These families, as Jean Borie has noted, all conform to the same pattern and evince the same values. They are all fat and absorbed in complacent, selfish pleasure, and they are all given an only child, who is a daughter. Borie defines the abiding characteristics of this repeated image of the 'mauvais foyer' as: 'clôture absolue et égoïste, rejet du monde extérieur, chaleur très forte, grande importance de la nourriture, de la digestion et du sommeil, grand calme de la vie, respect absolu de la famille comme valeur, renoncement complet aux satisfactions sexuelles "normales"'.[21] Above all, they are associated with the theme of sterility, of sexual abstinence in the name of a factitious decency. Lisa's body is as if swathed in the protective wrapping of her huge white apron; the scornful abstinence of Mme Charles is balanced by the greater generosity of her team of prostitutes; the vaginal constriction of Mme Campardon is echoed by the mysterious malady of Mme Mazelle.

There is a passage in *Le Ventre de Paris* which might serve as a symbolic representation of the relationship suggested by the novel between sexuality and sterility. It is the passage which describes what follows Lisa's discovery of Gradelle's fortune. Lisa invites Quenu into her bedroom for the first time, depositing the pile of gold and silver coins in the middle of the bed, between them. They count the money in silence. The image encapsulates their ensuing marriage, for the money keeps them tacitly separated. Lisa's discovery signals a sexless, contractual relationship unaffected by any taint of physicality. The gold, in other words, absorbs all sensuality. They are brought together by chance of circumstance and sympathy of ideals. Lisa's ample body is reflected in her bed: 'Le lit surtout était surprenant, avec ses quatre matelas, ses épaisseurs de couvertures, son édredon, son assoupissement ventru au fond de l'alcôve moite. C'était un lit fait pour dormir' (I, 656).[22] The last, brief sentence is devoid of ambiguity.

Although *La Joie de vivre* is interesting mainly for biographical and philosophical reasons, it is also pertinent to Zola's social themes. Bourgeois egoism is treated as a pathological phenomenon in this novel, in which the Chanteau family (another family of *rentiers*) remorselessly exploit the inherited wealth of their ward, Pauline Quenu (the daughter of Lisa). The monstrous egoism of the rapacious Mme Chanteau, who is reminiscent of Mme Josserand in *Pot-Bouille*, is matched by the self-absorption of her gout-ridden husband; the greed and social ambition of Mme Chanteau are set off by the innocence and altruism of Pauline.

It is usual to think of the bourgeoisie as costive or anal, preoccupied with accumulation and conservation. This conception is indeed confirmed by a reading of *Le Ventre de Paris*. Zola's portrayal of the bourgeoisie is largely determined, however, by the themes of dissipation and waste.[23] The earlier novels of *Les Rougon-Macquart*, from *La Fortune des Rougon* to *Nana*, emphasise the theme of orgiastic and nauseous excess, describing a process of disintegration in which the motif of wasteful appetites plays a prominent part. Gluttonous and frenzied excess leads to decay and ruin; consumption leads to destruction.

If Lisa Quenu represents the sterile parasitism of the *petite bourgeoisie*, Nana symbolises the decadence and depravity of the *haute bourgeoisie* and the aristocracy. The actress/prostitute is seen as both the product of a corrupt society and the catalyst of its destruction. The theme of the progressive contamination of high society by Nana is reflected in the personal disintegration of Count Muffat and the defection of his wife, Sabine. The life-style of Sabine takes on the ruinous extravagance of that of Nana, marked by images of waste, sterility and destruction. This is signalled by the transformation of the Muffat's mansion, and consecrated by a *fête* held to inaugurate the transformed mansion and to celebrate the engagement of Estelle, Sabine's daughter, to Daguenet, one of Nana's lovers. This occasion, which echoes an earlier reception given by Nana, is explicitly equated with the emergence of a new kind of licentious Imperial society, ironically underlined by the playing of the waltz, *La Blonde Vénus*: 'il semblait que ce fût quelque vent de la chair, venu de la rue, balayant tout un âge mort dans la hautaine demeure, emportant le passé de Muffat, un siècle d'honneur et de foi endormi sous les plafonds' (II, 1420).[24] Self-abandon turns the former austerity of Sabine's drawing-room into the promiscuity of *un lieu public*: 'Sabine, gâtée par la promiscuité de cette fille, poussée à tout, devenait l'effondrement final, la moisissure même du foyer' (Sabine, corrupted by the courtesan's promiscuity, and driven to every excess, completed the destruction and ruin of the family') (II, 1465). The Countess turns her home into a brothel. Images of decomposition and destruction correspond to an apocalyptic tone and an insistently moralistic vocabulary.

Houses in Zola are metaphorical reflections both of the moral life within them and of the bodies of their owners. The human body is often envisaged as a house, as in dreams.[25] At the centre of *Nana* is the vortex of Nana's body/house, focused by images of engulfment. Nana's body, like her house, swallows up fortunes and men: 'L'hôtel semblait bâti sur un gouffre, les hommes avec leurs biens, leurs corps, jusqu'à leurs noms, s'y engloutissaient, sans laisser la trace d'un peu de poussière' (II, 1433).[26] Images of waste, ruin, decay, nauseous excess, expenditure, disorder, destruction and voracity jostle together in passages of surrealistic extravagance. Nana's existence is characterised as 'un gaspillage effréné, un coulage féroce' ('frenetic expenditure, a torrent of wastefulness') (II, 1433). The final vision of one of the characters, as he surveys her house, is of a woman surrounded by débris and corpses: 'Au milieu de la débâcle de la maison, dans le coulage, dans le galop de massacre des domestiques, il y avait un entassement de richesses bouchant quand même les trous et débordant par-dessus les ruines' (II, 1466).[27]

Nana may thus be read as a lurid allegory of corruption and doom. At the end of the novel all those who have composed Nana's world cluster round her decomposing corpse. Her death coincides with the outbreak of the Franco-Prussian war, and the projected vision of the future looks forward to the ending of *La Bête humaine* and the imagery of *La Débâcle*. The atmosphere, heavy with a sense of foreboding, carries with it intimations of apocalyptic destruction, with the nightmarish image of the swelling crowds in the streets below, 'pareilles à des troupeaux menés de nuit à l'abattoir' ('like flocks of sheep driven to the slaughter-house at night') (II, 1480).

Although the novels which followed *Nana* are less specifically concerned with anti-Imperial polemic, they nevertheless describe or allude to the rottenness of the social fabric: *Pot-Bouille* describes the decomposition of a social class; *La Bête humaine* contains telling references to the corruption of the magistrature; *L'Argent* links the dissipation of Imperial society to a sense of social collapse; the retributive disasters of *La Débâcle*, which forms the historical conclusion to the cycle, are seen as the inevitable consequence of uncontrolled energy, self-consuming dissipation and the moral corruption of the representatives of social and political order. *Les Rougon-Macquart* as a whole depicts the breakdown of a society doomed to dissolution because of its reckless individualism and its unco-ordinated use of human energy. Running through the cycle is the theme of degeneracy, both social and pathological. The frenzied excesses of the Rougon-Macquart family contrast with the mute immobility of Tante Dide, who incarnates the fatal permanence of heredity, as if waiting at the lunatic asylum at Plassans for her corrupt race to destroy itself in wild agitation. The driverless train hurtling blindly through the night in *La Bête humaine* becomes an epic symbol of catastrophe. Full of singing soldiers bound for the crushing defeat of the Franco-Prussian war, the runaway train represents the nation rushing headlong towards destruction. It becomes, in other words, a striking figuration of the main motifs of Zola's indictment of Second Empire society: a self-destructive lack of control, radical instability, an absence of social leadership.

Society, then, is seen as a 'curée'. Zola's moralising satire is directed against the rapacious appetites, predatory greed and crass self-interest of the Rougons. His dissection of society reveals the moral corruption, egoism and hypocrisy of an acquisitive society. He exposes the sterility of bourgeois life and lays bare the materialist foundations of bourgeois ideology, of which the Second Empire was for him the epitomised political expression.

Leadership

What kinds of solutions does Zola propose to the problems of social anarchy and sterile materialism highlighted by his portrayal of Second Empire society? In what ways does he suggest that human energies may be co-ordinated and regulated, and put to productive use in the service of a stable and integrated social order? In what ways is the social pessimism of *Les Rougon-Macquart* mitigated by signs of hope? What part does the bourgeoisie play in the development of Zola's work towards the social optimism of *Les Quatre Évangiles*?

Zola was deeply sceptical of mass class action, revolutionary idealists and professional social reformers. He portrays socialists and revolutionaries as either naïve utopian dreamers or cynical opportunists.[1] The republicanism of Silvère (*La Fortune des Rougon*) and Florent (*Le Ventre de Paris*) is seen as a facet of temperament rather than the result of ideological conviction. Silvère's enthusiasm for the Republic is a sentimental reflection of his love for Miette; political idealism is symptomatic of an immature sexuality. The republicanism of Florent is portrayed as mere compensatory wish-fulfilment. The sickly Sigismond Busch (*L'Argent*), a former secretary of Karl Marx, lives in a world of abstract theory; his utopianism relegates him to the status of dreamer whose reveries have no influence on concrete events. The strong element of religious exaltation in the socialism of these revolutionaries was naturally antipathetic to Zola's positivist outlook, and he stresses the reinforcement of their idealism by their haphazard reading in socialist literature, underlining, for example, Etienne Lantier's autodidact inadequacy: 'Sur les moyens d'exécution, il se montrait plus vague, mêlant ses lectures, ne craignant pas, devant des ignorants, de se lancer dans des explications où il se perdait lui-même' (III, 1279).[2] Muddled thinking is thus associated with practical ineptitude: the republican insurgents in *La Fortune des Rougon* blunder into the trap set by the Rougons undeterred by the fact that they have no bullets for their rifles, while the political conspiracy in *Le Ventre de Paris* is treated as sheer farce.

The problems of proletarian leadership are posed with particular acuity in *Germinal*. Etienne Lantier, the leader of the miners' strike, is indeed the only working-class militant in *Les Rougon-Macquart* whom Zola intends us to take seriously as a political type. Although Etienne's political beliefs are taken seriously, Zola contrasts his ingenuousness with the political awareness of the anarchist Souvarine, who, unlike Etienne, sees clearly enough that the mine-owners are using the strike to break the miners' resistance. Etienne's dismay as the consequences of the abortive strike become apparent brings home to him the responsibilities of leadership, while the disaffection of the miners heightens his fears of his own inadequacy. Rejection by the miners and the recurring comparison between the strikers and a blind natural force reflect the fickleness of the masses and the fragility of Etienne's control over his followers. Before the strike fails, however, Zola describes Etienne's gradual slide into a rigid sectarianism and his loss of sensitivity to violence; and he also stresses the insidious attractions of both power and popularity once Etienne – already set apart from the miners by his intellectual superiority – establishes a position of authority over his fellow workers. Idealism fades into opportunism as thoughts of a political career begin to form in his mind. The personal rivalry between Etienne and Rasseneur, a moderate who opposes Etienne's militancy, becomes a salient theme of the novel. And Etienne's sense of estrangement from the miners is emphasised by his underlying complicity with Rasseneur; after Rasseneur has saved Etienne from the angry mob and has reasserted his influence over them, both rival leaders shrug their shoulders in virtual contempt at the herd-like instincts of the strikers and – an eloquent detail – have a drink together. When Etienne finally leaves the *coron* it is to join Pluchart, the peripatetic trade-union official who is as parasitic as any bourgeois.[3] The moral of Etienne's gradual *dégradation* is thus, in the words of Aimé Guedj, that 'toute conscience populaire qui s'individualise, se détache du peuple et passe à la bourgeoisie' ('all working-class consciousness which becomes individualised is detached from the people and absorbed into the bourgeoisie').[4] Zola's study of the psychology of Etienne and his relationship with the miners is also indicative of his abiding concern with social leadership and power. Zola's conception of the proletarian social reformer is at once patronising and dismissive: ineffectual or incompetent, his revolutionaries are portrayed as inadequate leaders both of their own class and, potentially, of society.[5]

Zola's distrust of proletarian revolutionaries is matched by his distaste for organised bourgeois politics. The fifteen months he spent as a parliamentary reporter for *La Cloche* in 1871 and 1872 had a lasting effect on his view of party politics. His day-by-day accounts of political happenings at Versailles emphasised the inconsequentiality of the debates and the inadequacy of the participants.[6] Nowhere is Zola's hatred of politics more evident, however, than in *Une Campagne*, the series of newspaper articles he wrote for *Le Figaro* in 1880–1. Politicians are depicted in these articles as either misguided imbeciles or intriguing knaves.[7] Republican politics, ravaged by factional conflicts, instability and the cynical pursuit of power and privilege, are characterised, Zola says, by a 'fétichisme de la médiocrité':

> Voici dix ans que nous pataugeons dans l'absurde. . . Nous mourons de politique, de cette politique tumultueuse et encombrante que la bande des médiocres, affamés de bruit et de places, ont tout intérêt à entretenir, pour y pêcher en eau trouble. Je ne vois qu'un salut: supprimer les médiocres, afin de supprimer leur tapage.[8]

Again, what plainly concerns Zola is the inadequate leadership provided by republican politicians.

Zola himself was not a profound or systematic political thinker; no more discernible an ideology than a firm republicanism and a general liberalism emerges from his political journalism, which is either evocative *reportage* or strident polemic. He was indeed less interested in dogma than in the efficient management of national affairs. Thus, parallel to his stress on the rottenness of the body politic, is his advocacy of the application to social problems of the positivist/Naturalist spirit, which is founded on a passionate faith in science: 'La République sera naturaliste ou elle ne sera pas' ('The Republic must espouse Naturalism if it is to survive').[9] The use of the scientific method, he argues, will lead to a form of government based not on dogma or on *a priori* principles, but on the objective 'laws' evolved from empirical experimentation and observation. Moreover, this 'technocratic' form of government, based on social engineering, involves an élitism by which the nation's most able men of science and the arts would be called upon to assume the responsibilities of office: 'Imaginez-vous que je voudrais une République des supériorités; moins de gâchis, moins de petits hommes et des appétits moins gros' ('Imagine that I would like to see a Republic of superior talents; less incompetence, less inferior types and smaller appetites').[10] The main components of Zola's scientific government are thus efficient leadership and the rational organisation of society in order to eliminate waste. A prime constituent of good leadership is thus good organisation. The élite to which Zola refers should ensure the smooth administration of a well-ordered and harmonious society based on the principles of balance and equilibrium. This need for order also implies due respect for authority and recognition of the need for moderation. Zola had a strong sense of order, both ideological and formal. His own life of mechanical literary production, interrupted only by his affair with Jeanne Rozerot and the sensational hiatus of the Dreyfus Affair, embodied the virtues of discipline, method and routine; as we have seen, it is as a consequence of uncontrolled energy as well as of *désoeuvrement* that the Rougon family eventually destroys itself.

An element of ambiguity arises from the contrast between Zola's positivist ideology, which leads to an optimistic vision of a well-ordered society based on science, and his detailed observation of the anarchic nature of a society based on the survival of the fittest. Zola's scientific faith, in other words, is at odds with his Darwinian view of humanity. Moreover, his commitment to social justice might seem to be in conflict with his own dogmatic temperament and with his admiration of those forceful characters who succeed in imposing their will on others. Zola's megalomania is clearly reflected in the pomposity of his theoretical writings, his highly combative journalism, and the vigour of his assault on the reading public.[11] The whole of Zola's fiction may in fact be read as an attempt to reconcile the themes of Darwinism and social responsibility. The motif of 'la curée' in his fiction, and his depiction of the persistence of a primordial 'bête humaine', reveal his recognition of the Darwinian aspects of human behaviour and his pessimistic awareness of the disruptive presence of instinctual appetites. It is precisely this awareness that leads him to realise the need for some form of responsible social leadership. In Zola's ideal society (realised in *Travail*), vital forces, operating within a rationally ordered framework, will be regulated and yet released – creatively channelled rather than being allowed to feed upon themselves. His sceptical attitude towards the principle of universal suffrage, because of the physical and moral inequality of individuals,[12] reflects his Darwinian view of society and implicitly confirms his belief in the rule of the masses by an élite.

Despite the evidence of both his fiction and his journalism, Zola's preoccupation with social leadership has been obscured – probably by his intervention in the Dreyfus Affair and the humanitarian eloquence of *L'Assommoir* and *Germinal*, which have tended to promote a simplified view of Zola as champion of the oppressed and spokesman of the workers rather than an advocate of responsible bourgeois leadership.[13] For Zola's scepticism about the workers' capacity for self-determination is matched by certain positive indications that his conception of the social role of the bourgeoisie is less negative than might be supposed. Zola's positivist faith in progress through science is accompanied in *Les Rougon-Macquart* by a latent messianism which is fully realised in *Les Quatre Evangiles*. This latent messianism takes the early form of fascination with power and admiration of energy. Early prototypes of the messiah are social adventurers and figures of power like Saccard I (*La Curée*), the Abbé Faujas, Eugène Rougon, Octave Mouret and Saccard II (*L'Argent*) – all of them variations on a single character-type, and all of them members of the bourgeoisie. The defining characteristics of these leader figures (which makes them stand out in stark contrast to Zola's timid and ineffectual revolutionaries as well as to the corruption and complacency of other types of bourgeois in the *Rougon-Macquart*) are an obsessive will to power and a ruthless determination to survive and succeed. They are all remarkable individualists.

La Conquête de Plassans is a novel about power. While the narrative of *La Fortune des Rougon* centres on the Rougons' seizure of power and the establishment of the family hegemony over Plassans, *La Conquête de Plassans* describes the 'conquest' of Plassans by the secret agent of the Imperial regime and the power exercised over an unstable woman, Marthe Mouret, by a strong-willed man. The forceful character of Faujas is constantly emphasised: 'L'abbé Faujus tendit les bras d'un air de défi ironique, comme s'il voulait prendre Plassans pour l'étouffer d'un effort contre sa poitrine robuste' ('The Abbé Faujas stretched out his arms in an ironical challenge, as though he would take Plassans and squeeze the breath out of it against his strong chest') (I, 916). Eugène Rougon, like Faujas, is portrayed as an exceptional individual who dreams of supremacy over the masses:

> Etre au-dessus de la foule où il ne voyait que des imbéciles et des coquins, mener le monde à coups de trique, cela développait dans l'épaisseur de sa chair un esprit adroit, d'une extraordinaire énergie. Il ne croyait qu'en lui, avait des convictions comme on a des arguments, subordonnait tout à l'élargissement continu de sa personnalité. Sans vice aucun, il faisait en secret des orgies de toute-puissance. (II, 131)[14]

Like Faujas, Rougon is large and broad-shouldered, and his physical strength reflects his strength of will: 'Malgré elle, la jeune fille [Clorinde] avait baissé les yeux sur les grosses mains de Rougon. . . Mais il s'était redressé, il semblait casser des pierres entre ses doigts fermés. Clorinde l'admirait' (II, 77–8).[15] The stress of his bull-like appearance also corresponds to his 'mépris du troupeau humain' ('contempt for the human herd') (II, 132). Eugène's dominating personality, set off by the pettiness and mediocrity of his gang of spoils-seeking supporters, becomes the entire focus of the novel: as Mallarmé noted, *Son Excellence Eugène Rougon* is 'moins le roman d'un régime politique que le roman d'un homme' ('less the novel of a political regime than the novel of an individual').[16] Zola is less concerned in this novel with describing the mechanisms of the political power structure and satirising the general lack of civil liberties than with depicting the psychology of power and leadership.

Zola's fascination with power is reflected in the political struggles described in *La Fortune des Rougon* and *La Conquête de Plassans* as well as *Son Excellence Eugène Rougon*; and it is also reflected in the ambitious commercial projects of Octave Mouret, the financial exploits of Saccard, and the sexual magnetism of Nana. If Eugène Rougon embodies the power of office, then Nana embodies the power of sex and both Saccard and Octave

Mouret the power of money. The mythical magnification of these characters – Rougon's domination over the whole country, the apotheosis of Nana at the races, Mouret's masterful exploitation of his female clientèle, Saccard's virtuosity as a financier – expresses this obsession.[17]

Rougon, Faujas and Octave Mouret – Saccard is the exception in this respect–are not only ruthless in the pursuit of their aims but also retain full control over their appetites. They embody the values of order and control in both their public and private lives. This is reflected in the resolute asceticism of Rougon and Faujas, and in the calculated philandering of Octave Mouret, who, like Maupassant's Bel-ami, uses sex to advance his career and conquer Paris. Both Mouret and Rougon have contracted marriages of convenience. Zola's fascination with the value of self-control is dramatised in the rivalry between Rougon and the beautiful adventuress, Clorinde Balbi. The success of Rougon, like that of Faujas, is built on the sublimation of his desires, a conservation of vital energies. The theme of success achieved through self-control reflects Zola's preoccupation with controlled energy – or rather, more specifically, his preoccupation with the organisation of vital forces into an integrated pattern.

Zola's latent admiration of Faujas, Eugène Rougon and the Saccard of *La Curée* develops into a more explicit approval of the Octave Mouret of *Au Bonheur des Dames* and the Saccard of *L'Argent*. This approval is connected with Zola's attempt in *Au Bonheur des Dames* and *L'Argent* to reconcile his Darwinian view of life with a need for responsible social leadership. In these two novels, as well as in *Germinal*, Zola specifically addresses himself to the world of capitalism, portraying the general economic structure of society through the careers of the dynamic entrepreneur, Mouret, and the arch-capitalist financier, Saccard.

Au Bonheur des Dames is an important text, for it marks Zola's desire to broaden his social perspective and embrace the whole of socio-economic reality through his description of the establishment and growth of the first great Parisian multiple store. The commercial phenomenon of the store is treated in dramatic Darwinian terms; it is seen as a gigantic living organism which inexorably swallows the little shops around it, while its internal functioning is determined by the competitive rivalry of employees: 'cette lutte des appétits, cette poussée des uns sur les

autres, était comme le bon fonctionnement même de la machine,
ce qui enrageait la vente et allumait cette flambée du succès dont
Paris s'étonnait' (III, 542).[18] The department store is thus conceived of as a microcosm of capitalist society. The ambiguity of
Zola's attitude to capitalism as an economic system reflects his
overriding concern with leadership and efficiency. Far from
advocating a radical reform of the capitalistic foundations of
society, he writes lyrically of private enterprise and the bold new
forms of capitalism, for he sees in them the triumph of Life:
capitalism is creative; the department store is seen as an inevitable product of progress and economic modernisation, and
Octave Mouret, the quintessential bourgeois, the 'self-made
man' whose success is built on bold administrative innovations,
is admired (like the Saccard of *L'Argent*) for his vitality. Admiration of Mouret's qualities of energy and dynamism is brought
out through the contrast established between him and his brilliant old school-companion, Vallagnosc. The contrast between
Mouret's spectacular business career and the stagnation of his
friend at the Ministry of the Interior is paralleled by the opposition between Vallagnosc's Schopenhauerian pessimism[19] and
Mouret's vigorous identification with the rapid social transformations around him: 'Vraiment, il fallait être mal bâti, avoir le
cerveau et les membres attaqués, pour se refuser à la besogne, en
un temps de si large travail, lorsque le siècle entier se jetait à
l'avenir' (III, 452).[20] Although a ruthless careerist, Mouret is
proud of being in tune with the times. And his role as a leader is
underlined by military and regal imagery ('comme tous les
grands capitaines, au moment de livrer sa bataille' ['like all great
captains when joining battle'] [III, 477]; 'il régnait sur toutes
avec la brutalité d'un despote' ['he reigned over them all with
the brutality of a despot'] [III, 797]).

Denise Baudu, the shop-assistant whose role as Zola's delegate in the novel is similar to that of Mme Caroline in *L'Argent*,
affirms that, although the growth of the big store forces the
old-fashioned shopkeepers out of business, the Darwinian laws of
social progress must be accepted: 'elle avait conscience que cela
était bon, qu'il fallait ce fumier de misères à la santé du Paris de
demain' ('she was aware that all this was a good thing, that this
manure of distress was necessary to the health of the Paris of the
future') (III, 748). A highly moralistic element is embodied in
Denise and her gradual acquisition of authority and influence

within the shop, for Mouret's ruthlessness is tempered by her humanitarian concern. It is important to note, however, that she embodies sheer rationality, a desire for order and efficiency, as well as compassion: 'Elle ne pouvait s'occuper d'une chose, voir fonctionner une besogne, sans être travaillée du besoin de mettre de l'ordre, d'améliorer le mécanisme' ('She could not do something herself or see a task being carried out without being obsessed with the need to put method into it, to improve the system') (III, 727). Denise becomes an apologist of free enterprise capitalism on the grounds of rationality and progress: 'Elle était secrètement pour les grands magasins, dans son amour instinctif de la logique et de la vie' ('with her instinctive love for logic and life, she was secretly on the side of the big shops') (III, 574). She argues that the lower prices offered by the big stores are clearly better for the public and that the big stores spell the elimination of all needless intermediaries: 'les intermédiaires disparaissaient, agents de fabrique, représentants, commissionnaires, ce qui entrait pour beaucoup dans le bon marché' ('the middle-men, factory agents, travellers, commission agents, were disappearing – which was an important factor in reducing prices') (ibid.). The reforms she urges – security of employment, the establishment of a pension scheme and a holiday system, the fostering of leisure activities and an educational programme – reflect her concern with efficiency as well as social justice:

> Etait-ce humain, était-ce juste, cette consommation effroyable de chair que les grands magasins faisaient chaque année? Et elle plaidait la cause des rouages de la machine, non par des raisons sentimentales, mais par des arguments tirés de l'intérêt même des patrons. Quand on veut une machine solide, on emploie du bon fer; si le fer casse ou si on le casse, il y a un arrêt de travail, des frais répétés de mise en train, toute une déperdition de force. (III, 728)[21]

Practical expediency – the elimination of waste and inefficiency within the capitalist system – is clearly as important as moral concern; reformism goes hand in hand with utilitarianism. The marriage between Octave (energy, drive) and Denise (moral responsibility, social purpose, efficiency) is a piece of artificial social symbolism which, however, marks a significant step in the development of Zola's social vision towards the utopianism of

Travail. For the price of Denise's hand is the internal reorganisa-
tion of the store along humanitarian lines – which looks forward
to the Fourieristic system of social co-operation which will form
the basis of Luc Froment's ideal community. *Au Bonheur des
Dames* thus represents an attempted marriage between bourgeois
individualism, rationalised efficiency and the common good.
Similar themes are developed in *L'Argent*, which centres on the
world of the Bourse and the inner workings of the capitalist
economy.

In *Germinal* (written two years after *Au Bonheur des Dames* and
six years before *L'Argent*) Zola attacks social inequalities and the
exploitative nature of capitalist society by maximising the stark
contrasts between the pathetic lives of the miners and the *aisance*
that characterises bourgeois existence. Critics have often pointed
out the detailed counterpointing of the poverty-striken Maheu
household and the cosy self-indulgence of the Grégoires, the
shareholders, who are portrayed in a heavily ironic manner. The
motifs that define the Grégoires' existence are egoism, complacency, well-being, food, warmth and idleness. In his description
of the visit of La Maheude to La Piolaine to ask for money, Zola
stresses the stereotyped class attitudes of the Grégoires: their
assumption of moral superiority, the unspoken reproaches that
the miners have too many children and drink too much (hence
their gift of discarded clothes but their refusal on principle to
give money), and their ludicrously self-justifying reflections that
the miners benefit from free coal and low rents. The visit round
the *coron* by Mme Hennebeau and her bourgeois friends (Part II,
Chapter 3) is built on the contrast between the harsh realities
of the miners' living conditions and the comfortable clichés
mouthed by the visitors. Zola's ironic treatment of the Grégoires'
complacency and insensitivity allies them with the Charles in *La
Terre* who are similarly self-enclosed, sentimental, and blandly
unaware of anything beyond the immediate family circle. The
irony suddenly disintegrates when Cécile is murdered by Bon-
nemort: their blindness is paid for by the death of their daughter
at the hands of the gnarled symbol of the exploited workers.

Zola's compassion for the miners is beyond question; but the
bourgeois representatives of capitalism, although they are all
concerned with preserving their own class interests, are far from
being uniformly evil. The mine managers are not presented as
cynically exploitative monsters but as victims of economic cir-

cumstance. Zola stresses the divided responsibilities of Hennebeau, the salaried manager of the big Montsou company. Hennebeau's nephew, the engineer Négrel, is an anti-proletarian cynic, deceitful and gruffly authoritarian, but he keeps the respect of the miners because of his energy and physical courage. After the collapse of the mine he risks his life to save the trapped miners; his courage is clearly contrasted with the inhumanity of Souvarine. However, the most sympathetic bourgeois in *Germinal* is Deneulin, the progressive, hard-working, paternalist owner of a small colliery. Like Négrel, he is respected for his energy and courage. Although authoritarian, he is an excellent manager of men: 'Lui, ne trônait pas au loin, dans un tabernacle ignoré; il n'était pas un de ces actionnaires qui paient des gérants pour tondre le mineur, et que celui-ci n'a jamais vus; il était un patron, il risquait autre chose que son argent, il risquait son intelligence, sa santé, sa vie' (III, 1392–3).[22] He is allied with the miners not only through the compassion he shows towards them but through the fact that, like them, he is crushed by the big company of Montsou. Thus, it is important to recognise that, although Zola wished to base his novel on stark contrasts, the bourgeoisie is not presented as monolithic; there are conflicts within the bourgeoisie as well as between the classes. The opposition between the idle, unregenerate Grégoires and the energetic, enlightened Deneulin emerges with particular clarity at the great dinner held at La Piolaine to celebrate the engagement of Cécile and Négrel after the failure of the strike. The dinner quickly turns into a celebration of the victory over the miners, and the smug self-congratulation of M. Grégoire is contrasted with the melancholy of Deneulin, whom the strike has ruined: 'C'était le glas des petites entreprises personnelles, la disparition prochaine des patrons, mangés un à un par l'ogre sans cesse affamé du capital' ('It was the death-knell of small private enterprise, of proprietors soon doomed to disappear, devoured one after the other by the insatiable maw of capital') (III, 1523). Zola laments the triumph of conservatism and egoism, ironically juxtaposing the defeat of the man of energy with the victory of the selfish Grégoires, thus underlying both his condemnation of parasitic elements in the bourgeoisie and his approval of entrepreneurial vigour.[23] In other words, the opposition between miners and bourgeois does not correspond to the antithesis between work and parasitism.

The ambivalence of Zola's portrayal of the bourgeoisie is a prominent feature of *La Débâcle* (1892). It is illustrated in the contrast between Delaherche, the rich manufacturer of Sedan whose support for the Emperor crumbles the moment his factory is threatened by the war, and Weiss, his sympathetic and patriotic employee. Whereas Delaherche favours surrender, so that his factory might be saved, Weiss dies courageously in defence of his property. Similarly, the shallow and adulterous Gilberte Delaherche is opposed to the devoted, idealised Henriette Weiss. But the main opposition of characters is that between Jean Macquart, a peasant, and Maurice Levasseur, a bourgeois. One of the principal themes of the novel is the bond of friendship that develops between Jean and Maurice, a friendship which transcends distinctions of class and expresses their common humanity. Each of them in turn saves the life of the other. But the temperamental differences between them are radical; the two heroes symbolise the contradictory qualities of the nation itself. Jean is level-headed, practical-minded, stolid and dependable. Maurice is generous-spirited and humane, but is weak-willed and easily influenced. He is both a product and a symbol of the unstable, effete society of the Second Empire. In a somewhat confused piece of symbolism, he is easily won over by the demagogic extremists of the Commune and dies – accidentally bayoneted by Jean! – on the barricades. Zola's rejection of the Commune and of revolutionary violence is emphatic. Although Jules Vallès paid homage to him as 'un communard de la plume' ('a Communard of the pen'),[24] he gives relatively little narrative attention of the Commune in *La Débâcle* and portrays it not as a heroic struggle but as destructive anarchism, a convulsive sympton of national decay and frustrated patriotism.[25] This negative account of the Commune is reinforced by the characterisation of Chouteau, the lazy, seditious soldier who, early in the novel, glibly advocates desertion, purveys garbled 'revolutionary' ideas and reappears later as a Communard. The exasperated idealism of Maurice is thus matched by Chouteau's sheer irresponsibility. The apolitical Jean, who remains a Versaillais, is incensed by the blind destruction of the Commune:

> . . .Il y avait encore les récits des abominations de la Commune, qui le jetait hors de lui, en blessant son respect de la propriété et son besoin d'ordre. Il était resté le fond même de

la nation, le paysan sage, désireux de paix, pour qu'on recommençât à travailler, à gagner, à se refaire du sang. (V, 883)[26]

The themes of leadership and organisation are treated in a very specific manner in *La Débâcle*. The novel is, after all, an elaborately documented account of the military defeat of France in 1870, which is ascribed to an unmitigated failure of national leadership. One of Zola's aims in the novel was to demonstrate the Darwinian proposition that the machine-like efficiency, firm discipline and good leadership of the Prussian army could not but defeat its disorganised, ill-equipped and incompetently led adversary: 'il n'était plus un homme, si borné fût-il, qui n'éprouvât le malaise d'être mal conduit, attardé à tort, poussé au hasard dans la plus désastreuse des aventures' ('there was not a man left, however dim-witted, who did not feel uneasy about being badly led, held up for no reason, thrust somehow into the most disastrous adventure') (V, 489). He further suggests that the future lies with Jean, the traditional French peasant. But it is surely legitimate to argue that Jean is in some ways more of a bourgeois than Maurice. The qualities he embodies, and which Zola endorses, are those of the *petite bourgeoisie*: 'Il était du vieux sol obstiné et sage, du pays de la raison, du travail et de l'épargne' ('He came from the old, unchanging, careful soil, from the land of reason, hard work and thrift') (V, 716). Against the collective folly of the age Zola sets the traditional bourgeois values of moderation, thrift and hard work, to which are added an impulse towards order (noted above with regard to Denise Baudu), qualities of leadership and efficiency (demonstrated in Jean's excellence as a platoon-commander), and respect for discipline and authority (reflected in his response to the Commune). The *embourgeoisement* of Jean is indicated in *Le Docteur Pascal*, where we learn that he has obtained a *licence*, married a peasant girl and become a small landowner. This brief glimpse of Jean as a patriarchal bourgeois farmer – for it is noted that he now has a small family – establishes him as a prototype of Mathieu Froment in *Fécondité*, who builds a 'New France' in the African colonies.

The answer to the problems of France, then, is not revolution but conservatism. Although Zola had a strong sense of social justice and responsibility, his vision is conservative in its impulse towards order and rationality, and in the considerable respect he implies for authority. Faith in the traditional bourgeois values of self-discipline, hard work and moderation is allied to a messianism whose germs are already visible in the early novels of the *Rougon-Macquart* series. Thus, an important determining factor in Zola's social and political vision is the theme of leadership; his treatment of the social role of the bourgeoisie is defined by the problems of leadership, authority and order. While Zola saw the bourgeoisie as a class as unfit to rule, he had little faith in the ability of the proletariat to help themselves: the workers are capricious, the revolutionaries disorganised and incompetent. Although a sharp critic of the anarchy and inhumanity of uncontrolled capitalism, Zola was unable to accept the remedies of utopian socialists. On the other hand, he does not globally condemn the bourgeoisie; his satire is directed against the bourgeois as parasite, while he implicitly sees hope for the creation of a new social order in certain bourgeois figures who, although partly presented in a framework of satire, are admired for their energy, enterprise and leadership. *Les Rougon-Macquart* reflects the development of Zola's attempt to combine dynamism with responsibility and rationality, to reconcile his worship of the will with his desire for a satisfying moral and social order. The myth of leadership is fully developed in the utopianism of his final works.

Utopia

Like Marx, Zola is more powerful and persuasive in his delineation of capitalist society than in the detailed elaboration of a future utopia. The prolixity of much of Zola's later writing provoked Henry James into remarking that in these last works everything is absent but quantity.[1] Nevertheless, despite the lack of imaginative conviction and the crude intellectual framework of *Les Trois Villes* and *Les Quatre Evangiles*, it is vital to recognise the thematic continuity between these novels and *Les Rougon-Macquart*. The themes of the later novels are partly determined by the social and intellectual climate of the last two decades of the nineteenth century; the 'cultural crisis' they reflect was about the idealist reaction against positivism and the attempts by writers like Bourget and Brunetière to show the moral dangers of a mechanistic world-view and to assert the limitations of science as an explanation of the universe. But Zola's later fiction, while plainly influenced by this wider context of intellectual issues, also makes discursively explicit the developing tendencies of *Les Rougon-Macquart*, expressing Zola's growing visionary idealism. These works represent a movement from description to diagnosis, from the anatomy of social abuses to the prescription of humanitarian remedies. Thus, although a detailed examination of *Les Trois Villes* and *Les Quatre Evangiles* is beyond the scope of this study, it is necessary to consider what becomes of the bourgeoisie in Zola's utopia and the ways in which the later novels shed light on the evolving social patterns of the *Rougon-Macquart*. Since it would be inappropriate to consider the post-*Rougon-Macquart* novels at length, I will focus attention on *Travail*, which is the most comprehensive and pertinent expression of Zola's final views on the ideal society.[2]

A basic aspect of the continuity between *Les Rougon-Macquart* and the later novels (immediately verified by a comparison between *La Curée* and *L'Argent*) is the increasing prominence in the representation of social reality of mythic structure in the later volumes of *Les Rougon-Macquart*. The strong mythopoeic elements in Zola's imagination have been widely recognised. An essential corollary of Zola's mythopoeism, which becomes very plain in the post-*Rougon-Macquart* novels, is his urge towards a total, synthesising philosophical vision of the world. Just as he situates man within a total context of shaping influences, so he tends increasingly to relate the personal and social action of his novels to a larger, transcending framework of cosmic truths. As the case of *L'Argent* illustrates, the patterns of myth in Zola interpenetrate with the concrete historical events which form the background to the cycle. In *L'Argent* the World Fair of 1867 (the apotheosis of the Imperial régime) and the *krach* of the Banque Universelle reflect the myth of catastrophe. Correspondingly, the theme of heredity is made to fit into the historico-mythical pattern; Zola establishes a parallelism between the physiological vitiation of the Rougon-Macquart family and the convulsive decline of the Second Empire. The rise of the bourgeoisie in the early novels, and the satisfaction of their appetites, are succeeded by the themes of disintegration and destruction. *Nana* describes a society plunging towards disaster, while *Pot-Bouille* evokes the decomposition of a whole social class.

The central myth of Zola is that of regenerative optimism. Zola's historical world-view, in other words, may be defined as a vision of life as a cyclical process of degeneration and regeneration which, as Guy Robert has suggested, is analogous to Nietzsche's myth of Eternal Return.[3] Zola describes a world full of violence, horror and apocalyptic disasters; the emergence of his myth of regenerative optimism depends, indeed, on a progressive multiplication of symbolic catastrophes, which are accompanied by increasingly explicit hope in their purifying potential. The mythical thought patterns of Zola's work are defined by a series of binary opposites; his myth of regenerative optimism consists in an archetypal struggle between the contrary but complementary forces of Life and Death. The myth of catastrophe, which assumes increasing importance after *Nana* and (especially) *Germinal*, is opposed by a myth of hope, sterility by fecundity, degeneration by regeneration. The theme of catastrophe as the necessary agent of renewal is expressed with great explicitness in *La Débâcle*, in which the holocaust of war and the upheaval of the Commune are transformed into symbols of national death and regeneration. The portrayal of the horrors of war is integrated into the familiar Zolaesque conception of natural evolution. The myth of decadence is worked out in *Le Docteur Pascal*. Zola gives the novel a cosmic dimension by stressing that Pascal's personal revitalisation through the transfiguring powers of love and fecundity signifies a new relationship with the universe. The themes of decadence and renewal are focused by the symbolic eclipse of Maxime's son, the haemophiliac Charles, by the son of Pascal and Clotilde. The liquidation of the Rougon dynasty is figured in the hereditary degeneracy of little Charles, who bleeds slowly to death before his insane great-great-grandmother, Tante Dide, who has been committed to the lunatic asylum at Plassans. Zola's utopian vision of progress towards a future golden age is linked in *Le Docteur Pascal* to an express belief in the enduring value of participation in the life-struggle, the redemptive value of work and the essential beneficence of nature. Although the novel reads more like a summarising conclusion than a creative achievement, it may be considered a pivotal work in the sense that Clotilde's nostalgia for transcendental meanings, together with Pascal's awareness of the insufficiency of science alone to cure the social ills so clearly documented in his own history of the Rougon-Macquart family, announce the quasi-religious nature of Zola's later fiction. The title of *Les Quatre Evangiles* itself, as well as the explicit concerns of *Les Trois Villes*, indicates that these novels may be read as a form of religious discourse. *Le Docteur Pascal* is also pivotal in as much as Pascal becomes a symbolic John the Baptist preparing the way for the Messiah. The birth of his posthumous son, 'messie que le prochain siècle attendait' ('the messiah awaited by the new century') (V, 1219), is seen as a kind of cosmic victory and a guarantee of continuity and renewal. His son is the social messiah whose destiny will be traced in the careers of Pierre and Luc Froment.

The organising principle of *Travail* – and the matrix of Zola's fiction – is the theme of fecundity, which shapes both Zola's sense of community and his vision of human relations. Zola's vitalist cosmogony corresponds to his mystique of human love, and the themes of sexuality and social reform are drawn together by the concept of creativity. The interlocking of social and sexual themes is mirrored in the fact that Ragu is Luc's political oppo-

nent as well as his sentimental rival (recalling the relationship
between Chaval and Etienne in *Germinal*). Luc's consciousness of
a 'mission', his dream of a new humanity, and his search for a
solution to the 'social problem', are persistently linked to the
pathetic figure of Josine, who incarnates the suffering of her
class: 'Luc. . . se disait qu'en cette malheureuse retentissait toute
la débâcle du travail mal organisé, déshonoré, maudit' ('Luc . . .
said to himself that in this poor creature resounded the whole
collapse of labour, badly organised, dishonoured and accused') (p.
566).[4] It is the haunting image of Josine which lifts Luc out of his
despondency after the trial, and it is through his union with Josine
that he is able to fulfil his role as social apostle: 'Seul, l'amour ferait
l'harmonie de la Cité. C'était sa communion intime avec le peuple
des déshérités, cette Josine délicieuse, qu'il avait faite
définitivement sienne. L'union était scellée, l'apôtre en lui ne
pouvait rester infécond, il avait besoin d'une femme pour racheter
l'humanité' (p. 751).[5] That human and social creativity are two
sides of the same coin is reflected in the symbolic links established
between procreation and social regeneration (a theme already
treated at exhaustive length in *Fécondité*). Fertile love is seen as the
sine qua non of the new community, the principle without which the
radical material transformations and social improvements
envisaged by Luc would be impossible. It is as if the birth of Josine's
child signals the magnificent expansion of La Crêcherie and the
apocalyptic destruction by fire of L'Abîme: 'On ne fonde rien sans
l'enfant, il est l'oeuvre vivante, élargissant et propageant la vie,
continuant aujourd'hui par demain. C'est le couple qui seul
enfante, qui seul sauvera les pauvres hommes de l'iniquité et de la
misère' (p. 788).[6] The paternity of Luc is invested with immense
prestige. Thus, as the old bourgeois order withers away, sovereign
love hastens social reconciliation, for the proliferation of marriages
between the children of bourgeois and workers helps to fuse the
classes.

Work is equated with fecundity, which becomes both a moral
imperative and a principle of social organisation. Creative
energy as the basis of the new community, the use of the human
passions within a harmonious and rationally organised society,
will promote both social efficiency and personal fulfilment. The
idea of a harmonious City spells greater efficiency in that Luc's
rational exploitation of the human passions along Fourierist
lines implies a system of values and laws which involves the

elimination of waste and the suppression of all non-productive, parasitic elements:

> Il suffirait de réorganiser le travail, pour réorganiser la société toute entière, dont il devait être l'obligation civique, la règle vitale . . . Une ville, une commune, n'était plus qu'une immense ruche, dans laquelle il n'y avait pas un oisif, où chaque citoyen donnait sa part d'effort à l'oeuvre d'ensemble dont la cité avait besoin pour vivre. (p. 654)[7]

It is not difficult to classify the bourgeois characters in the novel in the light of Zola's preoccupation with human and social creativity. Those opposed to Luc are identified, in the terms of the scheme of values elaborated in the novel, as unregenerate parasites. On the lowest level, the small retail traders, represented principally by the apoplectic butcher, Dacheux, and the greedy hardware merchants, the Laboques, manifest the rapaciousness and egoism of *les honnêtes gens* as adumbrated in *Le Ventre de Paris*. Dacheux, with his strident demands for social order and strong government, recalls Lisa Quenu: 'Il s'occupait de politique, était avec les riches, les forts, très redouté, borné et sanguinaire' ('A narrow-minded, hot-tempered man, and greatly feared, he busied himself with politics, being on the side of the rich and powerful') (p. 550). It is these small retailers who, led by Laboque, instigate a campaign of vilification against Luc in a desperate attempt to defend their economic interests by exploiting popular prejudice: 'C'était l'autorité, la propriété, la religion, la famille, qu'il s'agissait de défendre. Beauclair entier finissait par en être, les fournisseurs lésés ameutaient leurs clients, la bourgeoisie suivait, dans sa terreur des idées neuves' (p. 711).[8] Their casuistry merely masks their fear of the economic threat represented by La Crècherie, while their position as intermediaries within the capitalist system represents an obvious form of economic parasitism:

> Toute une déperdition de force et de richesse s'engouffrait chez eux, dans leur honnêteté relative de commerçants, qui volaient selon usage, avec la joie chaude, chaque soir, sur les besoins des autres. Des rouages inutiles, qui mangeaient de l'énergie, et dont grinçait la machine, en train de se détraquer. (p. 553)[9]

The expansion of La Crècherie and the co-operation between enlightened bourgeois and willing workers spell, of necessity, the disappearance of a parasitic class; the final sections of *Travail* celebrate the productive capacities of a community from which such a class has been removed, work having been reorganised in the interests of both efficiency and humane values. We thus recall Denise Baudu's advocacy in *Au Bonheur des Dames* of the elimination of needless middlemen and the severity with which Zola treats the parasites of capitalism in *L'Argent*.

Oisiveté and *jouissance*, idleness and pleasure pursued with no sense of social purpose, are primary forms of parasitism. The Mazelles, plump, smug and complacent *rentiers*, refer back, with their 'inertie bonasse' ('good-natured inertia') (p. 861) to their counterparts in earlier novels, the Grégoires in *Germinal* and the Charles in *La Terre*, and represent a kind of parasitism marked by moral blindness; while the history of the Qurignon family shows the destructive consequences of *jouissance*. The erosion of the Qurignons' dynastic fortune reveals that the creative energy of Jérôme Qurignon, the self-made man who expanded his father's factory into a thriving industrial complex, has been largely wasted, not only because of external economic circumstances but by the dissipation, mismanagement, congenital disabilities, suicides and deaths of his descendants:

> En trois générations, la réserve de puissance créatrice qui avait demandé tant de siècles de misère et d'efforts, venait d'être dévoré goulûment. Tout de suite, l'exaspération nerveuse, l'affinement destructeur s'étaient produits, dans la curée chaude de la sensation. La race, gorgée trop vite, éperdue de possession, culbutait en pleine folie de la richesse. (p. 604)[10]

This passage reads like a condensed account of the decline of the Rougon-Macquart family. The lessons of bourgeois degeneracy are that idleness is a sin, class exploitation is wasteful and self-destructive, and parasitism subverts the efficiency and humane organisation of the working community.

Zola suggests, however, that collective action by the workers offers no hope of social reform. He stresses the irresponsibility, conservatism and inertia of the workers, who play a negligible part in the social transformation represented by La Crècherie.[11]

Ragu and Fortuné embody the alienation of the worker under the capitalist system, the latter physically and morally stunted by the purely mechanical nature of his work, the former rendered brutally insensitive by his working conditions. The archetype of working-class resignation is the fatalistic Père Lunot; accepting the *patronat* as a fact of nature, he is unable to contemplate the possibility of social change. A corollary of the worker-slave mentality is simple regret at not possessing the privileges of the bourgeoisie. Ragu, although brutal and violent, remains politically inert, dreaming only of supplanting his bourgeois masters in order to enjoy similar idleness. La Toupe, the irascible wife of Bonnaire, is reminiscent of Mme Josserand in her bourgeois concern with appearances and desire for wealth.

In contrast to the degraded and dehumanised Ragu stand Bonnaire, the master puddler, and old Morfain, whose family has tended the furnace at La Crècherie for three generations. Bonnaire, an excellent worker, is proud of the skill and responsibility he exercises. Morfain, even more than Bonnaire, represents the ancestral nobility of work:

> Et Morfain, vivant dans son creux de roches, tout à la peine et à l'orgueil de son effort, apparaissait à Luc comme le descendant immédiat de ces ouvriers primitifs, dont le lointain atavisme se retrouvait en lui, silencieux, résigné, donnant ses muscles sans une plainte, ainsi qu'à l'aube des sociétés humaines. (p. 647)[12]

But the logic of Zola's vision in *Travail*, which is antipathetic to Morfain's attitude of stoic suffering, forces him to become increasingly critical towards the stubborn slave-mentality displayed by this modern Vulcan. Passive acceptance of his allotted role corresponds to tragic scepticism of all technological improvements; when the installation of electrical furnaces makes him redundant, he commits suicide by snapping an electric cable with his bare hands.

Zola's critique of the political apathy of the workers is matched by explicit disapproval of the working-class ideologies of his revolutionary activists.[13] He attempts in various ways to discredit his politicised workers, the anarchist Lange and the collectivist Bonnaire. Luc clearly respects the noble ideals of Bonnaire, but the high esteem in which he holds him is sharply qualified ·by his apprehensiveness about Bonnaire's confused thinking and the practical implications of his collectivism:

> Où il s'embrouillait, c'était sur la façon pratique d'arriver, par des lois, à cette socialisation, c'était surtout sur le libre fonctionnement du système, lorsqu'il serait mis en pratique, toute une machine compliquée de direction et de contrôle, qui nécessiterait une police d'Etat vexatoire et dure. (pp. 586, 588) [*sic*][14]

The anarchist, Lange, is portrayed as a fanatical and, above all, isolated figure. Through Luc, Zola expresses his hatred of the revolutionary violence espoused by both Lange and (with less specific emphasis) Bonnaire: 'C'était peut-être qu'il répugnait personnellement aux violences révolutionnaires, ayant mis sa foi scientifique dans l'évolution ininterrompue, qui a devant elle l'éternité pour faire son oeuvre' (p. 672).[15]

The vital corollary of this lack of faith in the workers as a force for social change is Luc's blatant status as a patriarchal leader. Zola's utopian hopes of human redemption correspond to his myth of a New Man. His preparatory notes for *Le Docteur Pascal* reveal his desire to conclude the series, and thus the whole social odyssey of the Rougon-Macquart, with an expression of hope in his 'enfant inconnu' ('unknown child'): 'C'est beau de fermer la série sur cet espoir en l'éternelle nature, en l'éternelle vie: espérer que l'être va naître qui recommencera l'expérience, qui sur ce vieux monde caduque, en fera naître un nouveau'.[16] The ending of *Le Docteur Pascal* focuses on Clotilde's lyrical reflections of the role her newborn child might eventually fulfil: 'Puisque la nation était à refaire, celui-ci ne venait-il pas pour cette besogne?' ('Since the nation was to be rebuilt, had not this child come to fulfil this task?') (V, 1219). The New Man who comes to restore order, to rebuild and redeem, arrives not as a working-class militant but as a bourgeois reformer.

It is thus important to note that, although the bourgeoisie of Beauclair is generally degenerate, Zola by no means proposes a blanket condemnation of the bourgeoisie as a class. Jérôme Quirignon focuses *déchéance* from something positive and valuable rather than absolute class condemnation; he speaks of decline and abuse rather than of ineluctable historical forces. The sympathetic Mme Mitaine is an exception to the rule of *petit-bourgeois* venality, while the nobility of Suzanne Boisgelin, an old friend of Luc, contrasts with the mediocrity of her husband. And although Delaveau, the manager of L'Abîme, is presented as a stubborn authoritarian opposed to worker-participation and trade unions, some sympathy is expressed for him; described as 'travailleur sage, sobre, continent, qui avait la haine de l'oisiveté et de la jouissance, destructives de toute sante créatrice' ('a sensible and sober worker who hated idleness and excessive enjoyment since he knew that they destroyed all creative health') (p. 766), considerable stress is placed on his qualities as an energetic and able administrator.

The information provided in the opening chapter about Luc's character and past history immediately establishes him as the epitome of the philanthropical bourgeois reformer:

> L'effrayant problème des hontes et des tortures du salariat s'était souvent posé à lui, il avait sondé à fond l'iniquité atroce, l'effroyable chancre qui achève de ronger la société actuelle, passant des heures de fièvre généreuse à rêver au remède, se brisant toujours contre le mur d'airain des réalités existantes. (pp. 546–7)[17]

His compassion for the workers is marked by a paternalistic and sentimental tone, which is reinforced by the pointed rhetorical questions that reflect his own *prise de conscience* as a possible liberator of the people: 'Etait-ce donc en Messie qu'une force ignorée le faisait tomber dans ce coin de pays douloureux, pour la mission rêvée de délivrance et de bonheur?' ('Was it as a Messiah that an unknown force had cast him into this woeful region to fulfil his long-dreamt-of mission of deliverance and happiness?') (p. 549). His messianic role is underlined not simply by the narrative action of *Travail* but by its tone of Biblical revelation and its use of Christian images and allusions. Luc's ordeal at the time of his trial and his knifing by Ragu are both described as 'calvaries' (pp. 721, 785).[18]

An obvious but important corollary of Luc's messianism is the stress Zola lays on (to use Marxist terminology) subjectivism, that is, the efficacy of individual action and initiative in the instigation of social change: 'Il était seul, il voulait agir seul, il mettait toute sa foi dans l'action. Il était l'homme qui ose, et cela suffirait, sa mission serait remplie' (p. 675).[19] It is feasible that this emphasis on Luc's status as a 'man of destiny' was reinforced by Zola's own spectacular demonstration of the efficacy of individual initiative by his intervention – as a leader of opinion – in the Dreyfus Affair. In this sense Luc and Marc Froment may be seen as reflections of Zola himself; *Vérité*, which describes the individual heroism of Marc Froment, is, after all, a transposition of the Dreyfus Affair. But this contingent historical factor must not obscure the continuity of Zola's fiction. For the individualism so apparent in *Travail* and the later novels is prefigured, as we have seen, by Zola's general interest in characters of outstanding determination, energy or enterprise; in particular, the thematic structure of *L'Argent*, with its stress on the themes of leadership, energy and responsibility, points to the links between the Napoleonic Saccard and the charismatic Luc.

The term 'charisma' is not misapplied, for it denotes Luc's exceptional qualities of leadership, his exemplary energy, his inspirational role in the construction of the ideal community, his patriarchal authority, and the virtual hero-worship of which he is the object:

> Il était partout à la fois, enflammant les ouvriers dans les halles de l'usine, resserant les liens fraternels des grands et des petits dans la maison commune, veillant à la bonne administration dans les magasins. On ne voyait que lui par les avenues ensoleillées de la Cité naissante, au milieu des enfants et des femmes, aimant à jouer et à rire, en jeune père de ce petit peuple qui était le sien. Tout naissait, grandissait, s'organisait à son geste, grâce à son génie, à sa fécondité de créateur, dont les deux mains ouvertes faisaient tomber des semences, partout où il passait. (p. 761)[20]

Luc's patriarchal prestige as the founder, benefactor and benign ruler of the perfect city-state increases with the passing years:

> Il était le Fondateur, le Créateur, le Père, et tout ce peuple en joie, tous ces convives à toutes ces tables, où l'on fêtait, avec le Travail, les fécondités de l'été, étaient son peuple, ses amis, ses parents, sa famille sans cesse élargie, de plus en plus fraternelle et prospère. Et une acclamation accueillit le voeu d'ardente tendresse qu'il portait à sa ville, monta dans l'air du

soir, roula de table en table, jusqu'aux lointaines avenues. Tous s'étaient mis debout, levaient à leur tour leur verre, buvaient à la santé de Luc et de Josine, le couple de héros, les patriarches du travail, elle, la rachetée, glorifiée comme épouse et comme mère, lui, le rédempteur, qui, pour la sauver, avait sauvé de l'iniquité et de la souffrance le misérable monde du salariat. (p. 938)[21]

The presence of Luc's three female companions heightens his patriarchal status. The self-abnegating Suzanne and Soeurette provide him with moral support and practical assistance in his social task, complementing Josine, the revered Mother of his numerous children, who, in their turn, provide dynastic continuity. The self-abnegation of Suzanne and Soeurette (for their relationship with Luc is non-carnal) is matched by Josine's placid willingness to share her husband with two other women in the interests of his cause; the transcendence of personal claims by the glory of personal service to their master underlines their essential subservience. This subservience (which would hardly commend itself to feminist readers of Zola) is accompanied by a rhetoric of adoration; quasi-religious veneration of Luc, reinforced by a virtual vow of chastity on the part of Suzanne and Soeurette, corresponds to the pattern of Biblical symbolism, together with more general religious elements, which pervades the novel. Female veneration is most marked in the case of Josine, rescued by Luc from a life of hunger and degradation. Their love, described entirely in terms of Luc's ineffable compassion and Josine's undying gratitude, is presented less as a personal relationship than as a piece of social symbolism which reinforces Luc's messianic project and his superior role as the redeemer of society.

The reader is informed that the economic organisation of La Crècherie is based on profit-sharing and worker-participation. Although Zola provides no practical details concerning the distribution of wealth and rewards, capitalist economics, in the form of shares and profits, are retained; this is illustrated by the nature of the economic association between La Crècherie and the farmers of Les Combettes. The constantly repeated formula used to denote the economic structure of the City is Capital, Travail, Talent: 'Jordan apporterait l'argent nécessaire, Bonnaire et ses camarades donneraient les bras, lui [Luc] serait le cerveau qui conçoit et dirige' ('Jordan would provide the money required, Bonnaire and his mates would provide the labour, and his would be the brain that plans and directs') (p. 670). The ideal which La Crècherie fulfils is that of capitalism with a conscience, an ideal which reinforces the fact of Luc's bourgeois philanthropism. The question of worker-participation, however, is more problematical. Although little is said of the political structure of Luc's organic society, it is plain that it is deeply paternalistic. Zola's brand of socialism in *Travail* is one in which governmental organisation, unions and political parties seem hardly to figure at all. The workers do not seem to share in the administration of the City, Luc remains the dominant figure, and power seems concentrated entirely in his hands. In other words, there seems a striking lack of democratic control or delegation of duties. The internal hierarchy of La Crècherie is again highlighted by the negotiations with Les Combettes, which are conducted solely by Luc, the uncontested leader of the City. The only character whose prestige is comparable to that of Luc is Jordan, the gifted technician who embodies the fact that Zola's scientific faith is central to his millenaristic dreams.[22] Thus, whereas the predominant viewpoint in *Germinal* is that of the exploited workers, in *Travail* it is that of the bourgeois reformer, the isolated individual. The working classes, far from occupying the centre of *Travail*, figure most schematically in the novel. While Etienne Lantier struggles against the bourgeoisie, Luc, a bourgeois, conducts a campaign on behalf of the working class.[23] The vision of society implicit in *Travail* relates only marginally and obliquely to contemporary socialism. Although the novel's point of departure is the apocalyptic expectations resulting from the crisis of industrial capitalism, the ideological basis of the social reforms advocated is not scientific socialism but a form of bourgeois paternalism.

The myth of leadership and the institution of a paternalistic society in *Travail* thus provoke questions about the problems of authority, personal freedom and the relationship between the individual and the state.[24] It is significant that female adoration, together with the devotion of the workers, is matched by a strain of rather priggish pomposity in Luc. For his self-approving virtuousness corresponds to the fact that he is the repository of all authority – in other words, a kind of benevolent dictator. Moreover, the elaborate rationalisation of society implies a total correspondence between personal fulfilment and social utility. Social utility is the ideology which guides and channels human energies in Luc's ideal society. Each individual must serve a social purpose. The crafts and hobbies of individual citizens are intended to be useful to the state. In this sense, Zola's social vision displays a latent authoritarianism. Similarly, although Zola's educational philosophy is based on the promotion and free expression of individual talent, it is assumed that private interests will invariably blend with the communal welfare and operate within a harmonious framework of careful social planning. Hence the emphasis on the unremitting gaiety of the citizens; pleasures are communal and popular contentment is expressed *en masse*.

Sex

Zola's sexual and social themes intersect at many points, and his perception of the bourgeoisie is clearly marked by preoccupations of a sexual nature. The conventional image of Zola in the nineteenth century, which still lingers on today, was that of a crude materialist drawn to the squalid and scabrous aspects of life. Henry James, in an article on *Nana*, wrote that Zola's narrowness of vision is to be explained by the 'singular foulness of his imagination'.[1] To persistent charges of obscenity Zola replied that, as a Naturalist, he must grasp the totality of existence. His theoretical writings contain many assertions that it was only through an unidealised and comprehensive portrayal of reality, no matter how sordid, that 'truth' could be perceived and social justice obtained. Moreover, frankness and freedom of vision were necessary complements to the novelist's new scientific role. It is evident, however, that the theme of sex in Zola goes far beyond the expression of a theoretical *parti pris* and that Zola's concern with sex is not merely prurient or voyeuristic. It is now generally acknowledged that the theme of sexuality is a vital shaping factor in Zola's creative vision. The sexual, social and mythical themes of his fiction are inextricably interwoven, and bourgeois attitudes to sexuality cannot be treated in isolation.

In *La Fortune des Rougon* the motifs of sexual loss and separation are closely linked to the novel's social and political themes. The naïve dreams of Silvère and Miette are contrasted with the squalid calculations of the bourgeois Rougons. Zola relates the theme of an unfulfilled and doomed sexuality to the theme of social and political corruption by identifying Silvère and Miette with the Republic and their deaths with the suppression of liberty. In Zola's satirical portrayal of the decaying bourgeois society of the Second Empire in such novels as *La Curée*, *Nana* and *Pot-Bouille*, social corruption is reflected in sexual promiscuity and sterility. The portrayal of sexuality in *Germinal* underlines the respective social situations of miners and bourgeois, while in *Au Bonheur des Dames* the condition of Denise's hand in marriage is a new benevolence on the part of Octave in the running of his department store. In *L'Argent* Mme Caroline's acceptance of her liaison with Saccard is related to the novel's social optimism, and this looks forward to the social and sexual themes of the later novels, in which social optimism corresponds to the cult of fecundity. The sexual problem in Zola cannot be resolved into black-and-white class terms in so far as Zola's workers are no less promiscuous than his bourgeois. But while sex among the working classes is portrayed as the only pleasure which costs nothing, Zola takes a serious view of adultery and promiscuity among the bourgeoisie and upper classes, generally portraying it as a waste of energy and a loss of will. Furthermore, sexual hypocrisy is a prominent bourgeois trait but is not a characteristic of the working classes; and moral guilt in sexual matters (as portrayed in *Une Page d'amour*, for example) is also restricted to the middle and upper classes.

In a newspaper article entitled 'L'adultère dans la bourgeoisie' (*Le Figaro*, 28 February 1881)[2] Zola outlined the three causes which, according to him, led bourgeois women into adultery. These causes are: nervous instability, a result of upbringing and surroundings (the hysterical Valérie Vabre in *Pot Bouille*); the mentality nurtured by a misguided education by parents obsessed with social status (the vain Berthe Josserand); and stupidity, that is, profound ignorance of life, also nurtured by a cloistered education (the ingenuous Marie Pichon). *Pot-Bouille* provides a fictional demonstration of this article; indeed, the prominence of didactic summarising passages which underline the determinism of social upbringing mars the total effect of the novel. The book shows how bourgeois husband-hunting, founded on social ambition and materialist motives, leads to loveless marriages and to adultery. Mme Josserand regards her daughters as objects to manipulate in the quest for rich husbands, instructing them in the techniques of genteel seduction. Berthe, after her marriage, recalls

les trois hivers de chasse à l'homme, les garçons de tout poil aux bras desquels on la jetait, les insuccès de cette offre de son corps sur les trottoirs autorisés des salons bourgeois; puis, ce que les mères enseignent aux filles sans fortune, tout un cours de prostitution décente et permise, les attouchements de la danse, les mains abandonnées derrière une porte, les impudeurs de l'innocence spéculant sur les appétits des niais; puis, le mari raccroché sous un rideau, excité et tombant au piège, dans la fièvre de son désir. (III, 334)[3]

Bourgeois vanity and cupidity are seen as sources of conjugal disunity, for women motivated by social ambition, like Félicité Rougon and Eléonore Josserand, debase marriage by regarding their husbands as vehicles for the furtherance of their own materialist ends. Marriage is a commercial association and a prospective husband merely a financial proposition. Aided by her own example, Mme Josserand has instilled in her daughters a low conception of men as base objects, 'dont l'unique rôle devait être d'épouser et de payer' ('whose sole role in life was to marry and to pay') (III, 80). The fruits of Berthe's education appear with her growing incompatibility with Auguste after only three weeks of marriage: 'C'était le heurt de deux tempéraments, de deux éducations différentes, un mari maussade, méticuleux, sans passion, et une femme poussée dans la serre chaude du faux luxe parisien, vive, saccageant l'existence, afin d'en jouir toute seule, en enfant égoïste et gâcheur' (III, 225).[4] Auguste, the victim, is resentful of her expensive social life, while Berthe quickly becomes a harsh, reflected image of her mother, equally adept in the art of the stereotyped riposte and the ferocious tirade. Her thirst for social distinction leads her to despise her husband for his inability to satisfy her needs: 'elle . . . l'accablait de ce mépris de l'homme, qui était comme la base de son éduca-tion' ('she showed him how profound was her contempt for men, a contempt upon which her entire education had been based') (III, 226). She turns to a lover to provide the gifts her husband cannot afford, but Octave also risks becoming the victim of her education as he progressively merges into the role of Auguste:

Elle, . . . d'une indifférence de fille grandie en serre chaude, ne semblait aimer de l'amour coupable que les sorties furtives, les cadeaux, les plaisirs défendus, les heures chères passées en voiture, au théâtre, dans les restaurants. Toute son éducation rehaussait son appétit d'argent, de toilette, de luxe gâché . . . (III, 258)[5]

The modest Marie Pichon has been brought up according to the highest principles, instilled into her by her smug *petit-bourgeois* parents, the Vuillaumes. In order to foster 'l'honnêteté', expounds Mme Vuillaume, children should be kept under constant domestic surveillance and protected from all pernicious influences. A daughter must always keep her eyes lowered in the streets, 'pour éviter les mauvais spectacles' ('so as to avoid seeing anything improper') (III, 66); she should be educated at home and in her mother's presence because innocence is corrupted in boarding-schools; the reading of newspapers and books should be forbidden (Marie was permitted to read George Sand's seemingly innocuous *André* a few months before her marriage). In the case of Marie, the blank ignorance of childhood has inevitably extended into marriage.[6] Her Romantic sentimentalism is excited by morning mass at Saint-Roch and by her reading of Sand. The consequences of her education are heavily underlined, for Chapter IV culminates in her joyless surrender to Octave, 'entre l'assiette oubliée et le roman' ('between the dirty plate and the novel') (III, 76). It is noted that the novel suffers some damage in the process. Angèle Campardon is also educated at home, since 'les demoiselles apprennent de vilaines choses dans les pensionnats' ('little misses learn the most awful things at boarding-school') (III, 18). And we learn from Zola's working notes (and not from the novel) that Mme Juzeur, who was abandoned without explanation by her husband ten days after their wedding and remains conspicuously impervious to Octave's advances, was 'élevée dans un couvent où le saphisme fleurit' ('brought up in a convent where lesbianism was rife').[7] The theme of bourgeois education is treated elsewhere in Zola. The morbid sexual curiosity of Renée Saccard is seen in terms of the licentious milieu of Imperial society and the perverting effect of that bourgeois institution, a convent education. Pauline Quenu's innocent acceptance of life in *La Joie de vivre* contrasts with the sexual ignorance inflicted on her by her stepmother; the shock caused by the onset of puberty is overcome by her surreptitious reading of her cousin's medical books.

Causes of bourgeois adultery which Zola did not categorise in his *Figaro* article but clearly portrays in his novels are *désoeuvrement* and socially-inspired curiosity. This kind of adultery is illustrated in Renée Saccard (*La Curée*), Juliette Deberle (*Une Page d'amour*), Mme Desforges (*Au Bonheur des Dames*), Mme Hennebeau (*Germinal*) and Gilberte Delaherche (*La Débâcle*).

It is arguable[8] that Zola's portrayal of bourgeois sexuality is ideologically demystifying in the sense that, in novels like *La Curée*, *Nana* and *Pot-Bouille*, he exposes as myth the reactionary supposition (voiced by conservative critics like Brunetière)[9] that the bourgeoisie, unlike the workers, are able to control their natural instincts and that their social supremacy is consequently justified. These novels expose the fallacy of bourgeois public decency and moral superiority. *Pot-Bouille*, in which the main object of Zola's satire is bourgeois sexual hypocrisy, stands out as Zola's most sustained and vituperative attack on the moral pretence of the bourgeoisie. The essence of Octave Mouret's 'sentimental education' is that he learns to distrust appearances. Overriding concern with appearances is treated incidentally in *Germinal* and *La Terre*. The public self-possession of Hennebeau, the mine-manager, contrasts with his private misery. His discovery that his wife is sleeping with her nephew, Négrel, at first enrages him; but he ignores her infidelity, reflecting that it is better to be cuckolded by his bourgeois nephew than by his proletarian coachman. Private humiliation is preferable to public scandal. In *La Terre* Zola emphasises the ironic discrepancy between the assiduously maintained respectability of the retired bourgeois couple, M. and Mme Charles, and the fact that their wealth derives from their management of a brothel for the middle classes in Chartres. One of the best comic scenes in the novel is that in which their innocent, convent-bred granddaughter is told of the origin of her dowry and immediately reveals that she is looking forward to taking over the management of the establishment so that she can introduce more efficient and more profitable methods.

The theme of social hypocrisy in *Nana* is associated with Zola's treatment of the traditional theme of the courtesan in a new and personal way. Unlike Hugo, Musset and Dumas fils in *La Dame aux camélias*, he did not address himself to the rehabilitation of the courtesan through love and sacrifice, but to the theme of the prostitute as agent of corruption. Zola insists on Nana's pernicious social role and on her role as diabolic incarnation of the Fatal Woman. This movement away from Romantic idealisation was characteristic of the Second Empire treatment of the courtesan. But Zola differs from his contemporaries in that there is no corresponding affirmation of bourgeois virtues in his treatment of the theme; on the contrary, *Nana* focuses the social and moral corruption around her, exposing the underlying depravity of those presumed to be morally and socially superior. The prostitute subverts class differences by bringing out the universality of sexual instincts.

The themes of social hypocrisy and the polluting power of Nana are reflected in the central metaphor of the theatre. The theatrical motif defines the tone of Nana's world and articulates symbolically the social criticism which the novel contains. The metaphor of play-acting emphasises that the Second Empire is a hollow charade, and highlights the factitiousness of high society itself, which becomes progressively absorbed into the brittle world of the theatre and the *demi-monde*. The interaction between the *demi-monde* and high society is seen in Nana's ambition to become the social queen of Paris, and her corrupting power is reflected in her imitation by Sabine and the exposure of the emptiness of the Countess's pretensions to morality. The world of the theatre and the world of high society imitate each other, and this symbolic process of assimilation is clinched when the Prince of Wales visits Nana in her dressing room; real royalty and a burlesque king, played by old Bosc, toast each other in mock solemnity.

Zola's attitudes towards marriage and sexual morality are shaped by his strong sense of social duty and social order, and by his preoccupation with controlled energy. Personal behaviour is seen in terms of social equilibrium and the natural order. He demands that women should take seriously their social tasks and is critical of those who do not adequately fulfil their roles as good wives and mothers. He underlines the disastrous consequences of a wife's neglect of her domestic or maternal duties. The hysterical religiosity of Marthe Mouret, reinforced by hereditary neurosis, leads to the destruction of her home, alienation from her husband and indifference to her children. The conflict between sexual passion and maternal duty in *Une Page d'amour* leads to the death of Hélène's daughter.[10] In *Pot-Bouille*, Camille Vabre, Angèle Campardon and Gustave Duveyrier, neglected by their egocentric parents, are left to the corrupting influence of the servants. In *Au Bonheur des Dames* Mme Marty ruins her schoolteacher husband with her extravagant purchases in Mouret's store. On the other hand, an example of wifely devotion carried to the heroic extreme of attempted self-sacrifice is provided by Henriette Weiss, who makes her way through the battlefield at Sedan and attempts to die with her husband at the hands of a Prussian firing-squad. Practical, staunch, hard-working, and exemplary *ménagères*, Zola's ideal women are sources of constant support to their husbands. The ideal of woman as helpmate was clearly expressed in an article entitled 'Femmes honnêtes' (*Le Figaro*, 18 April 1881),[11] in which Zola, to balance his previous piece on 'L'adultère dans la bourgeoisie', declares his admiration of the good qualities of the bourgeoisie as reflected in certain bourgeois women: intelligence, shrewdness, practical ability, hard work, sobriety, honesty, uprightness. These bourgeois virtues (exemplified in Mme Hédouin in *Pot-Bouille*) are embodied, he says, in those capable and intelligent bourgeois women who help their husbands in their work and thus contribute to the national welfare. Zola's sexual politics thus mirror his messianic social vision in the sense that, despite the importance of the theme of female emancipation in his later fiction, his concept of the role of women is patriarchal. His ideal woman, seen as a loyal wife, devoted mother and efficient *ménagère*, is defined by her relationship to her mate. Caroline Hamelin's admiration of Saccard and Clotilde's adoration of Pascal provide thematic links between *Les Rougon-Macquart* and the later fiction, in which the adoring, submissive role of women reinforces the patriarchal social structure of Zola's utopia. Domineering women in Zola (Félicité Rougon, Lisa Quenu, Eléonore Josserand, Mme Chanteau) are never sympathetic.

It is important to note that all of Zola's ideal heroines are or become bourgeois women, that his delineation of the ideal feminine type reflects his approval of certain bourgeois values (hard work, sobriety, *honnêteté*, order, moderation), and that, throughout most of his career, he held conventional, bourgeois views on marriage, the family and sexual morality. As we have seen, he attached great importance to conjugal fidelity: 'Une société tombe lorsque la femme mariée fait concurrence à la fille' ('A society is doomed when married women compete with courtesans').[12] Despite his description of the hollowness of marriage in novels like *La Curée*, *Pot-Bouille* and *Une Page d'amour*, he saw marriage and the family as sources of social stability. In *La Curée* he wanted to show 'à quel effroyable écroulement on en arrive, lorsque les moeurs sont pourries et que les liens de la famille n'existent plus' ('the terrible social breakdown that occurs when all standards of morality are eroded and family bonds no longer exist').[13] The bourgeois marriage of the novelist Sandoz, in *L'Oeuvre*, is seen as an essential condition of productive work. Henriette Sandoz, even-tempered, unpretentious, and an excellent *ménagère*, creates an atmosphere of undisturbed domestic calm and order. The firm conviction of Denise Baudu is that the only natural and legitimate consequence of love is marriage, which, she believes, is a necessary condition of stability and security. The novelette element in *Au Bonheur des Dames* culminates in the conversion of Octave Mouret from a cynically exploitative view of women to the idea of marriage as 'la santé nécessaire, la force et l'ordre même de la vie!' ('the health necessary to life, its very strength and order') (III, 801).

A significant evolution in Zola's attitude to marriage is discernible in *L'Argent*. Caroline Hamelin does not share Denise Baudu's resolute rejection of extra-marital sexuality. Although acknowledging the desirability of marriage, she sees her sexual liaison with Saccard as a kind of vital necessity, almost a natural law. What is now emphasised is not the sanctity of love, but the sanctity of life. Caroline justifies her yielding to Saccard in vitalist terms, as a *natural* act, which she links to an awareness of the ambiguity of all human conduct and an acceptance and affirmation of life's intrinsic goodness. She sees in her love for Saccard a necessary part of life's creativity. *L'Argent*, together with Zola's rejection in *Le Docteur Pascal* of the Christian view of marriage (Clotilde's baby may be a messiah, but he is also illegitimate), marks an important step towards the acceptance in the post-*Rougon-Macquart* works of a virtuous (and fertile) *union libre* as an acceptable substitute for bourgeois marriage. Luc and Josine, like Pascal and Clotilde, remain unmarried; and in Luc's new community marriage is abolished. It must be remembered, however, that marriage is celebrated in both *Fécondité* and *Vérité*, and that the *union libre* of La Crècherie is identical to bourgeois marriage in all but name.

Zola's acceptance of the *union libre* does not, of course, signify sexual licence; he continues to attach great importance to fidelity, family life and responsible parenthood. The bourgeois ethic of moderation informs Zola's attitude to sexuality in the sense that, throughout his work, he contrasts the desirability of moderation with the destructiveness of uncontrolled sexual passion. His ideal heroines are characterised by their *sagesse* and their

well-balanced attitudes to sex. They are invariably constant in
their affections. Zola accentuates the moral opposition between
the virtuous Denise Baudu and the promiscuity of her surroundings. *Au Bonheur des Dames* is, indeed, the narrative of a moral
triumph; Zola fully endorses Denise's (somewhat smug) resistance to the advances of Octave because of what she sees as his
opportunist infatuation. Zola's view was that sexuality, although
not illegitimate, must be regulated and disciplined. Abstinence
and excess are condemned in favour of the control of instinctual
desires in the interests of personal stability and social order.
Women who either represent or are victims of the disruptive
effects of passion include Renée Saccard, Marthe Mouret,
Hélène Grandjean, Nana, Christine (*L'Oeuvre*) and Baroness
Sandorff.

In opposition, then, to the avatars of the *mangeuse d'hommes* and
to frivolous, selfish or ambitious *mondaines* is a group of female
characters who, altruistic and self-sacrificing, represent the values of hope, stoicism and fecundity, and reflect Zola's ideal of
woman as a source and nourisher of life. This series of ideal
women includes Denise Baudu, Pauline Quenu, Henriette Sandoz, Caroline Hamelin, Henriette Weiss, Clotilde Rougon,
Marie (*Paris*) and Josine (*Travail*). These women embody a healthy constancy and an optimistic faith in life in the face of suffering and injustice. Sane and balanced, consoling rather than con-
suming, they dispense calm, protection and security. They are,
in other words, mother-figures: the virtues of Zola's ideal women
(compassion, kindness, self-abnegation) are matriarchal ones.[14]
And their quasi-maternal attitudes are reflected in their compassionate response to social injustice. Denise and Caroline in particular have a keen sense of social duty and social purpose. The
principle of charity is the essence of Pauline Quenu, who distri-
butes food and money to the impoverished local fisherfolk. Her
generosity contrasts with the sterile avarice of her mother, Lisa
Quenu. Her self-abnegation is such that, although in love with
her cousin, Lazare, she relinquishes him to Louise and resigns
herself to nursing their sickly son; her charitable works are a
patent substitute for love and maternal fulfilment. Charity,
hope, stoicism and self-abnegation are the principal characteristics of Caroline Hamelin. But the fact of her childlessness,
echoed by that of Princess d'Orviedo, remains an inconsolable
tragedy. In *L'Argent* philanthropy is still defined by its compensatory value. It is not until the final novel of the cycle, *Le Docteur*

Pascal, that woman's maternal vocation is fulfilled. In *Le Docteur Pascal* Zola states unequivocally, and for the first time in *Les Rougon-Macquart*, that the only true end of sexuality is procreation. *Le Docteur Pascal* and *Fécondité* are the chief expressions of Zola's belief that the end of love is child-bearing and that all else is selfish, frivolous and unnatural. Bourgeois egoism and dissipation are associated with the theme of sterility. Promiscuity, closely related to the sin of indolence, is seen as misdirected sexual energy. Maternity is given a quasi-religious aura in Zola's later works. Virginity and sterility are calamities, while the principle of fecundity is assimilated to Zola's myth of regenerative optimism; it is the motor of social progress, the guarantee of hope and continuity. Celebration of continuity through a pattern of eternal return is identified with the personal salvation of Pascal. Clotilde, by giving him a child, restores to him the vitality and youth he had thought lost; his impersonal quest for scientific truth thus becomes a highly personal discovery of the regenerative powers of fecundity. Similarly, in *Travail*, it is the birth of Luc's child that signals the prodigious growth of La Crècherie. Zola's social and sexual themes are thus linked through the notion of the creative use of the passions.

Fécondité, which Zola considered to be the résumé and culmination of his whole work, is Zola's response to France's declining birth rate and the increasing use of contraceptive techniques. It is a turgid anti-malthusian tract which advocates fecundity as a civic virtue. Birth control, abortion and wet nursing are seen as predominantly bourgeois practices. The novel condemns the bourgeoisie's perversion of nature and punishes it with family disintegration. 'Bourgeois' direction of the sexual act away from its natural end, the transmission of life, corresponds to the symbolic degeneracy and sickliness of certain bourgeois children throughout Zola's fiction: the androgynous Maxime and his haemophiliac son in *La Curée*, *L'Argent* and *Le Docteur Pascal*, Saturnin in *Pot-Bouille*, the delinquent Victor in *L'Argent*, the Beauchênes' son in *Fécondité*. Zola's disapproval of birth control is related to the theme of waste (one of the projected titles of *Fécondité* had been *Le Déchet* [*Waste*]) in the sense that birth control is a waste of potential life while procreation is seen as a source of increased national resources. One of the theses of *Fécondité* is that having numerous children will contribute to the national wealth and welfare; in other words, it will have a social purpose.

Finally, it must be emphasised that Zola's attack on promiscuity is not that of Christian morality, nor (as we have seen) is his ultimate view of marriage that of Christianity. The doctrine of original sin conflicts with Zola's belief in the intrinsic goodness of life and the ultimate beneficence of nature, while the Christian values of renunciation and chastity are incompatible with his myth of fecundity. In *La Faute de l'abbé Mouret*, Zola's deeply anticlerical adaptation of the Genesis myth which centres on the antithesis between religion (sterility) and nature (fecundity), he expresses his hatred of Catholicism for its negation of life, its suppression of natural sexual instincts, and the rule of celibacy. Archangias (like Faujas in *La Conquête de Plassans* and Cognasse in *Vérité*) is a priest in whom chastity is heightened to the point of misogyny. The drama of Serge Mouret looks forward to the odyssey of Pierre Froment, the unifying figure of *Les Trois Villes*. Froment is a priest who has lost his faith and who, after unsuccessfully attempting to instigate ecclesiastical reform, leaves the Church to marry. He rejects the Catholic moral system as deeply repressive: 'Jésus est destructeur de tout ordre, de tout travail, de toute vie. Il a nié la femme et la terre, l'éternelle nature, l'éternelle fécondité des choses et des êtres. Puis, le catholicisme est venu bâtir sur lui son effroyable édifice de terreur et d'oppression.'[15] Zola's work from *Le Docteur Pascal* onwards represents a systematic attack on the obscurantism of the Church, its politically reactionary nature, its hostility to science, and its inability to come to terms with the deepening social problems of the modern world. The social irrelevancy of the Church is noted in *Germinal* and *La Terre* in the miners' distrust of the Abbé Ranvier and the empty church of the Abbé Godard. The Church is also hypocritical in that its charitable aims are belied by its essential concern with power. *Lourdes* evokes the commercialisation of the Church while in *Rome* Zola describes a Papacy ossified by dogma and dominated by a thirst for power. In *La Conquête de Plassans* he had described the political machinations of the Church, attempting to use the new Bonapartist régime as an ally, while in *Pot-Bouille* (as in *Le Ventre de Paris*) it is seen as a bulwark of established society, casting a cloak of respectability over the decomposing world of the bourgeoisie.[16] The Abbé Mauduit reappears in *Travail* as the Abbé Marle: 'Il acceptait . . . les invitations à la Guerdache sans illusions sur les vertus de la bourgeoisie, et il y déjeunait ou y dînait en quelque sorte par devoir, afin de cacher sous le manteau de la religion les plaies qu'il savait là (p. 610).[17] The Church is of course deeply opposed to Luc's utopian society. But the most virulent expression of Zola's anticlericism is *Vérité*, his last and posthumous novel, which describes the conflict between Catholicism and liberal education. In this novel Zola transposes the main elements of the Dreyfus Affair to a Catholic school, where a Jewish schoolmaster is falsely acccused of the pederastic murder of a young schoolboy and the killer is eventually revealed to be one of the teaching monks at the school. Marc Froment, the *instituteur* who proves the schoolmaster's innocence, is presented in extravagantly heroic terms as a magus-like leader who devotes his life to bringing enlightenment to the masses through secular education. *Vérité* is a fierce attack on both the Roman Catholic Church and the Christian religion, coupled with the advocacy of an improved primary education as a means to deliver France from the ignorance and obscurantism imposed by Catholic education. Both *Travail* and *Vérité* culminate in the collapse of the Church and the triumph of Zola's vitalist ideology. Thus, although Zola's work represents a defence of certain bourgeois values, he became increasingly hostile to the established forms of bourgeois religion; and it is important to note that in his final works he attributed great importance to the role of education, which is, after all, the means of inculcating what are bourgeois values, but in a social framework that, it is hoped, will not allow the vices of bourgeois life to take root.

Part II

FOUR PERSPECTIVES

La Curée: Speculation and Dissipation

...Pendant trois annécs, j'avais rassemblé des documents, et ce qui dominait, ce que je trouvais sans cesse devant moi, c'étaient les faits orduriers, les aventures incroyables de honte et de folie, l'argent volé et les femmes vendues. Cette note de l'or et de la chair, cette note du ruissellement des millions et du bruit grandissant des orgies, sonnait si haut et si continuellement, que je me décidai à la donner. J'écrivis La Curée. Devais-je me taire, pouvais-je laisser dans l'ombre cet éclat de débauche qui éclaire le second Empire d'un jour suspect de mauvais lieu? L'histoire que je veux écrire en serait restée obscure.

Il faut bien que je le dise, puisqu'on ne m'a pas compris, et puisque je ne puis achever ma pensée: La Curée, c'est la plante malsaine poussée sur le fumier impérial, c'est l'inceste grandi dans le terreau des millions. J'ai voulu, dans cette nouvelle Phèdre, montrer à quel effroyable écroulement on en arrive, lorsque les moeurs sont pourries et que les liens de la famille n'existent plus. Ma Renée, c'est la Parisienne affolée, jetée au crime par le luxe et la vie `a outrance; mon Maxime, c'est le produit d'une société épuisée, l'homme-femme, la chair inerte qui accepte les dernières infamies; mon Aristide, c'est le spéculateur né des bouleversements de Paris, l'enrichi impudent qui joue à la Bourse avec tout ce qui lui tombe sous la main, femmes, enfants, honneur, pavés, conscience. Et j'ai essayé, avec ces trois monstruosités sociales, de donner une idée de l'effroyable bourbier dans lequel la France se noyait.[1]

This extract from the letter Zola wrote to Louis Ulbach, editor of
La Cloche, on the suspension of the newspaper serialisation of *La
Curée* evokes the three main characters in the novel, vividly illustrates Zola's determination to place their private destinies firmly
within the context of the greedily acquisitive bourgeois society of
Second Empire Paris, and clearly states the novel's principal
themes and images: speculation, dissipation, moral corruption,
misdirected energy, madness, freneticism, degeneration and
waste. The 'physiological' themes of 'l'épuisement prématuré
d'une race' ('the premature extinction of a race') and 'le détraquement nerveux d'une femme' ('the nervous breakdown of a
woman')[2] are subsumed by the Balzacian themes of social change
and bourgeois venality.[3] *La Curée* proclaims the falseness and
hollowness of a society governed by money; and its satire of
speculative frenzy and sexual excess is grounded in moral reprobation and horror at the futile and uncontrolled expenditure of
energy.

I

La Curée is virulent social polemic. It might be described as
journalistic, not so much because of the infusion into the text of
quantities of careful documentation, but because of the extreme
topicality of its themes for the reader of 1871, the *emphase* of its
tone, and its deployment for satirical purposes of vivid and
arresting images. 'It is as a crusading journalist', observes Harry
Levin, 'that [Zola's] resemblance to Dickens comes out most
clearly.'[4] Although the Empire had fallen by the time of the
novel's publication, Zola referred to *La Curée* as 'ce livre de
combat' ('this combative book'), and asked Louis Ulbach, 'Me
faudrait-t-il donner les noms, arracher les masques pour prouver
que je suis un historien, non un chercheur de saletés? C'est
inutile, n'est-ce pas? Les noms sont encore sur toutes les lèvres.'[5]
The serialisation of the novel was stopped by the Government –
ostensibly for immorality, but almost certainly for political
reasons.

    The satire of *La Curée* springs from a sense of moral revulsion
at the degradation of the epoch; Zola's sociological observations
rest, in other words, on certain moral attitudes. The articles Zola
wrote for various republican newspapers (*La Tribune, Le Rappel*
and *La Cloche*) from 1868 to 1870 contained biting attacks on the

dissipations of Imperial high society, the fraudulent financial operations which accompanied the *haussmannisation* of Paris, and the régime's lack of concern for social justice.[6] These articles are echoed by the tone and style of many passages in *La Curée*. Comparisons with Hugo's *Les Châtiments* (1853) are unavoidable. Zola was adding his own, radicalist voice to the republican and liberal voices (like Picard, Guéroult and Ferry) who, increasingly during the 1860s, demanded parliamentary control of public finances and attacked the licentiousness of Imperial society and the autocratic nature of the régime; he stresses the moral decadence of contemporary society, however, rather than its political injustices.

Zola's characters are thus incarnations of a certain society and its values. Saccard and Renée embody the two major preoccupations of Second Empire Paris: money and pleasure. Moreover, the twin themes of *l'or* and *la chair*, the description of Saccard's frenetic quest for wealth and the narration of Renée's incestuous passion for her stepson, are thematically integrated in a blatantly insistent way.[7] Zola's treatment of both property speculation and incest reveals a vision of alienation, dehumanisation and wasted energies in a society dominated by money. He stresses that Renée's desires must be seen as the necessary product of Second Empire Paris; her incest is only explicable in terms of its historical and social context: 'Dans le monde affolé où ils vivaient, leur faute avait poussé comme sur un fumier gras de sucs équivoques' ('In the maddened world in which they lived, their sin had sprouted as on a dunghill oozing with equivocal juices') (I, 481). Speculation and incest are closely related on the level of the narrative: Saccard exploits Renée ('une enseigne dorée à ses spéculations') ('a sign-board to his speculations') (I, 429), using her physical charms to further his business projects; and the theme of incest interlocks with the eventual transfer of property to Saccard. The novel's metaphoric language establishes links between Renée's existence and monetary considerations; *La Curée* depicts, through the destiny of Renée, the destructiveness and hollowness of a society based on purely materialist values. It is not fortuitous that the novel's final sentence refers to the enormous, unpaid bill left behind by Renée's death. Finally, long passages of recapitulation and exposition (Chapters II and III) help to 'explain' the protagonists in terms of their past lives, explicitly linking their individual existences with their social background; similarly, Zola constantly correlates narrative developments with their social settings – a backdrop of balls and dinner-parties emphasises the connections between the life of the individual and that of the group.

The very violence of Zola's denunciation of the Second Empire makes it important to note that he is not making in *La Curée* a general statement about the bourgeoisie as a whole. Although he stresses bourgeois corruption, his portrayal of the bourgeoisie remains ambiguous. Jean Borie remarks of Renée: 'Son histoire illustre bien certaines des ambiguïtés des *Rougon-Macquart:* le monde bourgeois y est à la fois valorisé par le rêve nostalgique d'une décence familiale, d'un bonheur abrité à l'écart (ici la maison de l'île Saint-Louis où, autrefois, la pureté de l'enfant répondait à la sévère probité du père) et dénoncé comme le théâtre de la curée mortelle des appétits'.[8] A basic structural feature of the novel is the symbolic contrast between the Hôtel Saccard and the Hôtel Béraud – suggesting antagonisms within the bourgeoisie and the loss of true bourgeois values. The apogee of Saccard's fortunes corresponds to the construction of the mansion in the Parc Monceau, which is characterised by its vulgar opulence and its pretentious conglomeration of architectural styles: 'C'était un étalage, une profusion, un écrasement de richesses' ('The display of decoration was profuse to oppressiveness') (I, 331). It is a garish emblem of the age: 'cette grande bâtisse, neuve encore at toute blafarde, avait la face blême, l'importance riche et sotte d'une parvenue' ('this great structure, still new and absolutely pallid, showed the wan face, the purse-proud foolish importance of a female parvenu') (I, 332). Saccard's new mansion, with its associations of disorder and excess, is opposed to the chill austerity of the house of Renée's parents on the Ile Saint-Louis. The corruptions of the present are thus opposed to the lost rectitude of the past; traditional bourgeois values, associated with the motif of childhood, have been displaced by the new bourgeois *arrivisme* of the Second Empire. The two *hôtels* are the two poles between which Renée's existence oscillates: purity and corruption, past and present. The perversions of the hothouse are contrasted with the blissful days spent in the children's room in Renée's former home. Renée, who is not without a moral conscience, is torn between two separate and incompatible worlds; the visits to the Hôtel Béraud are interludes which prick her conscience and provoke self-reflection. She thus not only embodies the dissipations of Imperial society but also evokes the moral values of another kind of bourgeoisie; the milieu of Second Empire Paris has corrupted the 'instincts de vieille et honnête bourgeoisie qui dormaient au fond d'elle' ('instincts, slumbering within her, of the honest old middle-class') (I, 334). Zola wrote in his working notes: 'Sa famille représente cette vraie bourgeoisie de Paris, cossue, riche, calme, droite, toute entière aux vieux usages' ('Her family represents the true middle class of Paris, well-to-do, rich, calm, upright, entirely traditionalist').[9] The Saccard *ménage* represents the replacement of the idea of the bourgeois family by that of a kind of debasing commercial association: 'L'idée de famille était remplacée chez eux par celle d'une sorte de commandite où les bénéfices sont partagés à parts égales' ('The family idea was replaced with them by a sort of partnership whose profits are divided in equal shares') (I, 426). Renée's father, survivor from a former age, is the only character in *La Curée* whom Zola describes in unambiguously positive terms.

Images of debasement and degeneration thus translate Zola's satirical vision. Louis Bonaparte, the cardboard dictator, is a debased imitation of Napoleon Bonaparte, the mythic hero. The ostentatious architectural style which characterised the Second Empire, and of which the newly-rich vulgarity of Saccard's mansion is an excellent example, is described as 'ce bâtard opulent de tous les styles' ('that fecund bastard of every style') (I, 332). Hereditary degeneration is symbolic of moral degeneration: Louise de Mareuil is sickly and moribund, while Saccard's offspring is the parasitic and epicene Maxime. Zola makes plain the symbolic and mythical significance of Maxime, whose degeneracy is described as the result partly of heredity, partly of a decadent society:

La race des Rougon s'affinait en lui, devenait délicate et vicieuse. Né d'une mère trop jeune, apportant un singulier mélange, heurté et comme disséminé, des appétits furieux de son père et des abandons, des mollesses de sa mère, il était un produit défectueux, où les défauts des parents se complétaient et s'empiraient. Cette famille vivait trop vite; elle se mourait déjà dans cette créature frêle, chez laquelle le sexe avait dû hésiter, et qui n'était plus une volonté âpre au gain et à la jouissance, comme Saccard, mais une lâcheté mangeant les fortunes faites; hermaphrodite étrange venu à son heure dans une société qui pourrissait. (I, 425)[10]

Zola translates a sense of degeneration through the theme of debased mythology. *La Curée* contains a large number of mythological echoes and references to classical antiquity. Parody and burlesque are used as satiric devices; images of the decadence of the Roman Empire are employed to depict the decomposition of Second Empire society.[11] Saccard's *concierge* inhabits 'un petit temple grec' ('a little Greek temple') (I, 330); the Medea of myth has become Sidonie, a vulgar procuress, 'ratatinée dans sa robe noire de magicienne' ('shrivelled up in her black sorceress's dress') (I, 556), who 'poisons' Renée with her false advice; the 'belles épaules' of Renée, 'si connues du tout Paris officiel' ('beautiful shoulders, so well known to all official Paris') (I, 475), are imaged as 'les fermes colonnes de l'Empire' ('the firm pillars of the Empire') (ibid.), but the dizzy movement of M. de Saffré's erotic dance, 'les "Colonnes" ', suggests that these columns are close to collapse. Renée, surrounded by the 'symphonie en jaune mineur' ('symphony in pale yellow') of the 'petit salon' ('little room') (I, 351), is compared to Diana. Her self-contemplation, self-disgust, and mounting sense of alienation in the final chapter correspond to the dominance of a retrospective and static view, and also the theme of debased myth, in which she figures in projection as a modern Phèdre. The narrative parallels between the tragedy of Phèdre and the story of Renée are transparent and deliberate: 'Décidément, c'est une nouvelle *Phèdre* que je veux faire' ('Certainly, it is a new *Phèdre* that I wish to produce').[12] The horror of Renée's self-recognition when she sees *Phèdre* at the Théâtre Italien with Maxime-Hippolyte is reflected in internal monologue: 'Comme son drame était mesquin et honteux à côté de l'époque antique!' ('How mean and shameful was her tragedy by the side of the idyll of antiquity!') (I, 509). The tragedy of *Phèdre* becomes the melodrama of Renée, while Hippolyte has become an effete young dandy. Renée's mind dwells on the idea of debasement after she leaves the theatre:

Tout se détraqua dans sa tête. La Ristori n'était plus qu'un gros pantin qui retroussait son peplum et montrait sa langue au public comme Blanche Muller, au troisième acte de *La*

Belle Hélène; Théramène dansait le cancan, et Hippolyte man-
geait des tartines de confiture en se fourrant les doigts dans le
nez. (I, 510)[13]

Falseness and factitiousness are primary features of the
bourgeois world described in *La Curée*. One of the first things
Saccard does when he arrives in Paris is invent a false name in
order to spare his brother any embarrassment. His use of a
pseudonym typifies his role as a swindler. Artificiality is suggested by the opening description of the Bois de Boulogne (an
artificial lake), which is seen as a kind of theatrical décor: 'Ce
coin de nature, ce décor qui semblait fraîchement peint, baignait
dans une ombre légère, dans une vapeur bleuâtre qui
achevait de donner aux lointains un charme exquis, un air
d'adorable fausseté' (I, 322).[14] Destruction of the authentic and
natural corresponds to the theme of degeneration: the lawns in
the Parc Monceau, for example, are described as 'pans de velours' ('patches of velvet') upon which 'les promeneuses . . .
traînaient leurs jupes, mollement, comme si elles n'eussent pas
quitté du pied les tapis de leurs salons' ('the ladies on foot trailed
their skirts languorously, as though they had not lifted a foot
from the carpets of their drawing-rooms') (I, 496). The theatrical motif is continued in the mythological *tableaux* mounted by
M. Hupel de la Noue at the *bal travesti*, with Maxime and Renée
playing Narcissus and Echo, and Saccard as Plutus. Second
Empire society, given over to the worship of money, provides an
iconographic representation of itself in these *tableaux vivants:*

> Une nouvelle grotte se creusait; . . . elle devait se trouver au
> centre de la terre, dans une couche ardente et profonde, fissure
> de l'enfer antique, crevasse d'une mine de métaux en fusion
> habitée par Plutus . . . Et les yeux des spectateurs
> s'accoutumaient avec ravissement à ce trou béant ouvert sur
> les entrailles enflammées du globe, à ce tas d'or sur lequel se
> vautrait la richesse d'un monde. (I, 548–9)[15]

No emotion or passion can be real in the society Renée
inhabits. Renée seeks 'authentic' experience in an artifical society, but instead she plunges into perversion. The themes of perversion, corruption and inversion reinforce the theme of degeneration. There are the allusions to the lesbianism of the Mar-

quise d'Espanet and Mme Haffner, the covert homosexuality of Baptiste, and the precocious depravity of Maxime. At the centre of the novel, however, is the theme of incest. Renée and Maxime are morbidly fascinated by the scabrous, and their discussions of perverted and 'criminal' love prefigure their own incestuous relationship. Maxime says: '"Moi, je voudrais être aimé par une religieuse. Hein, ce serait peut-être drôle!. . . Tu n'as jamais fait le rêve, toi, d'aimer un homme auquel tu ne pourrais pas penser sans commettre un crime?"' (I, 328).[16] Whereas the Phèdre of legend suppressed and denied her passion, Renée seeks perverse enjoyment in virile domination of her partner; she seeks escape from boredom in the 'joies cruelles d'un amour qu'elle regardait comme un crime' ('cruel delights of a passion which she regarded as a crime') (I, 483), pursuing in that 'crime' the 'jouissance rare et extrême qui seule pouvait réveiller ses sens lassés, son coeur meurtri' ('rare and supreme enjoyment which alone was able to rouse her tired senses, her wounded heart') (ibid.). Renée conforms with almost caricatural perfection to the characteristics of the literary stereotype of the *belle dame sans merci* as defined by Mario Praz in *The Romantic Agony:* a cruel sensuality, a forceful and violent masculinity matched by the frailty and passivity of her partner: 'Renée était l'homme, la volonté passionnée et agissante. Maxime subissait. Cet être neutre, blond et joli, frappé dès l'enfance dans sa virilité, devenait, aux bras curieux de la jeune femme, une grande fille, avex ses membres épilés, ses maigreurs gracieuses d'éphèbe romain' (I, 485).[17] The attributes of the Fatal Woman and the themes of perversion and sadism are focused by the erotic symbolism of the hothouse exotica.[18]

The themes of degeneration, dehumanisation and factitiousness are closely associated with images of sterility. Maxime, although totally corrupt, remains strangely sexless. It is planned that he should marry Louise de Mareuil, a grotesque emblematic figure whose sexless quality is strongly emphasised. Physical degeneration, identified with a tainted heredity, must inevitably lead, in the case of the sickly Louise, to an early death: 'Contrefaite, laide et adorable, elle était condamnée à mourir jeune' ('Deformed, ugly, and adorable, she was doomed to die young') (I, 434). Social decay, sexual promiscuity, corruption, money, sterility and death are closely associated in Zola's imagination. An archetypal figure of sterility and death is Saccard's sister, the *entremetteuse*, Sidonie, who provides her brother with his 'pre-miers fonds'. With knowledge of every scandal, she embodies, like her brother, the mercenary obsession of the age: 'La femme se mourait en elle; elle n'était plus qu'un agent d'affaires, un placeur battant le pavé de Paris, ayant dans son panier légen-daire les marchandises les plus équivoques, vendant de tout, rêvant de milliards' (I, 371).[19] Her function as *entremetteuse* cor-responds to her sexlessness ('cet hermaphrodisme étrange de la femme devenue être neutre et entremetteuse à la fois') ('this extraordinary hermaphrodism of a woman grown sexless, man of business and procuress in one') (I, 373) and to images of death. Her role in the case of Renée highlights the fact that the latter's marriage is a transaction associated with death. A condition of Saccard's speculative success is precisely the 'death' of Renée's unborn child, which is anticipated by Sidonie and proves to be the vital factor in Saccard's schemes involving the property at Charonne; 'On lui avait acheté deux cent mille francs son nom pour un foetus que la mère ne voulut pas même voir' ('He had received two hundred thousand francs to give his name to a foetus which its mother would not even look at') (I, 386). The significance of Renée's handing over to Saccard the property at Charonne is twofold: first, it expresses the final loss of bour-geois probity, for the property had belonged to Renée's Aunt Elisabeth; and secondly, it means that Rénée's life is placed firmly under the sign of sterility, for she had sworn to leave the property to any child she might have had.

II

The celebrated descriptions of the hothouse and its monstrous tropical flora, associated with the motifs of sadism, perversion and the Fatal Woman, are not successful because they have an excessively lurid flavour and are not satisfactorily absorbed into the novel's thematic structure; but the other symbolic descrip-tive sequences round which the novel is built are more effective, for they constitute a general social statement. The long descrip-tive passages in *La Curée* do not simply reproduce but help to define the social reality with which the novel deals. The style of *La Curée* provides striking confirmation, albeit in an extravagant manner, that the coherence of Zola's novels rests on their dense

metaphorical structures. Despite Zola's theoretical commitment
to minute descriptive accuracy, nothing is further from the truth
than the idea that his Naturalism is synonymous with
inventory-like descriptions based on sheer enumeration or accurate documentation; his descriptions provide not merely the
framework or the tonality of his world but express its very meaning. Moreover, the surface diversity of the *Rougon-Macquart*,
Zola's division of the world into categories and social groups, is
belied by the strong unifying impression given by the dominant
themes and characteristic imagery of his novels. The richness of
the metaphorical structures of Zola's fiction also contrasts with
the relative slightness of his plots and the general lack of psychological complexity of his characters. Although certain patterns of plot, character and situation recur insistently (victims,
violence, catastrophe, death), the anecdotal element is not of
overwhelming interest or importance. If one summarises *La
Curée*, one realises how little action there is in it, considering its
length; one thinks of the novel as a series of tableaux rather than
incidents. The narrative structure centres on the incestuous
involvement of Renée with her stepson and her entrapment in
the ruthless financial machinations of her husband; but the
weight of the novel is born by the repetition, modulation and
symphonic variations of dominant images and motifs, the evocation of mood in terms of concrete symbols and décor, sensations
and texture. The originality of *La Curée* lies in the deployment of
a highly expressive metaphoric language to translate a certain
vision of society; and an explication of the novel's richly textured
prose must concentrate on the recurrence and interlinking of the
motifs of the city, *le regard,* nudity, mirrors, childhood, fire,
water, excess, madness and movement.

The *haussmannisation* of Paris becomes in *La Curée* a symbol of
the general corruptions and injustices of contemporary society.
Haussmann's large-scale transformation of the capital gives *La
Curée* one of its main themes and much of its symbolic décor.
Throughout the Rougon-Macquart cycle, indeed, the topo-
graphical frame of Paris embodies a network of associated
images which define Zola's central themes, encapsulate the
moods of his characters and provide a metaphorical projection of
their dreams and desires. Saccard's materialistic dreams are
equated with conquest of the city; on the very evening of his
arrival in the captial, he walks for hours in the compulsive need

to 'battre de ses gros souliers de provincial ce pavé brûlant d'où il comptait faire jaillir des millions. Ce fut une vraie prise de possession' ('to tread with his clodhopping shoes the burning stones from which he hoped to extract millions of money. It was like taking possession') (I, 359). The city has no realistic identity but, in the tradition of Romantic anthropomorphism of Balzac and Hugo, is transformed into a poetic presence, a landscape of fantasy and nightmare. Above all, the background of the city mirrors Zola's desire to link the lives of his characters to their social context. Like the Halles in *Le Ventre de Paris*, the city in *La Curée* becomes a vast, amplified symbol of the rottenness of contemporary society; Paris itself embodies the excesses and tawdry extravagance of the Imperial régime:

A cette heure, Paris offrait, pour un homme comme Aristide Saccard, le plus intéressant des spectacles. . . Selon l'heureuse expression d'Eugène Rougon, Paris se mettait à table et rêvait gaudriole au dessert. La politique épouvantait, comme une drogue dangereuse. Les esprits lassés se tournaient vers les affaires et les plaisirs . . . Il y avait, au fond de la cohue, un frémissement sourd, un bruit naissant de pièces de cent sous, des rires claires de femmes, des tintements encore affaiblis de vaisselle et de baisers . . . Il semblait qu'on passât devant une de ces petites maisons dont les rideaux soigneusement tirés ne laissaient voir que des ombres de femmes, et où l'on entend l'or sonner sur le marbre des cheminées. L'Empire allait faire de Paris le mauvais lieu de l'Europe. Il fallait à cette poignée d'aventuriers qui venaient de voler un trône, un règne d'aventures, d'affaires véreuses, de consciences vendues, de femmes achetées, de soûlerie furieuse et universelle. Et, dans la ville où le sang de décembre était à peine lavé, grandissait, timide encore, cette folie de jouissance qui devait jeter la patrie au cabanon des nations pourries et déshonorées (I, 367).[20]

One of the keynotes of Zola's talent is a gift for hallucinatory descriptive passages which combine fantasy and concreteness as themes and images converge in moments of heightened vision. The reader of *La Curée* is constantly struck by the frequency of passages characterised by hyperbolic language and a concentration of the central images round which the novel is organised. Cumulative effects constitute a distinctive technique of Zola, and

the characteristic tone of many passages in *La Curée,* suggesting
déchaînement and loss of control, is one of fever and delirium. In
the passage quoted above, which illustrates vividly the dramatic
and metaphorical function of the city, sensuous and materialistic
dreams culminate in a tone of apocalypse and destruction.

Paris both entices and destroys Renée.[21] The opening chapter
of *La Curée* describes her entry and absorption into the city. As
the gas-burners in the Place de l'Étoile light up, 'elle croyait
entendre des appels secrets, il lui semblait que le Paris flamboyant des nuits d'hiver s'illuminait pour elle, lui préparait la
jouissance inconnue que rêvait son assouvissement' (I, 329).[22]

The description of the visit of Renée and Maxime to the Café
Riche is a striking example of Zola's use of the concrete presence
of the city and boulevards as an image of complicity and corruption, and as a mirror of the desires and destinies of his characters.[23] Descriptions of the boulevards seem to stimulate Renée's
erotic feelings: 'Ce large trottoir que balayaient les robes des
filles, et où les bottes des hommes sonnaient avec des familiarités
particulières, cette asphalte grise où lui semblait passer le galop
des plaisirs et des amours faciles, réveillaient ses désirs endormis' (I, 446).[24] The description of the meal and the ensuing
incest is orchestrated according to certain recurrent motifs (the
fascination of the boulevard, the watcher, the mirror and the
prostitute) which give clearly patterned expression to Renée's
vague feelings. The psychological progression of the whole
episode is articulated mainly through the shifting focus between
Renée and the boulevard. During the scene, Renée goes to the
window, and looks out over the boulevard, three times (I,
449–51, 453, 457). On the first occasion, both Renée and Maxime lean out to see an animated impressionist scene, full of noise,
light and laughter. The café tables stretch out into the middle of
the road; men and women sit drinking and laughing against the
noisy background of the crowd and passing omnibuses. This
nocturnal scene has an intoxicating effect on Renée. After the
meal, she leans out of the window again, lost in dream. There is
less traffic, the shops are closed, only the cafés are open, and the
gaslamps are being extinguished:

> Renée ne quitta la rampe qu'à regret. Une ivresse, une lan-
> gueur montaient des profondeurs plus vagues du boulevard.
> Dans ce ronflement affaibli des voitures, dans l'effacement des

clartés vives, il y avait un appel caressant à la volupté et au sommeil. Les chuchotements qui couraient, les groupes arrêtés dans un coin d'ombre, faisaient du trottoir le corridor de quelque grande auberge, à l'heure où les voyageurs gagnent leur lit de rencontre (I, 454).[25]

The description is marked by parallel movements of rise and decline. As outer animation declines and the last pedestrians disappear, Renée's inner excitement mounts. Final silence coincides with the consummation of incest. Afterwards, Renée again goes to the window:

> ... c'était dans les ténèbres du boulevard qu'elle trouvait quelque consolation. Ce qui restait au ras de l'avenue déserte, du bruit et du vice de la soirée, l'excusait ... Les hontes qui avaient traîné là, désirs d'une minute, offres faites à voix basse, noces d'une nuit payées à l'avance, s'évaporaient, flottaient en une buée lourde que roulaient les souffles matinaux. Penchée sur l'ombre, elle respira ce silence frissonnant, cette senteur d'alcôve, comme un encouragement qui lui venait d'en bas, comme une assurance de honte partagée et acceptée par une ville complice. (I, 457–8)[26]

The explicitness of 'hontes', 'vice' and 'ville complice' is matched by the concretisation of atmosphere in the characteristic phrases, 'cette senteur d'alcôve' and 'une buée lourde que roulaient les souffles matinaux'. The implied comparison between the city and a huge brothel echoes both the earlier reference to 'quelque grande auberge' ('some great inn') (I, 454) and the previous comparison between the kiosks and 'des veilleuses espacées dans un dortoir géant' ('night-lights spaced along a giant dormitory') (I, 457). The interpretation of Renée's destiny is thus contained in the selective detail of its description.

An atmospheric sense of general promiscuity informs the Café Riche episode; the constant alternating focus between the secrecy of the private room and the background of the boulevard gives a generalising social significance to the scene. Throughout the novel, Zola attempts repeatedly to establish correspondences between sexual and social corruption by placing frenetic debauchery and the incestuous relationship between Renée and Maxime within the framework of the transformation of Paris.

Expanding outward movement, from the Hôtel Saccard to the whole of *le nouveau Paris*, implies that perdition is identified with the city: '[Ils avaient] une sensation de perfection dans la vie de la rue . . . Chaque boulevard devenait un couloir de leur hôtel' ('[They had] a feeling of perfection in the life of the streets . . . Every boulevard became a corridor of their house') (I, 497).

The motif of spying helps to pattern the Café Riche episode and to evoke a sense of guilt and self-consciousness. The image of the watcher is introduced by the reference to the silhouettes of women behind the white curtains of the private rooms at Brébant's, and by Maxime's stories of adultery and deceit. The reference to spying is continued in the image of the tired faces of the men on the top deck of the Batignolles omnibus, looking up at Renée and Maxime 'du regard curieux des affamés mettant l'oeil à une serrure' ('with the curious glance of famished people peering through a keyhole') (I, 451). Similarly, the knowing glance of the waiter embarrasses Renée. Maxime sends him away as they sit down to eat, but he walks phlegmatically in and out as he serves the dessert, and then returns for a moment to shut the curtains before Renée yields to Maxime.

The motif of observation figures strongly in the novel. Renée is frequently seen watching others, which evokes her boredom and frustration. The novel begins with a description of Renée and Maxime examining the people in the other carriages. A few pages later, Renée herself attracts all eyes at a dinner party given by her husband. Zola stresses that her existence is of a most public nature: 'un amant l'avait quittée, avec scandale, aux yeux de tout Paris' ('a lover had jilted her openly, before the eyes of all Paris') (I, 410). The opening chapter culminates in the scene in which Renée watches Maxime and Louise from the hothouse. But it is usually Renée herself who is observed; and the principal function of the motif of *le regard* is to express her dispossession of her inheritance and of her own self-identity. She is as if surrounded by the grinning faces of her ravishers, corrupters and accusers. She is disturbed by the black figure of Baptiste, whose silent stare seems continually to accuse her. His glance echoes that of the waiter at the Café Riche. Saccard is characterised by his thin-lipped smile (I, 460, 465, 468), while the 'sourires discrets' ('discreet smiles') (I, 471) of Mme Sidonie accompany her attempt to divest Renée of her property. Larsonneau is similarly portrayed as a smiling, merciless financial executioner.

The motif of *le regard* is reinforced by images of nudity, which reflect Renée's self-alienation, her reduction to object-like status, and her final destruction at the hands of Saccard. At the Tuileries ball, Renée is embarrassed by the ogling eyes of the Emperor and the General. In the following chapter, at the Ministry ball, she is a triumph: 'les hommes se bousculèrent pour la voir' ('men jostled each other to see her') (I, 475). Even more daringly *décolletée* than before, she seems to represent the epoch. Eugène Rougon is quick to note the eloquence of her nudity: her low-cut dress, he thinks, cannot fail to carry off a crucial vote in the Chamber of Deputies. Towards the end of the novel, at the *bal travesti*, Renée appears in the most audacious costume she has yet worn:

> un maillot couleur tendre . . . lui montait des pieds jusqu'aux seins, en lui laissant les épaules et les bras nus; et, sur ce maillot, une simple blouse de mousseline, courte et garnie de deux volants, pour cacher un peu les hanches. Dans les cheveux, une couronne de fleurs des champs; aux chevilles et aux poignets, des cercles d'or. Et rien autre. Elle était nue. (I, 555)[27]

The theme of nudity is coupled with the use of mirrors in the evocation of Renée's destruction and loss of identity.[28] The motif of the mirror heightens Renée's self-consciousness as a public figure and underlines her sense of futility. An immense mirror covers the wall of the first landing in Saccard's mansion: 'Renée montait, et, à chaque marche, elle grandissait dans la glace; elle se demandait, avec ce doute des actrices les plus applaudies, si elle était vraiment délicieuse, comme on le lui disait' (I, 333).[29] It is the image of Renée contemplating herself in the mirror, 'se perdant dans une subite rêverie' ('lost in a sudden reverie') (I, 406), which enraptures Maxime. In the private room at the Café Riche, 'elle jouissait profondément de ce mobilier équivoque, qu'elle sentait autour d'elle; de cette glace claire et cynique, dont la pureté, à peine ridée par ces pattes de mouche ordurières, avait servi à rajuster tant de faux chignons' (I, 448–9).[30] Renée's self contemplation in the high wardrobe mirror in the penultimate chapter brings together the themes of nudity and the mirror, and, although marked by a banal internal monologue, represents her climactic awareness of her own destruction and sol-

itude. She stares at her reflection in amazement, 'toute préoc-
cupée par l'étrange femme qu'elle avait devant elle' ('quite taken
up with the strange woman she beheld before her') (I, 572). The
bourgeois Renée with the golden childhood and Renée the corrupt society figure are thus brought into confrontation. Renée's
dispossession of her fortune and her personal 'violation' are like
a slow re-enactment of her distant, quite literal rape. This is
linked to the development of the nudity theme, which culminates
in the repeated, despairing question, 'Qui l'avait mise nue?'
('Who had stripped her naked?') (ibid.), and in Renée's final,
hallucinated vision of Saccard and Maxime stripping her naked.
The theme of nudity thus corresponds to her self-disgust and her
vision of defilement. Dominant themes and images are linked in
a moment of revelation: 'Elle savait maintenant. C'étaient ces
gens qui l'avaient mise nue. Saccard avait dégrafé le corsage, et
Maxime avait fait tomber la jupe. Puis, à eux deux, ils venaient
d'arracher la chemise' (I, 575).[31] She recognises her value in the
eyes of Saccard as an economic investment, a manipulated
object:

> Renée, en regardant les deux apparitions sortir des ombres
> légères de la glace, recula d'un pas, vit que Saccard l'avait
> jetée comme un enjeu, comme une mise de fonds, et que
> Maxime s'était trouvé là, pour ramasser ce louis tombé de la
> poche du spéculateur. Elle restait une valeur dans le porte-
> fueille de son mari . . . (I, 574)[32]

Renée's sense of guilt and her disgust at her own nudity are
intensely associated with objects. The profusion of objects and
discarded clothes in her luxurious dressing room, which seems
an extension of her naked body, now seem strange and oppressive:

> . . . la baignoire exhalait l'odeur de son corps, l'eau où elle
> s'était trempée, mettait, dans la pièce, sa fièvre de femme
> malade; la table, avec ses savons et ses huiles, les meubles,
> avec leurs rondeurs de lit, lui parlaient brutalement de sa
> chair, de ses amours, de toutes ces ordures qu'elle voulait
> oublier. Elle revint au milieu du cabinet, le visage pourpre, ne
> sachant où fuir ce parfum d'alcôve, ce luxe qui se décolletait
> avec une impudeur de fille, qui étalait tout ce rose. La pièce

était nue comme elle; la baignoire rose, la peau rose des tentures, les marbres roses des deux tables s'animaient,
s'étiraient, se pelotonnaient, l'entouraient d'une telle
débauche de voluptés vivantes, qu'elle ferma les yeux, bais-
sant le front, s'abîmant sous les dentelles du plafond et des
murs qui l'écrasaient (I, 576).[33]

It is a commonplace of Zola criticism to note that he created a
world in which men and women are crushed by things; but some
of the ways in which he communicates his vision, and some of its
implications, have been insufficiently explored. Renée's existence, as we have seen, is defined by frustration, ennui and
corruption; her dissipation corresponds to her lassitude, her
moods of dreaming passivity and her vague yearnings. The
opening pages of *La Curée*, which introduce us to Renée, establish
an equation between 'l'ecocurement du luxe' ('the fulsomeness
of luxury') (I, 328) and 'le vide de son être' ('the void of her
existence') (I, 324); the outward splendour of her life contrasts
with her despairing sense of futility. Exhaustive descriptions of
material objects, of the sumptuous physical décor of bourgeois
existence, express a vision of a society which, dominated by the
profit motive, reduces people to the status of things. If we adopt
the Goldmann/Lukács theory that the essence of the novel as a
genre is a search for authentic values in an inauthentic society,
then we will conclude that the importance of Renée's vision
before the mirror lies in her recognition of the inauthenticity of
Second Empire society, her awareness (to use Marxist terminology) of her own reification.[34] She realises that, in the eyes of
society, she is seen and valued in commercial terms, as a mere
marketable commodity, another glittering artifact; she exists in a
society which eliminates human values and denies her separate
identity as a person. As we have seen, her primary function at
the dinner party given by Saccard in Chapter I is to display his
wealth by wearing expensive jewels, while her plunging neckline
will have important legislative advantages for the régime.
Moreover, the conditions of Renée's dowry virtually make her a
real-estate investment for Saccard: 'il la regardait un peu comme
une de ces belles maisons qui lui faisaient honneur et dont il
espérait tirer de gros profits' ('he looked upon her in a measure
as upon one of those fine houses which did him credit and which
would, he hoped, yield him a large profit') (ibid.).

The motifs of guilt, transgression, corruption, defilement, destruction and death correspond to nostalgia for a lost paradise, for the innocence and purity of childhood. *L'homme zolien*, thrust into a state of rupture and alienation both from his environment and from himself, longs for unity and harmony; the motif of childhood expresses this desire for escape. The motif of childhood and images of the past are particularly prominent in *La Curée*, which may indeed be read as a novel of lost innocence. In *La Curée*, as Jean Borie has observed, 'la bourgeoisie et le corps [in the person of Renée] sont déchus de l'idylle enfantine, livrés aux loups du capitalisme et de la sexualité' ('the bourgeoisie and the body have lost touch with the childhood idyll, and are delivered to the wolves of capitalism and sexuality').[35] Renée's apartment, the hothouse and her childhood room in her parents' house on the Ile Saint-Louis all become different kinds of refuge.

Renée's self-alienation corresponds, as we have seen, to self-disgust; contemplation of her naked body in the wardrobe mirror fills her with anger and shame: 'un mépris de sa chair l'emplissait d'une colère sourde contre ceux qui la laissaient ainsi' ('contempt of her flesh filled her with mute anger against those who had left her thus') (I, 572); and sensing that she has become old ('Comme elle était vieille!') ('How old she looked!') (ibid.), her thoughts are cast back to her childhood as images of the past suddenly rise up before her: she sees herself when she was seven years old in the dark Hôtel Béraud, one Christmas when her aunt bought some new dresses for her and her sister. This description recalls the detailed evocation of her childhood at the end of Chapter II: 'dans cette maison morte, dans ce cloître, il y avait un nid chaud et vibrant, un trou de soleil et de gaieté, un coin d'adorable enfance, de grand air, de lumière large' ('in this lifeless house, in this cloister, there was one warm nest full of life, a corner of sunshine and gaiety, a nook of childhood, of fresh air, of bright light') (I, 401). The children's room, reached through a maze of stairways and corridors, forms a sort of belvedere overlooking the Seine. Full of sunlight and laughter, this room becomes a hidden refuge in which Renée and her sister spend their holidays: 'la chambre devint un paradis' ('the room became a paradise') (ibid.). At the end of the novel, immediately following the description of the shimmering, triumphant procession in the Bois de Boulogne, Renée revisits the Hôtel Béraud for the last time – returning, that is, to her childhood. The children's room is now empty and silent. The themes of loss, purity and corruption crystallise as she opens the window and leans out: 'Renée étouffait, au milieu de cet air gâté de son premier âge. Elle ouvrit la fenêtre, elle ragarda l'immense paysage. Là rien n'était sali' ('Renée was stifled amid this tainted atmosphere of her childhood. She opened the window, she looked out upon the boundless landscape. There nothing was soiled') (I, 598). The city which Renée had surveyed from her window as a child is a place which had not yet subjected her to its corrupting influence.

III

If Renée's life retracts, ending in dereliction and death, the existence of Saccard, embodiment of speculation, seems to describe a process of constant and triumphant expansion. Saccard is characterised by remarkable dynamism, restless energy, huge ambition, egocentricity, cynicism, an utter lack of principles, single-mindedness, and the profligacy involved in his financial swindles. An obvious way of exploring Zola's imaginary universe is to study it from the Bachelardian perspective[36] of the material images which inform its texture and meanings; the cardinal themes of profligacy and waste, for example, are reinforced by images which suggest ephemerality and dissolution. The relationship between speculation on the one hand, and destruction, dissolution and impermanence on the other thus corresponds to the interlinking of images of gold, fire and liquidity: 'Aristide Saccard, depuis les premiers jours, sentait venir ce flot montant de la spéculation, dont l'écume allait couvrir Paris entier' ('From the very beginning Aristide Saccard felt the advent of this rising tide of speculation, whose spume was in the end to cover the whole of Paris') (I, 367). It is the time of 'cet agio formidable sur la vente des terrains et des immeubles, qui allumait, aux quatre coins de la ville, la bataille des intérêts et le flamboiement du luxe à outrance' ('that formidable piece of jobbery in the sale of real property, which gave rise in every corner of the town to the conflict of interests and the blaze of unrestrained luxury') (I, 368). Saccard begins to lay his plans: 'il savait que la pluie d'or qui en battait les murs tomberait plus dru chaque jour' ('he knew that the shower of gold which was beating down upon the walls would fall more heavily every day') (I, 387).

   The passage in which Saccard and Angèle look out over Paris from a restaurant window on the Buttes Montmartre evokes Saccard's dream of turning the city into gold. Marine images ('cet océan de maisons aux toits bleuâtres, pareils à des flots pressés') ('that sea of houses with blue roofs, like surging billows') (ibid.) correspond to the throbbing life of the city and to images of fire, light, fluidity and melting: 'Oui, oui, j'ai bien dit, plus d'un quartier va fondre, et il restera de l'or aux doigts des gens qui chaufferont et remueront la cuve' ('Yes, yes, I said so, more than one district will be melted down, and gold will stick to the fingers of those who heat and stir the mortar') (I, 388). Saccard, carried away by the future transformation of the city, is pictured as an alchemist dreaming of producing gold out of bricks and mortar.

   The descriptions of Saccard's elaborate speculative manoeuvres, and of Renée's implication in them, are characterised by sustained fantasy and hyperbole. His period of mastery as a speculator is evoked by an extended image of an ever-expanding sea of gold coins in which he swims:

> Saccard s'affamait, sentait ses désirs s'accroître, à voir ce ruissellement d'or qui lui glissait entre les mains. Il lui semblait qu'une mer de pièces de vingt francs s'élargissait autour de lui, de lac devenait océan, emplissait l'immense horizon avec un bruit de vagues étrange, une musique métallique qui lui chatouillait le coeur; et il s'aventurait, nageur plus hardi chaque jour, plongeant, reparaissant, tantôt sur le dos, tantôt sur le ventre, traversant cette immensité par les temps clairs et par les orages, comptant sur ses forces et son adresse pour ne jamais aller au fond. (I, 416)[37]

The money flowing from his strongbox is seemingly inexhaustible: 'Ce fleuve d'or, sans sources connues, qui paraissait sortir à flots pressés de son cabinet, étonnait les badauds. ～' ('This flood of gold with no known source, which seemed to flow from his office in rapidly-recurring waves, astonished the gaping onlookers') (I, 420).

   Images of dissolution (water) and engulfment (fire) reflect Renée's alienation and loss of self. Like Emma Bovary, she has nothing firm or permanent to hold on to. Having run up huge debts, she is eventually dispossessed of all she has except for the property at Charonne, to which she remains obstinately attached: 'Dans cette fortune, qui avait les clameurs et le débordement d'un torrent d'hiver, la dot de Renée se trouvait secouée, emportée, noyée' ('In this fortune, which clamoured and overflowed like a winter torrent, Renée's dowry was shaken, carried off and drowned') (I, 436). The motif of drowning recurs in her climactic sense of self-disgust and self-alienation, as she contemplates her life since her marriage:

> Sa vie se déroulait devant elle. Elle assistait à son long effare-ment, à ce tapage de l'or et de la chair qui était monté en elle, dont elle avait eu jusqu'aux genoux, jusqu'au ventre, puis jusqu'aux lèvres, et dont elle sentait maintenant le flot passer sur sa tête, en lui battant le crâne à coups pressés. (I, 573)[38]

Images of liquidity, together with the motifs of gold and flesh, are linked to Renée's madness, as her sanity seems to be drowned, progressively and fatally, in a sea of gold.

Images of flames and sulphurous heat are closely associated with the frenzied embraces of Renée and Maxime in the hot-house. They evoke passion, excess and damnation; fire images complement images of *la curée*, fever and sensuality; and the themes of dissipation and speculation, gold and flesh, are linked by fire imagery, for Saccard is compared to a blacksmith twisting Renée 'dans les flammes de sa forge, se servant d'elle, ainsi que d'un métal précieux, pour dorer le fer de ses mains' ('in the flames of his forge, using her as a precious metal with which to gild the iron of his hands') (I, 575). The motifs of exoticism and the hothouse, and an intensification of images of heat and limit-less expenditure, correspond to the delirious self-abandonment which characterises the period of perversion with Maxime: 'elle eut un cauchemar d'étranges amours, au milieu de bûchers, sur des lits chauffés à blanc' ('she had a nightmare of strange pas-sions amid flaring logs on white-hot beds') (I, 470).

Renée's desire for oblivion also corresponds to images of fire and heat, which translate the sense of numbness and helpless-ness which progressively encloses her. Throughout the conversa-tions about money with Saccard and Sidonie following the incest, there is stress on heat and fire. The heat numbs Renée into a state of delicious torpor, taking away her self-awareness and dissipating her remorse. The fire becomes a refuge, a variation on the theme of return to the protection of childhood:

> Dans cet air brûlant, dans ce bain de flammes, elle ne souffrait presque plus; sa douleur devenait comme un songe léger, un vague oppressement, dont l'indécision même finissait par être voluptueuse. Ce fut ainsi qu'elle berça jusqu'au soir ses remords de la veille, dans la clarté rouge du foyer, en face d'un terrible feu qui faisait craquer les meubles autour d'elle, et lui ôtait, par instants, la conscience de son être. (ibid.)[39]

As Renée listens to the cajoling tones of Mme Sidonie, the room seems filled with a large red glow; she is lulled into a dreamlike state as Mme Sidonie extracts money from her. She is finally left alone by the dying fire, confused and exhausted, her head full of dancing figures, the voices of Saccard and Sidonie, and the fateful images of that day and of the previous night.

The principal structural features and narrative procedures of *La Curée* are fairly obvious. But although the close affinities of theory, technique and subject-matter between Zola and the Impressionists have received quite extensive treatment from critics,[40] the relationship between Zola's stylistic impressionism and his basic themes can be still further emphasised. It is especially important to recognise, for example, that the constant impressionism of detail which characterises Zola's descriptions corresponds to perpetual movement and agitation.

A novel by Zola is usually remarkable for its creation of a total atmosphere, for the concrete density of its texture, and for its pictorial and sensuous power. Zola had a markedly plastic imagination, a keen awareness of form, texture, colour and light. His descriptions display a detailed orchestration of sense-impressions; and it is natural that much of his imagery should be drawn from sensory experience, given his materialist conception of the influence of milieu, for it is on the level of sensations that man apprehends the world. Henry James was quick to note Zola's striking ability to render experience into palpable terms, into 'immediate vision and contact'.[41] The novels in which descriptive impressionism figures most prominently, apart from *La Curée* (1872), are *Le Ventre de Paris* (1873), *La Faute de l'abbé Mouret* (1875), *Une Page d'amour* (1878) and *Nana* (1880) – that is, the novels written when the Impressionists were at the height of their powers. *Le Ventre de Paris,* which is famous for its immense impressionist food-tableaux, reflects Zola's vigorous 'modernist' sympathies in art and his recent contact with the Impressionist painters. The narrative is carried forward, the themes developed, and the moods of the characters expressed, through sheer description and sensuous evocation. Ideas are presented schematically and with their emotional force. Florent brings an alert sensibility into the Halles, acting as the reader's 'eye'; his reactions are made more acute by his hunger, and his thin, black figure sets off the colourful descriptions he provokes. The presence of the painter, Claude Lantier, sanctions the stylistic and verbal luxuriance of the novel, its sumptuous pictorial set-pieces which merge into fantasy and hallucination.

One aspect of Zola's stylistic impressionism is the fact that his descriptions are shaped and limited by the subjective point of view of an observer. Rather than being introduced into the novel by a systematic Balzacian exposition or an omniscient global description of milieu, the reader is given the fragmentation and immediacy of an outsider's view: the confused impressions of Florent, for example, as he arrived in the Halles (or Gervaise in *L'Assommoir,* Etienne in *Germinal* and Jean Macquart in *La Terre*). We are offered the haphazard visual and sensuous impressions of the character as they develop, without the interpretation usually supplied by an omniscient author; or rather, the impression itself precedes identification and explanation. Effects of immediacy mean that the character and the reader are brought into direct confrontation with things rather than being distanced from them. And because of the weight Zola places on description, the natural order of things is reversed: objects and things become the real protagonists of his novels and the human element is only incidentally mentioned. Claude Duchet writes: 'Infidèle déjà à son projet "naturaliste", Zola fait moins dans *La Curée* une étude de personnages placés dans un milieu que l'étude d'un milieu placé dans des personnages' ('Already disregarding his "naturalist" project, Zola produces in *La Curée* less a study of characters placed in a certain milieu than a study of a milieu placed within certain characters')[42] It is indeed hardly possible to make a distinction between the foreground and the background in *La Curée*. Moreover, as we have seen, the long descriptions of houses, furniture, social gatherings, and so on, do not have a merely documentary function, but express a vision of an individual crushed by things, alienated from her environment.

The essence of Zola's impressionism in *La Curée* is movement and instability. The rigid and static quality of Zola's characters, which is reflected in their being accompanied almost always by a *description-leitmotiv* every time they appear (a brief physical notation or a reminder of their dominant character-trait) contrasts with the vibrancy of his descriptions. Lengthy descriptions naturally have the effect of suspending the flow of the narrative; but although there is relatively little narrative movement in *La Curée* the novel is not static but full of animation. Throughout the novel, the motifs of frenetic movement and dizzy excess correspond to the motifs of flux and dissolution. Recurring water imagery suggests both movement and dissolution, and combines with the play of light which decomposes surfaces, objects and buildings. Effects of decomposition and dissolution correspond to the fact that impressionist descriptions become a series of fused images, a homogeneous blur, in which the general impression eclipses particular detail. The volatility of the phenomenal scene in Zola, made up of fragmented and mingled sense perceptions, creates a sense of swarming multiplicity. The frequent use of abstract nouns renders the images even less concrete. Even inanimate things in Zola, as everyone knows, seem to be set in motion, to vibrate with a dynamic inner life.

The themes of money and pleasure are linked by the motifs of movement, *débandade* and waste. Renée's sensual experiments, her financial extravagance, and the massive and frenetic scale of Saccard's speculations, are characterised by a total lack of control. Renée and Saccard balance each other in that they both engage in excess; and this dizzy excess corresponds to perpetual movement: 'Saccard, après avoir quitté l'Hôtel-de-Ville, pouvant mettre en branle un roulement de fonds considérable, se lança dans la spéculation à outrance, tandis que Renée, grisée, folle, emplissait Paris du bruit de ses équipages, de l'éclat de ses diamants, du vertige de sa vie adorable et tapageuse' (I, 399).[43] Vertiginous expansion and the urge towards destruction correspond to the motifs of movement, flux and dissolution. We see an unstable world, characterised by a sense of irresistible pressures and fatal forces, moving with increasing speed towards destruction. The characteristic narrative rhythm of a Zola novel is one of accelerating movement. The recurring use in *La Curée* of the words 'folie', 'fièvre', 'galop', 'souffle', 'danse' and 'défilé' implies movement and speed. The city becomes even more closely associated with vice, temptation and degradation after Renée and Maxime have contracted their incestuous relationship; and the search for morbid pleasures in the streets of Paris, and their fascination with the new real-estate constructions, reach a frenetic pitch: 'Les amants avaient l'amour du nouveau Paris. Ils couraient souvent la ville en voiture' ('The lovers doted on the new Paris. They often drove through the town by carriage') (I, 496).

To excess and movement corresponds a kind of manic delirium in the characters. The key words and the general lexical tone of *La Curée* reflect a sense of madness and instability. Saccard's dreams of the future transformation of Paris merge into a hallucination of destruction, a vision of frenetic madness: 'Mais ce sera la folie pure, le galop infernal des millions, Paris soûlé et assommé!' ('But there will be a sheer orgy, a bacchanal of millions, Paris drunk and overwhelmed!') (I, 389–90). At times he seems to be half demented. Images of movement, fever and freneticism combine with recurrent images of fire and heat to evoke his frenzied speculative activity: 'cette danse des millions qu'elle [Paris] avait mise en branle' ('this dance of gold which it [Paris] had led off') (I, 418); 'ses fièvres chaudes, sa folie de la pioche et du moellon' ('its violent fever, its stone-and-pickaxe madness') (ibid.); 'La fièvre de spéculation sur les terrains, la hausse furieuse sur les immeubles' ('The fever of speculation on land, the wild inflation of property values') (I, 419); 'ce Paris brûlant et inassouvi' ('this burning and insatiable Paris') (ibid.).

The vast edifice of Saccard's schemes and ambitions corresponds to the actual buildings he inhabits and to his movement from one house to another. His ascendant fortunes are marked by changes in his dwelling; he leaves the Rue Saint-Jacques for an elegant rented flat in the Marais, and then, on his marriage, he moves into 'un superbe appartement, dans une maison neuve de la rue de Rivoli' ('an imposing flat in a new house in the Rue de Rivoli') (I, 386). Images of excess, nudity, fire and gold combine in the descriptions of his most spectacular dwelling, the mansion in the Parc Monceau. The life of individual buildings is defined by images of frenetic activity. The description of Saccard's apartment in the Rue de Rivoli, for example, is characterised by ceaseless movement and giddy excess:

Singulier appartement, que ce premier étage de la rue de Rivoli. Les portes y battaient toute la journée; les domestiques y parlaient haut; le luxe neuf et éclatant en était traversé continuellement par des courses de jupes énormes et volantes, par des processions de fournisseurs, par le tohu-bohu des amies de Renée, des camarades de Maxime et des visiteurs de Saccard. (I, 414)[44]

Saccard receives daily vast numbers of profiteers of the most varied kinds: 'toute l'écume que les tempêtes de Paris jetaient le matin à sa porte' ('all the scum that the tempests of Paris hurled at his door every morning') (Ibid.). The apartment becomes a public thoroughfare, a centre of promiscuous activity, which engulfs all who enter. Contrasting images of old and new, cold and heat, silence and noise, total immobility and dynamic movement, are expressed in the symbolic juxtaposition of Saccard's new mansion and the silent, austere house of Renée's parents, who, as we have seen, represent the lost respectability of a former age: 'Parfois, le mari et la femme, ces deux fièvres chaudes de l'argent et du plaisir, allaient dans les brouillards glacés de l'île Saint-Louis. Il leur semblait qu'ils entraient dans une ville morte' (I, 399).[45]

The very name of Saccard evokes both money ('sac d'écus') and the idea of destruction and ruin ('saccage'). Saccard's dynamism and his constant 'besoin d'expansion' ('need for expansion') (I, 360) find expression in the gutting of entire buildings and the destruction of whole quarters of Paris. The theme of speculation connotes both destruction and instability. Wild agitation corresponds to emptiness, activity to absence. Like his house, Saccard's precarious fortune is built on a void: 'D'aventure en aventure, il n'avait plus que la façade dorée d'un capital absent' ('Passing from adventure to adventure, he now only possessed the gilded façade of a missing capital') (I, 463). Images of an abyss, of collapse, subsidence and apocalyptic disaster express the total insecurity of his fortune: 'des sociétés s'écroulaient sous lui, de nouveaux trous se creusaient plus profonds, par-dessus lesquels il sautait, ne pouvant les combler' ('companies crumbled beneath his feet, new and deeper pits yawned before him, over which he had to leap unable to fill them up') (ibid.). The essence of Saccard is dissipation and self-destructive waste. The descriptions of his financial gymnastics and of his remarkable mansion are defined by increased movement, flux and delirium. Zola's art is in many ways an art of hyperbole. A hyperbolic vocabulary ('d'énormes bénéfices', 'sa fortune colossale') ('huge profits', 'his colossal fortune') (I, 436) corresponds to dizzy excess, increasing madness and fever: 'C'était la démence pure, la rage de l'argent, les poignées de louis jetées par les fenêtres' ('It was pure folly, a frenzy of money, handfuls of louis flung out of the windows') (ibid.). The stress on accelerated movement and animation points towards the disappearance of all constrictions or constraints, of all fixity and permanence: 'Le coup de vent de la vie contemporaine, qui avait fait battre les portes du premier étage de la rue de Rivoli, était devenu, dans l'hôtel, un véritable ouragan qui menaçait d'emporter les cloisons' (I, 437).[46] The mansion, like the apartment in the Rue de Rivoli, becomes a kind of public meeting-place, where nothing is hidden from the watching eyes of the servants.

> Au milieu de ces appartements princiers, le long des rampes dorées, sur les tapis de haute laine, dans ce palais féerique de parvenu, l'odeur de Mabille traînait, les déhanchements des quadrilles à la mode dansaient, toute l'époque passait avec son rire fou et bête, son éternelle faim et son éternelle soif. C'était la maison suspecte du plaisir mondain, du plaisir impudent qui élargit les fenêtres pour mettre les passants dans la confidence des alcôves. Le mari et la femme y vivaient librement, sous les yeux de leurs domestiques. Ils s'étaient partagé la maison, ils y campaient, n'ayant pas l'air d'être chez eux, comme jetés, au bout d'un voyage tumultueux et étourdissant, dans quelque royal hôtel garni, où ils n'avaient pris que le temps de défaire leurs malles, pour courir plus vite aux jouissances d'une ville nouvelle. (I, 437–8)[47]

The motifs of gold ('rampes dorées'), appetites ('son éternelle faim et son éternelle soif') and frenetic movement ('les déhanchements des quadrilles . . . dansaient', 'un voyage tumultueux et étourdissant', 'pour courir plus vite aux jouissances'), merge in a tone of unreality, heightened by the use of phrases in apposition.

The striking characteristic of representative passages is a rich intermingling of thematic imagery and the translation of themes and mood into graphically concrete terms. Associated images and metaphors succeed each other in hallucinatory fashion; metaphor crowds upon metaphor, reflecting a general sense of feverish and yet futile activity:

> Cependant la fortune des Saccard semblait à son apogée. Elle brûlait en plein Paris comme un feu de joie colossal. C'était l'heure où la curée ardente emplit un coin de forêt de l'aboiement des chiens, du claquement des fouets, du flamboiement des torches. Les appétits lâchés se contentaient enfin, dans l'impudence du triomphe, au bruit des quartiers écroulés et des fortunes bâties en six mois. La ville n'était plus qu'une grande débauche de millions et de femmes. Le vice, venu de haut, coulait dans les ruisseaux, s'étalait dans les bassins, remontait dans les jets d'eau des jardins, pour retomber sur les toits, en pluie fine et pénétrante. Et il semblait, la nuit, lorsqu'on passait les ponts, que la Seine charriât, au milieu de la ville endormie, les ordures de la cité, miettes tombées de la table, noeuds de dentelles laissés sur les divans, chevelures oubliées dans les fiacres, billets de banque glissés des corsages, tout ce que la brutalité du désir et le contentement immédiat de l'instinct jettent à la rue, après l'avoir brisé et souillé. Alors, dans le sommeil fiévreux de Paris, et mieux encore que dans sa quête haletante du grand jour, on sentait le détraquement cérébral, le cauchemar doré et voluptueux d'une ville folle de son or et de sa chair. Jusqu'à minuit, les violons chantaient: puis les fenêtres s'éteignaient, et les ombres descendaient sur la ville. C'était comme une alcôve colossale où l'on aurait soufflé la dernière bougie, éteint la dernière pudeur. Il n'y avait plus, au fond des ténèbres, qu'un grand râle d'amour furieux et las; tandis que les Tuileries, au bord de l'eau, allongeaient leurs bras dans le noir, comme pour une embrassade énorme. (I, 435)[48]

The themes of speculation and sensuality, *or* and *chair*, money and women, interact in this paradigmatic evocation of the frenzied social pursuits of the Second Empire. The interlinked motifs of the passage are the city, animality, appetites, fire, water, disorder and madness. The principal syntactic characteristic of the extract is the eclipse of human subjects by abstract nouns and things. The subject of the opening sentence is 'la fortune': subsequent subjects are 'la curée', 'les appétits', 'la ville', 'le vice'. A nominal syntax and the repetition of appositional phrases reinforce the dominance of things. The assumption of dominating importance by things and abstract nouns, the striking absence of any human agent or subject, suggests total *débandade* – the lack of any controlling or directing human consciousness. Images of 'la curée' in the third and fourth sentences suggest the reduction of men to animal level and the unbridled indulgence of instinctual appetites; fire and water images ('Elle brûlait', 'feu de joie', 'flamboiement des torches', 'le vice . . . coulait') suggest dissolution and impermanence; images of madness ('le détraquement cérébral', 'une ville folle'), coupled with the reference to feverishness ('le sommeil fiévreux'), heighten the sense of lost control; concrete images of disorder and dirt ('Et il semblait . . .') suggest moral reprobation at shameless abandonment, the comparison with 'une alcôve colossale', reinforced by the references to 'une grande débauche', 'le vice', and 'le cauchemar . . . voluptueux', suggest the wild promiscuity of the age; the 'il n'y avait plus' of the final sentence, and the coupling of 'furieux et las', suggest a dying fall, inner rottenness, enervation and exhaustion; while the convergence on the final image of Tuileries, 'allonge[ant] leurs bras dans le noir, comme pour une embrassade énorme', emphatically places Saccard's individual existence and the general social corruption within the context of the Imperial regime.

La Curée is not all movement. The opening description of the novel is one of arrested movement: the traffic-jam. Myriad impressionist details, notations of light and colour, and the noise of harnesses and hoofs, correspond to the description of the carriages moving forward again:

> Mille clartés dansantes s'allumèrent, des éclairs rapides se croisèrent dans les roues, des étincelles jaillirent des harnais secoués par les chevaux. Il y eut sur le sol, sur les arbres, de larges reflets de glace qui couraient. Ce pétillement des harnais et des roues, ce flamboiement des panneaux vernis dans lesquels brûlait la braise rouge du soleil couchant, ces notes vives que jetaient les livrées éclatantes perchées en plein ciel et les toilettes riches débordant des portières, se trouvèrent ainsi emportés dans un grondement sourd, continu, rythmé par le trot des attelages. (I, 321)[49]

The gentle movement of the carriage is identified with Renée's mood of delicious torpor, and with her vague, unformulated yearnings: 'cette oscillation molle . . . l'emplissait d'une torpeur délicieuse. Mille petits souffles lui passaient sur la chair: songeries inachevées, voluptés innommées, souhaits confus' ('this gentle oscillation . . . filled her with a delicious torpor. A thousand tremulous emotions passed over her flesh: dreams unrealised, nameless delights, confused longings') (I, 329). Her critical sense of alienation and isolation from the world in the penultimate chapter, clinched by the revelation of the forthcoming marriage of Maxime, takes place against a background of whirling movement – the *cotillon* of dancing guests, locked together in shrill hilarity. Circularity, movement and hallucination combine in Renée's climactic vision of her past life, which she sees turning round and round her. The immobility with which the novel opens thus contrasts with the frenzied movement of Chapter VI: 'Elle se le [Saccard] rappelait sautant les obstacles, roulant en pleine boue, et ne prenant pas le temps de s'essuyer pour arriver avant l'heure, ne s'arrêtant même pas à jouir en chemin, mâchant ses pièces d'or en courant' (I, 574).[50] Renée flees to the hothouse in despair and, through the open doors, sees the *cotillon* in the distance, forming a culminating image. The chapter ends as the music and dancing figures take on a note of delirious frenzy, reflecting the spinning turmoil of Renée's feelings:

> . . . elle voyait la furie des pieds, le pêle-mêle des bottes vernies et des chevilles blanches. Par moments, il lui semblait qu'un souffle de vent allait enlever les robes. Ces épaules nues, ces bras nus, ces chevelures nues qui volaient, qui tourbillonnaient, prises, jetées et reprises, au fond de cette galerie, où la valse de l'orchestre s'affolait, où les tentures rouges se pâmaient sous les fièvres dernières du bal, lui apparurent comme l'image tumultueuse de sa vie à elle, de ses nudités, de ses abandons. (I, 580)[51]

Iridiscent surfaces correspond, then, to perpetual motion. Flux and movement correspond to impermanence and instability. These, and associated impressionist techniques, are strikingly present in the description of the visit of Renée and Maxime to the Café Riche. The entire description is framed by journeys in a carriage. The opening image of Renée in the moving carriage (I, 442, 446) evokes the distance between Renée and the world, her exclusion as a spectator, and her accompanying mood of deep reverie and langour: 'Renée, la tête à la portière, resta silencieuse, regardant la foule, les cafés, les restaurants, dont la file interminable courait devant elle' ('Renée, with her head at the window, remained silent, looking at the crowd, the cafés, the restaurants, whose interminable line scudded past') (I, 446). As we have seen, the description of the dinner and the ensuing incest is punctuated by descriptions of the boulevard and the passers-by, as Renée looks out from the balcony of the café. Zola emphasises the dissolution of the city into a swarm of fragmentary impressions and blurred images, and he notes that even active movement ultimately produces a sense of sameness, emptiness and boredom:

> Et le défilé repassait sans fin, avec une régularité fatigante, monde étrangement mêlé et toujours le même, au milieu des couleurs vives, des trous de ténèbres, dans le tohu-bohu féerique de ces mille flammes dansantes, sortant comme un flot des boutiques, colorant les transparents des croisées et des kiosques, courant sur les façades en baguettes, en lettres, en dessins de feu, piquant l'ombre d'étoiles, filant sur la chaussée, continuellement. (I, 450)[52]

The pedestrians are compared to mechanical dolls, which echoes Renée's sense of détachment.

Circular movement and circularity of structure, combined with repetition and descriptive impressionism, correspond to Renée's sense of entrapment and to the general sense of evanescence. The circular motif is stressed in Chapter V, in which Renée's financial problems reach a crisis. In this chapter, Renée, in a desperate quest for money, visits her father and her aunt before being thrust back into the arms of the financial broker, Mme Sidonie, who attempts to persuade her to sell herself to M. de Saffré. At the end of the novel, Renée, now alone, revisits the Bois de Boulogne for the last time. Images of liquidity and gold combine in the long, intensely impressionistic descriptions of the brilliant light-effects in the Bois: 'Le soleil, haut sur l'horizon, coulait, emplissait d'une poussière d'or les creux des feuillages, allumait les branches hautes, changeait cet océan de feuilles en un océan de lumière' ('The sun, high on the horizon, swept down, filling the hollows of the foliage with a golden dust, lighting up the tall branches, changing that sea of leaves into a sea of light') (I, 592). The sunlight has changed the lake into a large, shining mirror of polished silver. The retrospective view, as memories and images of the past form in Renée's mind, reinforces the sense of loss and alienation; and Renée's isolation and revulsion are opposed to images of splendour, ease and contentment. Her immobility is set against the almost ritualistic, triumphant procession of carriages before her. The dominant sense of movement is focused on the image of turning wheels, which again recalls the opening chapter: 'elle apercevait la file des roues qui tournaient comme des étoiles d'or' ('she caught sight of the line of wheels revolving like golden stars') (I, 593). The spectacle is crowned by the sudden appearance of the Emperor, who disappears just as quickly in the sunlight. The scene with which the novel opens, Renée and Maxime returning from the Bois, is thus echoed by the final scene. Swiftness of movement has been replaced by slowness of movement, expectation by regret, langour and longing by solitude and dereliction.

Although *La Curée* does not represent a global condemnation of the bourgeoisie, it is heavily laden with implicit moralising. Zola satirises a society in which relationships between people are determined and ordered by money, and in which everything is placed on a monetary basis; the 'psychological' theme of Renée's incestuous passion and personal destruction not only counterpoints but interlocks with the 'social' theme of property speculation. The novel portrays the falsification and distortion of human relations produced by the cash nexus and, as such, may be regarded as an aggressive exposure of an alienating society. The mainspring of the novel, however, is the theme of dissipation. *La Curée*, viewed as a coherent totality, conveys a vision of appalling waste – waste of money and waste of energy; or rather, energy is misdirected and uncontrolled. Saccard is not rendered totally antipathetic by virtue of his remarkable dynamism; moreover, he is distinguished from his cronies, Mignon and Charrier, by his extreme prodigality. But the linguistic character and thematic structure of the novel focus on the profoundly destructive consequences of activities which are not subject to any control or constraint. Saccard, although dynamic, is a figure of disorder and destruction. The significance of *La Curée* in the context of this study, and the light it throws on Zola's conception of the bourgeoisie, thus lies in the mentality displayed by Saccard. The problem posed by the general *débandade*, the collective madness, of the age is how to control, confine and direct human energies, and how to define the values which must inform the attempt to organise and channel human vitality.

Une Page d'amour: The Ambiguities of Passion

Announcing the publication of *Une Page d'amour*, *Le Bien public* confidently assured its readers that 'ce roman pourra[it] être laissé sans crainte sur la table de famille' ('this novel could be left without fear for any member of the family to see').[1] The novel is one of the least read of the Rougon-Macquart series, display- ing none of Zola's most characteristic and powerful gifts as a novelist. Critics usually couple it, quite wrongly, with the insub- stantial and inferior *Le Rêve*. Its muted tone and style were part of Zola's deliberate design to 'faire opposition' ('produce a contrast') by inserting his 'oeuvre intime et de demi-teinte' ('intimate, half-tone work') (II, 799) between the blackness of *L'Assommoir* and the virtuosity of *Nana*. The novel was so uncharacteristic, in fact, that during its composition Zola was pursued by doubts as to its value, fearing that it might be *too* pallid and grey and make no impact.[2] If the tone is muted, however, it is not monochrome, nor is the portrayal of Hélène static. With *Une Page d'amour* Zola was consciously attempting to write a 'psychological' novel. Zola's general lack of psychological penetration is well known. The success of his characters depends largely on their dynamic integration into the total atmosphere and general rhythm of his novels. But the picture of shifting and conflicting emotional states in Hélène, above all unconscious ones, is more penetrating than critics have allowed. Moreover, the sexual psychology and sexual symbolism, revealing and con- centrating on the unconscious personality, arguably place *Une Page d'amour* in a central thematic position in the Rougon- Macquart series, since the novel gives specific dramatised expression to a theme which runs through nearly all of Zola's fiction: the disruptive nature of a sexuality seen as an irresistible fatality. An examination of the novel's structure and thematic imagery will reveal a fundamental opposition between *abandon* and *isolement* on the one hand, and erotic temptation and engulfing desire on the other.

Although *Une Page d'amour* is primarily interesting as a psychological study, its 'sociological' content is not negligible. Zola manages to convey a sharp critique of bourgeois values while deliberately eliminating a satirical tone and suggesting an innocuous surface. The novel deals directly with bourgeois adultery and bourgeois marriage, which are recurrent themes in *Les Rougon-Macquart* and receive notable expression in *Pot-Bouille*. It also reflects the emptiness of bourgeois life and the theme of moral laxity beneath respectable appearances; there is a difference of degree, not of essence, between the world of appearances in *Une Page d'amour* and *La Curée*. Minor social themes in *Une Page d'amour* which reappear in other novels (especially in *Pot-Bouille*) are the education of children (reflected in the cloistered life of Jeanne and the censorship imposed on Pauline Deberle, who is sent into the garden when the conversation becomes too *risquée*), arranged marriages (reflected in Hélène's early marriage to Charles Grandjean and in the desire to 'marry off' Pauline), *le bovarysme* (Hélène's reading of *Ivanhoe*) and the role of religion.

I

Technically, *Une Page d'amour* is one of the most Flaubertian of Zola's novels, especially in its use of symbols and echoing images and sensations. It is not that it possesses the intricate ironical structure of a Flaubert novel, but its texture, evoking relationships below the conscious level, is richer than a first reading might reveal. The text is full of counterpoint, of external signs and symbols, recurrent images and situations, which articulate, incite, prefigure and punctuate the development of Hélène's inner feelings.

The structure and imagery of the novel are shaped by the splits and oppositions within Hélène, by the basic tensions between probity and temptation, maternal love and sexual passion, past and present, Hélène's apartment and the impulse to leave it, simultaneous repulsion and attraction, guilt and elation. Zola is anxious to establish Hélène as a figure of exemplary moral stature, which is emphasised by adjectives like 'pure', 'chaste', 'correcte', 'grave', 'droite', 'raisonnable', 'ferme', and nouns like 'majesté', 'honnêteté', 'hauteur', 'pudeur'. In the first scene by the window, her rigid moral probity is seen in terms of her past life:

> Elle avait vécu plus de trente années dans une dignité et dans une fermeté absolues. La justice seule la passionnait. Quand elle interrogeait son passé, elle ne trouvait pas une faiblesse d'une heure, elle se voyait d'un pas égal suivre une route unie et toute droite. Certes les jours pouvaient couler, elle continuerait sa marche tranquille, sans que son pied heurtât un obstacle. Et cela la rendait sévère, avec de la colère et du mépris contre ces menteuses existences dont l'égoïsme trouble les coeurs. La seule existence vraie était la sienne, qui se déroulait au milieu d'une paix si large. (II, 850)[3]

But her proud 'honnêteté' is also associated with memories of the past's sterility, and, while holding Jeanne tighter, 'comme pour écarter des pensées qui menaçaient de la séparer d'elle' ('as though to drive away any thoughts that threatened to come between them') (II, 853), her heart 'melts' before the vibrant radiance of the landscape. Her 'honnêteté' is thus immediately opposed to slow *attendrissement*, which merges into a mood of dream, expectation and final intoxication. The use of the past and the underlining of ambivalence are pressed further in the second window-scene, which pictures Hélène's confusion after Henri's avowal of love. Fear and resentment are matched by an irresistible voluptuousness. The desire to escape from the reality of her passion, and indeed of all feelings, is followed by revolt against the emotional emptiness of her past, and surrender to her new happiness: 'elle réclamait la chute' ('she yearned, now, to fall from grace') (II, 906); 'quelle duperie, cette rigidité, ce scrupule du juste qui l'enfermaient dans les jouissances stériles des dévotes!' ('it all seemed a hollow sham now – that strict code, that conscientious virtue that condemned her to the sterile joys of pious women!') (ibid.).

Intimations of Hélène's growing love are frequently linked to fear and anxiety; and moments of two-sided feeling mark all periods of crisis. Hélène wants to tell the Abbé Jouve of her feelings, but 'elle tremblait que le prêtre ne réussît à la guérir' ('she dreaded lest the priest might succeed in curing [her]') (II, 926). Her anguish is itself part of a single intense experience: 'au fond d'elle, une joie débordante montait, de son angoisse elle-même. Elle chérissait son mal' ('in the depths of her heart, out of her very anguish, an uncontrollable joy was rising. Her pain was precious to her') (ibid.). When, under the weight of her secret, she finally reveals her love, she reacts in horror at the counsel of marriage with Rambaud. 'Vous appelez au secours', says the Abbé, 'et vous n'acceptez pas de salut' ('You call for help and reject salvation') (II, 973). While Mère Fétu is showing Malignon's secret apartment to Hélène, Hélène's feelings of irresistible fascination are mingled with shame and disgust: 'Alors, malgré sa répugnance, honteuse de ce qu'elle faisait là, Hélène la suivit' ('Then, despite her repugnance and the shame she felt at her own action, Hélène followed her', (II, 996).

The moral judgment expressed in the retrospective postscript clinches the profound ambivalence at the centre of the novel. For the ending is in no sense conclusive or explanatory; the Hélène contemplating her past from a distance is the *femme honnête*, contemplating some inexplicable, distant aberration: 'elle croyait juger une personne étrangère, dont la conduite l'emplissait de mépris et d'étonnement' ('she felt as if she were judging an utter stranger, whose conduct filled her with amazement and shame') (II, 1089). This total gap in her personality, seen as momentary self-alienation, elicits no nostalgia or regret, only incomprehension and self-censure. Zola attempts, characteristically, to place the events of the novel in the larger perspective of life's continuity. Suggestions of timelessness are given by the stark houses, 'comme moisies par des siècles d'humidité' ('as if centuries of damp had mildewed them') (II, 1088), and the horses and coaches, '[qui] semblaient se pourrir là depuis des temps très anciens' ('as if they had stood rotting there since time out of mind') (II, 1089). Hélène seems to have returned to her former state of tranquillity, emphasised by the echoing of identical phrases. The image of her life as a slow walk along a straight road is repeated. But her past has been established, albeit ambiguously, as an image of sterility; despite the final mention of the fishing rods, we cannot but see her marriage with Rambaud as a return (literally so, since they now live in Marseille) to the loveless emptiness of her first marriage, for Rambaud is an image of her first husband, he too kissing her cold, naked feet

on their wedding-night. Ambivalence is doubled by further
ambiguity with the undermining of moral judgment and emotional detachment by the dominant tone of sadness. The
resumption of the 'dialogue' with Paris brings us back to the
snow-covered landscape of the opening pages, with images of
immobility, silence, desolation and death. The image of Paris,
immense, indistinct and impassive encapsulates the final mood
of resignation and exclusion. The explicit equation between
Paris and life heightens the implied opacity of life itself:
'Hélène, une dernière fois, embrassa d'un regard la ville impassible, qui, elle aussi, lui restait inconnue' ('Then Hélène, for the
last time, let her eyes range over the impassive city, which she
would never know') (II, 1091–2). The novel thus ends not on a
stridently tragic note, but on a dilution of tension, a closing circle
of unresolved conflict.

II

Central ambiguities are closely linked to dominant metaphor,
elements of structure and rhythmical effects, which constantly
imply sexuality to be an insidious and fatal force, seen in terms of
eroded will, loss of self-awareness, sensual self-abandon and final
disaster. The progression is from a sentimental, romantic love to
overpowering sexual passion. Tensions of feeling do not spring
directly from the exigencies of Hélène's moral dilemma, but from
a sense of straining against a powerful fixation. She is not tormented because the affair is illicit; nor does she have any religious convictions which might make her consider her love a sin.
The character of Jeanne is to be seen as symbol and motif rather
than as an axis of moral choice. A lexical study of the novel
would reveal the frequency of words like 'rêverie', 'complais-
ance', 'attendrissement', 'assoupissement', 'mollesse', 'engourdissement', 'oubli', 'bercer', amollir', 'endormir', 's'abandonner', 's'anéantir' – all suggesting dissipation of resistance,
interior dissolution and loss of contact with external reality. The
first indirect meetings between Hélène and Henri take place in
Mère Fétu's garret, where Hélène's role as dispenser of charity
permits a sweet savouring of emotion, 'à laquelle elle cédait sans
résistance, tout amollie de pitié' ('to which she yielded freely,
disarmed by pity') (II, 830). In the Deberles' garden this

becomes an 'attendrissement continu' ('increasing tenderness') (II, 880), as the pleasant sense-impressions seem to draw her closer to Henri: 'Les allées, ratissées tous les matins, avaient une mollesse de tapis'('The paths, raked every morning, were like soft carpets to her feet') (II, 879). Hélène's passivity and the progressive erosion of her resistance to Henri are intimately related to the treatment of sensory perception. The savouring of unavowed passion corresponds with the Mois de Marie, in which Hélène's love is sublimated and diverted into religious worship. Her passion is seen as a sapping of the will, as her thoughts are stifled and her senses lulled by the atmosphere of the heated church: 'elle s'abandonnait au bercement du cantique, goûtait un bien-être dévot, que jusque-là elle n'avait jamais ressenti dans une église' ('she surrendered to the lulling rhythm of the hymn, enjoying a sense of spiritual well-being that hitherto she had never experienced in a church') (II, 917). The ambiguity of her passion is amply illustrated by her desire for a mute, unavowed love without commitments or words, which would provide its own satisfactions. The verb 's'abandonner', suggesting delicious surrender, is a recurring one. During the children's party, Hélène, standing in the brightness of the lamps and candles, 's'abandonnait, pendant que le souffle d'Henri chauffait sa nuque' ('relaxed unselfconsciously, with Henri's warm breath against her neck') (II, 895). Similarly, when she revolts against the constrictions of her life, we read: 'Henri pouvait la prendre, elle s'abandonnait. Alors, elle goûta un bonheur infini à ne plus lutter' ('Let Henri take her, she would surrender. Then she felt an infinite joy at giving up the struggle') (II, 906).

After her 'chute', Hélène's mood of mechanical passivity and sensuous absorption is evoked by her visit to the kitchen. Her nervous excitement is soothed into a kind of complacent oblivion as she watches Rosalie and Zéphyrin eating, 'affaissée sur la haute chaise de bois, s'oubliant dans une grande douceur' ('sunk back in the tall chair and feeling delightfully relaxed') (II, 1044). This echoes her sense of total detachment from her surroundings when she finally yields to Henri. The sensuous warmth suggested by the delight of the food, the inviting smells, and the transparent happiness of the two servants, evoke in Hélène a feeling of complicity as she becomes enveloped in the atmosphere of comfort and relaxation:

Elle se sentait comme enveloppée dans leur tendresse. Et elle continuait pour eux leurs rêves... Toutes les distances se trouvaient rapprochées, elle n'avait plus une conscience nette d'elle ni des autres, du lieu où elle était, ni de ce qu'elle venait y faire. Les cuivres flambaient sur les murs, une mollesse la retenait, le visage noyé, sans qu'elle fût blessée du désordre de la cuisine. Cet abaissement d'elle-même lui donnait la profonde jouissance d'un besoin contenté. (II, 1045)[4]

As in the description of the 'chute', the mingling of dream and sensuous detail produces a kind of absence, a loss of self-awareness, a descent to the unconscious level; and the ambiguity of Zola's stance is expressed in the explicit judgment of the last sentence, equating self-abandon and self-abasement, and half puncturing the whole impression evoked. Additional ironic significance is given to Hélène's entry into the kitchen by the early establishment of a clearly defined and distanced relationship between the two servants and herself. Her self-abandon signifies the closing of the distance formerly separating them, based on her own authority as *maîtresse de maison* exercising necessary supervision and constraint: 'Toutes les distances se trouvaient rapprochées'. This corresponds to a progression from order to disorder. Hélène's pride in her well-ordered household is associated with her 'honnêteté' and 'dignité'; and Rosalie takes no less pride in the resplendence of her kitchen. After Zéphyrin's arrival, each Saturday sees a cleaning of the kitchen in preparation for his weekly visit: 'il fallait voir le bel ordre, les casseroles et les pots par rangs de grandeur, chaque chose à son clou' ('everything was in apple-pie order, the pots and pans arranged according to size, each hanging on its right hook') (II, 862). In Part V, Chapter 1, however, they are oblivious to the disorder around them: 'Autour d'eux, la cuisine, qui n'était pas rangée encore, étalait la débandade de la desserte' ('Around them the kitchen was still strewn untidily with used dishes') (II, 1042).

The essential movement in the mind of Hélène is thus from progressive, sensuous *assoupissement* to fatal necessity. We see a sensibility apparently powerless: 'c'était une sensation de mollesse et d'apaisement, qui peu à peu devenait nécessaire à Hélène' ('she experienced a sensation of peace and relaxation that had gradually become indispensable to her') (II, 921). Our sense of the force of unconscious desire merges into a mounting impression of somnambulism with the approach of Hélène's 'chute', as she is possessed by the *idée fixe* of the anonymous letter and then by the resolution to prevent Juliette from keeping the rendezvous. The actual 'chute' is followed by a strange, numbed absence: 'Elle marchait dans un rêve . . .; elle songeait qu'elle n'avait ni remords ni joie. Cela était ainsi, elle ne pouvait faire que cela fût autrement' ('She moved as though in a dream . . .; it struck her that she felt neither remorse nor joy. That was how things were, and she could do nothing to alter them') (II, 1035). It is as if Jeanne's death brings her back to a state of consciousness.

Structurally, *Une Page d'amour* produces a sense of convergence towards an end, of fatal, almost logical, progression. The novel's rigorous architectural symmetry was immediately noted by contemporary reviewers. It follows Zola's usual method of systematic, linear construction; the narrative is carried forward in definite stages and the chapters, organically linked, are built round specific events or developments. And the internal construction of chapters, the accumulative disposition of concrete detail based on counterpoint, is determined by the need to produce a sense of convergence. The recurrent situations involving the Passage des Eaux, the Deberles' garden, the 'chambre rose', and Mère Fétu, perform a unifying function, frequently marked by a sense of isolation, enclosure, absorption and silence.

Superficial aspects of the novel's textural and formal qualities are matched by examples of premonition and prefiguration. The motifs of a fall and a slope, and images of verticality and descent, are used to prefigure Hélène's 'chute'. 'If a woman dreams of falling', wrote Freud, 'it almost inevitably has a sexual sense: she is imagining herself as a "fallen woman".'[5] In her regular visits to Mère Fétu, Hélène takes particular pleasure in descending the Passage des Eaux. Looking down, 'elle avait, d'en haut, une étrange sensation, en regardant s'enfoncer la pente raide du passage' ('she had a queer feeling when she stood at the top and looked down the steep slope of the passage') (II, 829). In the difficult descent she is delighted by the fresh shade and seclusion, while at the bottom, looking up, she has a vague sense of apprehension and fear: 'En bas, elle levait les yeux. La vue de cette pente si raide, où elle venait de se risquer, lui donnait une légère peur' ('Once at the bottom she would look back, and the sight of the steep slope down which she had ventured always

gave her a little shiver of fright') (ibid.). (We think of Gervaise
looking up at the tenement building in *L'Assommoir*, and later
looking down over the banisters of the sixth floor, 'se hasardant
là comme au bord d'un gouffre' ['hanging poised over the
abyss'] [II, 423]; we also recall the courtyard/sewer symbol in
Pot-Bouille.) The repeated cries of a cat trapped in an old well are
only too heavy with the implication of Hélène's ensnarement by
her own incipient dilemma. Similarly, the fall from the swing,
which forms the climax of Part I, signals in its elaborations wider
emotional developments: spontaneous joy gradually breaking
through Hélène's grave reserve, final release from mourning,
increased awareness of Henri, and a possible warning.

III

To identify the unifying metaphors of *Une Page d'amour*, and to
establish their ancillary images, is, as we have seen, to reveal a
play of oppositions. The symbolic décor of the novel expresses
the duality and tensions within Hélène, both conscious and
unconscious. This antithetical movement, in which *intimité* is
opposed to *ouverture*, spatial claustration to liberation, is articulated round the central metaphor of *la chambre*, with its linking
image of the window.[6] The closing chapters of the first three Parts
all begin with Hélène's gesture of opening wide the window. And
what better symbol of the central drama than Jeanne's replacement of her mother at the window? In Part V the distance and
alienation between Jeanne and Hélène are fixed in the image of
Jeanne at the window looking down at her mother in the garden;
later, Jeanne stays by the fire while Hélène goes out every day;
and when Jeanne is about to die Dr Bodin opens wide the window as she tries once more to look out over Paris. Central to the
role of the window motif in the expression of the novel's meaning
is its ambiguity, for it combines both immobility and movement,
fixity and reverie, marking the dividing-line between constriction and acceptance on the one hand, aspiration and escape on
the other. Images of narrow enclosure, isolation and solitude are
constantly contrasted with images of open space, immensity and
depth: 'Son coin de solitude ouvrait sur cette immensité' ('Her
solitude had this outlet on to immensity') (II, 822), 'l'inconnu de
la grande ville' ('the great city's mystery') (II, 905), 'une abîme

d'obscurité où l'on devinait un monde' ('an abyss of darkness hiding a whole world') (II, 965). The city is not seen in terms of the social life it contains, for its distance renders it a vast natural spectacle comparable to Le Paradou in *La Faute de l'abbé Mouret*.

Hélène's life of reclusion, the calm and order of her present existence, and her fragile feelings of security, are intimately associated with her bedroom: 'Elle aimait cette vaste chambre si calme, avec son luxe bourgeois, son palissandre et son velours bleu' ('She loved her great quiet room, with its homely luxury, its rosewood furniture and its blue velvet') (II, 821). The novel's opening paragraphs, which describe Hélène's apartment as she sleeps, evoke an atmosphere of bourgeois comfort and calm. The muted colours, the silence and the enveloping drowsiness are matched by the softness of the velvet curtains and bedcovers, and emphasised by the adjectives: 'une calme lueur' ('its dim quiet light'), 'sa tranquille attitude' ('her peaceful attitude'), 'un léger souffle' ('breathing softly') (II, 801). When Hélène returns after the 'chute' she seems to need to revisit all the rooms of her apartment, returning as if to the protective intimacy of a refuge: 'Tous les meubles étaient à leur place; elle les retrouvait, cela lui causait un plaisir' ('All the furniture was in its place; she recognised it, and that gave her pleasure') (II, 1035–6). But this 'refuge' itself embodies ambiguity, for enclosed space may bring frustration as well as security. Furnished by Rambaud, her bedroom reflects his stolid bourgeois simplicity: 'les rideaux lourds, les meubles sombres et cossus' ('the heavy curtains, the dark, substantial furniture') (II, 822). The room and furniture give the reassurance of familiarity, but the identification between them and Rambaud as a norm of security immediately suggests claustrophobic dullness. This is heightened in Part I, Chapter 5, in which Hélène looks out over Paris from her window. Her innocence and ignorance (of sexual passion and of life), and the limitations and refusal of experience, are identified with the apartment, as temptation is identified with descent: 'C'était comme si elles se fussent arrêtées au seuil d'un monde dont elles avaient l'éternel spectacle en refusant d'y descendre' ('It was as if they had stopped on the threshold of a world that lay forever outspread before them, and refused to enter it') (II, 854). The sentence is a key one. Distance and height imply safety; while at the same time the spectacle can always be enjoyed in contemplation. The persistent contemplation of Paris from a distant height

relates Hélène and Jeanne to the series of 'watchers' in Zola –
people who witness actions but do not participate in them – and
thus underscores the themes of exclusion, frustration and isolation which form the basis of the novel. Contemplation gives a
form of possession without participation. The themes of solitude
and alienation, of ignorance and of *l'inconnu*, are, moreover, more
than merely sexual in their implications. Hélène is detached
from life itself, with implications of life's impurity. This corresponds to her lack of contact with Henri, who remains a remark-
ably shadowy figure throughout. Hélène reflects at the end of the
novel that she has never really known him: 'Au dernier comme au
premier jour, il lui restait étranger. . . Il passait, son ombre s'en
était allée avec lui. Et leur histoire n'avait pas d'autre dénouement' ('He remained a stranger to her, on the last day as on the
first. . . He had passed out of her life and his shadow had gone
with him. And their story had no other ending') (II, 1090).

Hélène's alienation from life corresponds to a movement
towards suspension. Although her past is associated with a sense
of emptiness, we also feel her efforts to maintain a similar kind of
suspension in the present, to extend and preserve the timelessness of the present moment. This is expressed through the
themes of ignorance and dream (see below), and through
Hélène's pervasive moods of dreamlike contemplation, her passive absorption in present happiness, and the ambiguous pleasure of anticipation: 'Cela était très doux, de l'avoir là et de
l'ignorer' ('They were happy merely to have it [Paris] there,
boundless and undiscovered') (ibid.); 'Hélène rêvait . . . une
longue suite de jours semblables' (Hélène 'began to dream of a
long succession of such days') (II, 948); 'elle semblait mettre un
raffinement à retarder l'heure du second rendez-vous' ('she
seemed to take a subtle pleasure in postponing their second
rendezvous') (II, 1048). The image of Hélène on the threshold of
an unknown world, the balance between seclusion and exclusion, between temptation and the wish to remain insulated from
passion, emphasises the attraction of Paris, which, with its dark,
indistinct shapes, becomes a metaphor of sensual temptation,
inviting, but dangerous, mysterious and disturbing: 'Souvent,
Paris les inquiétait, lorsqu'il leur envoyait des haleines chaudes
et troublantes' ('Paris often made them feel uneasy, when some
sultry, heady wind reached them from the city') (II, 854).
Hélène and Jeanne have only gone down into Paris three times

in eighteen months, and Jeanne's questions underline Hélène's ignorance.

The constant undulating movement and myriad variety of the visual scene set off the intimacy and immobility of Hélène's apartment. The vast poetic symbol of the city is persistently evoked in images of liquidity, flux and ever-changing light. The opaque solidity of the furniture and the objects in the room emphasise the sense of fixity, which is opposed to the later, pervasive moods of floating, movement and suspension that characterise Hélène's dream-like states, and also to the images of dissolution, fluidity and erosion associated with the evolution of her feelings. The metaphor of space is linked also to the dimension of time: Hélène's room is associated with monotony and the regular succession of jejune *mardis*. Her life before her marriage is characterised as 'cette succesion de jours semblables' ('the endless sameness of her days') (II, 848); and before the climactic events of Part IV we are given the impression of time's steady flow: 'Au bout de la semaine, ils se connaissaient comme s'ils avaient vécu des années côte à côte' ('By the end of the week they knew one another as well as if they had lived side by side for years') (II, 830). This sense of time's fixedness contrasts with the accelerated narrative rhythm of Part IV, evoking immediacy and urgency as all converges towards the rendezvous. Apart from the last chapter, the novel's action takes place over a period of ten months, whereas the crucial period of crisis is concentrated into two days and nights, which occupy the whole of Part IV.

Images of verticality and depth (the house is 'bâtie à pic sur la hauteur' ['perched right on the edge of the hill']) (II, 845) set off the monotony and probity of Hélène's past life, evoked as a slow walk along a straight and even path. Open space, immensity and images of promise are juxtaposed with the dark, damp house of her childhood, with memories of the emotional aridity of her past, the monotony of childhood followed by twelve years of marriage to a man she never loved. Rambaud and Jouve, moreover, are clearly associated with Hélène's past through their previous acquaintance with her husband. Part I, Chapter 5, firmly establishes the tension of equations as the following: apartment – Rambaud – security – past – claustrophobia – emptiness ↔ Paris – open space – immensity – the unknown – temptation – descent – sensuality.

Zola thus builds up a coherent pattern of connotations. The second scene of contemplation by the window, precipitated by the doctor's avowal of love, adds a new element to the equation: Henri. Hélène's reactions to her bedroom, supported by the returning image of the past, mark the progress of her passion:

> En haut, dans sa chambre, dans cette douceur cloîtrée qu'elle retrouvait, Hélène se sentit étouffer. La pièce l'étonnait, si calme, si bien close, si endormie sous les tentures de velours bleu, tandis qu'elle y apportait le souffle court et ardent de l'émotion qui l'agitait. Était-ce sa chambre, ce coin mort de solitude où elle manquait d'air? Alors, violement, elle ouvrit une fenêtre, elle s'accouda en face de Paris. (II, 902)[7]

The double emphasis of the first sentence, the triple repetition of the second, the explicitness of 'ce coin mort', and the violence of her gesture, illustrate the turbulence of her feelings. She seems to see the room with fresh eyes, realising its oppressive limits. Its calm and immobility become suffocating negative values, frustrations associated with the past. The tensions between passion and constraint, calm and agitation, merge into violent revolt as the dullness of Paris after the rain is changed into a resplendent vision dominated by images of gold, fire and flames, and Hélène's fear and resentment give way to delicious self-abandonment: 'Eh bien! La passion était fatale, Hélène ne se défendait plus. Elle se sentait à bout de force contre son coeur' ('Then Hélène yielded to the fatality of passion. She could no longer defend herself against it; she had no strength left to fight against her own heart') (II, 906). The wish to escape from the confines of the bedroom becomes a desire for a deep, almost transcendent, passion which would be concentrated into a single, supreme moment: 'elle réclamait la chute, elle l'aurait souhaitée immédiate et profonde. Toute sa révolte aboutissait à ce désir impérieux. Oh! disparaître dans une étreinte, vivre en une minute tout ce qu'elle n'avait pas vécu!' (II, 906–7).[8] This is a formulation very typical of Zola, associated with the themes of dream and of a *lieu inconnu,* and looking forward to the images of engulfment surrounding Hélène's 'chute'.

The word 'inconnu' assumes focal significance in the text, complementing the familiarity of Hélène's apartment and focusing her moods of fascinated contemplation. Her apartment is opposed to the places in which her love is excited and satisfied – places which are unknown and unfamiliar, liberating from everyday attachments and associations. The scene of the first indirect meetings between Hélène and Henri is, as we have seen, Mère Fétu's garret,[9] in which stiff deference gives way to deep sympathy:

> . . . dans son salon, elle aurait gardé la froideur méfiante de sa nature. Mais là, ils se trouvaient loin du monde, partageant l'unique chaise, presque heureux de ces pauvres et laides choses qui les rapprochaient, en les attendrissant. . . Le taudis de la mère Fétu s'emplissait de lumière, dans cette communion de leur bonté. (II, 830)[10]

The garret concentrates and identifies *intimité*, total seclusion ('loin du monde', 'ce grenier perdu') ('far from the world', 'this remote garret') (II, 830, 831) and *attendrissement*. Hélène's 'chute' takes place in the secret *garçonnière*, which is close to Mère Fétu's garret: 'Cette pièce lui était inconnue, aucun objet ne lui parla' ('The room was strange to her, no object in it meant anything to her') (II, 1023). And in her confession to the Abbé Jouve, Hélène recognises that 'jamais elle n'aurait cédé à cet homme, si Jeanne était restée auprès d'elle. Il avait fallu qu'elle le rencontrât dans cette chambre inconnue' ('she would never have yielded to that man, if Jeanne had been at her side; it was only because she had met him in that strange room') (II, 1064–5). The word 'inconnu' is identified with sexual ignorance and curiosity when it is associated with Paris; and it acquires heightened significance in the final chapters ('la ville impassible, qui . . . lui restait inconnue' ('the impassive city which she would never know') (II, 1092), assimilated to the theme of *l'interdit sexuel*. The recurring sense of total isolation and enclosure corresponds to the moods of absorption and absence which characterise Hélène's reverie; and it anticipates the heightened detachment from reality which marks her final 'chute'. The 'loin du monde' ('far from the world') of page 830 becomes the 'hors du monde' ('out of the world') of page 1023. All such moments are matched by almost total silence: 'cette molle retraite, où les bruits de dehors n'arrivaient point' ('this luxurious hiding-place, remote from any sound of the outside world') (II, 987); '[le] silence et [le] demi-jour qui devaient régner dans la chambre rose' ('the silence and half-light that must prevail in the pink room') (II, 992).

Certain key words, combined with images, motifs and significant sensations help to define and modulate the central themes. These focal words contribute to the interplay of associations which marks the texture of the novel. This is visible, for instance, in connexion with the theme of *le regard* (see below) and the lexical complex suggesting the dilution of Hélène's resistance to a passion of which at first she is only vaguely aware. It is also evident in the images of verticality and depth associated with Paris, and the sense of falling and engulfment which characterises Hélène's 'chute' ('abîme', 'profondeur', 'vide béant', 'trou noir', 'immensité noire', 'engloutissement', 'anéantissement', 's'anéantir'). Linking imagery provides associative connexions which strengthen the novel's unity and poetic symbolism. There is an important network of images and vocabulary emphasising unconscious levels of feeling, the undercurrents of emotional desire implied by the theme of Hélène's reverie. Two recurring words of this kind are 'sourd' and 'vertige':

> C'était, dans son coeur, un sentiment de protestation indignée, d'orgueilleuse colère, mêlé à une *sourde* et invincible volupté (II, 903);

> . . . cette recherche pleine d'énervement et de *sourds* désirs (II, 987);

> Sa volonté lui échappait, des pensées inavouables faisaient en elle un travail *sourd* (II, 999);

> Au fond, elle avait une *sourde* honte, le poids de sa fille sur son épaule la faisait rougir (II, 1038);

> C'était sa jouissance, ces montées et ces descentes, qui lui donnaient un *vertige* (II, 843);

> . . . il y avait là un *vertige* où chancelait sa raison (II, 1090).[11]

The sexual significance of 'vertige' is clear. It is associated with falling, particularly with falling into the unconscious, and the sexual sense of this has already been noted. The accumulation of these focal words at various nodal points of the narrative corresponds to the convergence of central themes. They are also shot through with ambiguity: 'vertige' signifies loss of control as well as delicious self-abandonment; 'attendrissement' implies both unconscious desire and suspension; 'anéantissement' carries implications of destruction as well as ultimate satisfaction.

The theme of a *lieu inconnu* in which harmony and happiness will be achieved gives rise to several intense moments of dream. During Jeanne's second convalescence, Hélène's growing resentment of her daughter's jealousy is matched by a vision of wish-fulfilment: 'quelque rêve vague où elle se voyait marcher avec Henri dans un pays inconnue et charmant' ('one of those vague daydreams where she and Henri were wandering together in some unknown, enchanting landscape') (II, 948). The dream of union with Henri is a recurring one. The revelation of bourgeois morality at the Deberles' reception marks a similar release of fantasy. Accompanied by the tinkling of the piano, 'un rêve la berçait: Henri avait chassé Juliette, et elle était avec lui comme sa femme, dans des pays lointains dont ils ignoraient la langue' ('she yielded to a dream: Henri had sent Juliette away and she was living with him as his wife, in some far-off country whose language they did not know') (II, 983). Hélène's torment in the next chapter as to the whereabouts of the rendezvous merges into the feverish near-fantasy of half-sleep as she imagines a room in a cheap hotel, and then 'un appartement délicieux, avec des tentures épaisses, des fleurs, de grands feux clairs brûlant dans toutes les cheminées' ('a delicious apartment, thickly curtained, full of flowers, with great bright fires burning on every hearth') (II, 987); and suddenly the dream-image of Juliette and Malignon is replaced by that of Henri and herself: 'elle se voyait avec Henri, au fond de cette molle retraite, où les bruits de dehors n'arrivaient point' ('she saw herself with Henri in this luxurious hiding-place, remote from any sound of the outside world') (ibid.). Whereas the returning image of the past marks important stages of feeling, dream-moments often project us into an imagined future. Dream, constantly punctuating the narrative and closely linked to spatial imagery, lies at the heart of the novel, expressing unconscious desires and translating the central tensions upon which the novel is built. Hélène is frequently immersed in silent reverie. Moods of absorption merge into oneiric and somnambulist states. Moreover, the symphonic and symbolic descriptions of Paris, with their myriad anthropomorphism, offer dream-landscapes whose poetic symbolism has clear erotic significance.

IV

In counterpoint to the themes of isolation and enclosure, associated with Hélène, there is the world of superficial and ephemeral appearances associated with Juliette: the theatre, fancy-dress balls, amateur theatricals, the emphasis on transient and factitious decorative styles such as *japonaiserie*. Hélène's 'solid' and well-ordered apartment contrasts with Juliette's heavily decorated drawing-room and the ornateness of Malignon's *garçonnière*. Juliette's shallowness and her concern for appearances are reflected in the motifs of the theatre and play-acting, recalling the use of theatrical representation in *La Curée* and *Nana* to evoke the artificiality of high society. The background of Henri's declaration of love to Hélène is the colourful occasion of the children's fancy-dress ball; Juliette delights in the theatricality of the occasion (which includes a Punch and Judy show) and in the preparation of costumes. The heated bourgeois church attended by Juliette is decorated with flowers, recalling the profusion of flowers in Juliette's drawing-room and anticipating the aestheticism of the church in *Pot-Bouille*. When Hélène arrives at Juliette's house with the intention of preventing her from keeping the rendezvous with Malignon, she finds her rehearsing Musset's *Le Caprice*. The idea of an affair as a form of social *divertissement* is underlined by the calculated *mise-en-scène* of Malignon's *garçonnière*, and the motif of theatricality is reinforced by allusions to 'comédie imbécile' ('idiotic comedy') (II, 1007), 'jeu de coquette' ('flirtation') (II, 1015) and 'des amants d'opéra-comique' ('comic-opera lovers') (ibid.). When Hélène visits Juliette the day after the rendezvous, she finds her 'pâle et les yeux rougis comme une héroïne de drame' ('pale and red-eyed like the heroine of a melodrama') (II, 1047). Juliette's factitious grief on Jeanne's death is matched by Zola's sharply ironic emphasis on her desire to create 'des funérailles touchantes' ('a touching funeral') (II, 1072); the procession of children dressed in white echoes the scene of the children's ball. Juliette's shallowness is focused by the word 'indifférence'. Hélène is shocked and irritated by Juliette's complacency before the rendezvous: 'Elle souffrait de la façon indifférente dont Juliette la recevait' (II, 1003); 'cette indifférence, cette légèreté glaçaient Hélène, qui arrivait toute brûlante de passion' (ibid.); 'elle [Hélène] rêvait sa perte, pour voir si elle garderait toujours le sang-froid de son indifférence' (II, 1005).[12] Juliette, with her inconsequential *bavardage*, remains fundamentally indifferent to Jeanne's fatal illness: 'elle avait beau baisser la voix, prendre des mines apitoyées, sa jolie indifférence perçait, on la voyait heureuse et triomphante d'être elle-même en bonne santé' ('however much she dropped her voice and assumed compassionate airs, she failed to conceal her charming indifference. She was obviously happy and triumphant at being in such good health herself') (II, 1065–6). The theatrical motif, combined with the stress on Juliette's 'indifference', sets off the authentic feelings of Hélène.

Une Page d'amour is a good example of the heterogeneity of Zola's bourgeois world, and it contains a significant element of 'class' comment which anticipates some of the themes of *Pot-Bouille*. The values represented by Juliette Deberle are opposed to those embodied in Hélène. It is important to note that Juliette serves a narrative, moral and ideological purpose – otherwise why does Zola disturb his point of view and give us an omniscient view of Juliette and Malignon together when, elsewhere, she is almost invariably seen through the eyes of Hélène? This shift in perspective curiously anticipates and balances the transition to an omniscient view of Jeanne. Hélène's fatal passion contrasts with the shallowness of Juliette, who leads a life of frivolous socialising and whose receptions are similar to those organised by Mme Duveyrier in *Pot-Bouille*. When Hélène first meets Juliette, the latter's false charm and vapid drawing-room talk, full of empty superlatives and conventional enthusiasm, contrasts with Hélène's embarrassed reticence. Hélène has a conventional sense of bourgeois *convenances*, but the world of bourgeois rituals – Trouville, Worms, the latest boulevard play, society gossip – is clearly foreign to her. The contrast between Hélène and Juliette is associated with a more general opposition in Zola between the city and the country. Hélène is not a Parisian. She comes from Provence; Rambaud too is associated with Provence. Generally in Zola the country is identified with health, innocence and naturalness, the city with perversion and precocity; the natural innocence of Rosalie and Zéphyrin is thus opposed to the stale world of bourgeois adultery.

The opposition established at Juliette's initial reception is exploited at the later one, when Hélène discovers the rendezvous between Juliette and Malignon. Her upright morality is deeply shocked: 'C'était un coup de foudre pour elle, quelque chose

d'inattendu et de monstrueux' ('It had struck her like a thunderbolt; the thing was so unexpected, so monstrous') (II, 979).
Moreover, the images of sexual freedom enumerated by Mlle
Aurélie reveal to Hélène that she is the exception and make her
question her own scruples. In Mlle Aurélie she sees the smiling,
complacent face of bourgeois adultery:

> Hélène, d'un regard lent, faisait le tour du salon. Dans ce
> monde digne, parmi cette bourgeoisie d'apparence honnête, il
> n'y avait donc que des femmes coupables? Son rigorisme pro-
> vincial s'étonnait des promiscuïtés tolérées de la vie parisienne.
> Et, amèrement, elle se raillait d'avoir tant souffert, lorsque
> Juliette mettait sa main dans la sienne. Vraiment! elle était
> bien sotte de garder de si beaux scrupules! L'adultère
> s'embourgeoisait là d'une béate façon, aiguisé d'une pointe de
> raffinement coquet. (II, 981)[13]

Hélène's isolation renders her struggle more poignant and her
discovery marks another important stage in her *déchéance*, for the
chapter is sealed, as Hélène leaves, by her sudden surrender to
Henri's passionate embrace. (We remember the fatal kiss
exchanged between Gervaise and Coupeau in *L'Assommoir*.) the
fashionable and comfortable milieu of bourgeois Passy thus
becomes an influence inciting Hélène to adultery. She wonders
why she should not succumb to the accepted pattern of
bourgeois behaviour.

In his working notes, Zola described the posturing figure of
Juliette as: 'une bourgeoise aimant à recevoir, donnant des
dîners, etc., et glissant à la faute par désoeuvrement. L'adultère
parisien, sans drame aucun, fleuri et superficiel.'[14] Like Renée
Saccard, the coquettish Juliette is attracted to adultery by ennui
and socially-inspired curiosity: 'Jusqu'à ce jour, elle avait à peu
près fait tout ce que faisaient ses amies, autour d'elle; mais une
passion lui manquait, la curiosité et le besoin d'être comme les
autres la poussèrent' (II, 1015).[15] Juliette's life is defined by
social convention and fashionable taste. Hélène's deep need to
ignore and suppress her passion, associated with the suffering of
passion as a 'calvary',[16] is thus contrasted with the socially-
inspired curiosity which almost leads Juliette to succumb. Similarly, Hélène's sense of guilt and remorse is contrasted with
Juliette's superficial shame at having almost failed to keep up

appearances and with her equally superficial easy social acceptance of Malignon afterwards. Juliette's behaviour at Malignon's *garçonnière* and afterwards suggests that she can exercise a fragile control over her world of appearances in which the criteria one should not transgress are those of taste rather than of conviction; and her attitudes are characterised by a relative *insouciance* rather than intensity which can be touched by shame but not by guilt. Guilt in sexual matters is specifically bourgeois; it may be argued that is is more highly characteristic of a Protestant than a Catholic bourgeoisie but that, in either case, it depends on a high degree of personal individuation, whereas a 'shame' culture would be defined by the transgression of socially recognised norms (for example, taste in the case of Juliette) rather than the individual's own internalised moral code. Hélène's authentic feelings and awareness contrast with Juliette's superficial social code based on general acceptance and convention (often tacit) rather than on sincerity. It is interesting to note, from this point of view, the fact that Hélène, while a *bourgeoise* is marginal and highly individualised in comparison with the *bourgeoisie mondaine* represented by the highly 'socialised' Juliette. Hélène is perhaps more generally marginal, having, relatively speaking, improved her social position (for example, she is disturbed initially by the 'gros luxe' ['sombre luxury'] [II, 821] of her own apartment). She is also marginal in terms of religious observance (see II, 913, 921), and it is significant that the Abbé's advice appeals more to self-fulfilment and self-esteem than to social duty ('il ne prononça aucune phrase banale sur les devoirs') ('he uttered no conventional admonition about duty') (II, 971).

V

Une Page d'amour is pre-eminently a novel of silent tensions and conflict, emotional pressures and constraints, dreaming contemplation and entrancement; and this dominant atmosphere is systematically exploited in the theme of *le regard*, which expresses both tension, guilt and *intimité*. Images of surveillance serve as corollary and reinforcement of the sense of enclosure associated with Hélène's apartment. Our abiding image of Hélène is of a passive onlooker. Her characteristic pose is that of sitting at her high vantage-point overlooking Paris or silently contemplating those around her. The sheer recurrence of the words 'regards', 'regarder', 'yeux', 'face', 'visage' is as striking as the lack of verbal communication between the two principal characters.

When Zola first notes Henri's eyes examining Hélène, it is to postulate her *honnêteté* and to indicate the doctor's immediate physical attraction: 'elle gardait une majesté, une hauteur d'honnêteté et de pudeur qui la laissait chaste sous ce regard d'homme, où montait un grand trouble' ('there was something so majestic about her, such a lofty purity that she remained undisturbed by this man's now deeply troubled gaze') (II, 810). Their growing consciousness of each other in Mère Fétu's garret is seen partly in their eyes: 'leurs yeux se rencontraient' ('their eyes met') (II, 826). In these moments of *intimité*, 'debout l'un près de l'autre, se regardant bien en face' ('standing close together and looking one another in the eyes') (II, 830), Mère Fétu pursues them with noisy humility and crafty innuendo, and also with her small, prying eyes which record every reaction: 'elle ne les quittait plus du regard, allant de l'un à l'autre, avec un sourd travail dans les mille rides de son visage' ('she never took her eyes off them, glancing from one to the other while her profusely wrinkled old face twitched slyly') (II, 825–6). When they are left alone, the silence and their isolation cause them sudden embarrassment, and they watch each other or avoid each other's *regard*. Their embarrassment seems to be heightened by the round fanlight which peers down at them like a spying eye: 'Ils étaient bien seuls, cachés à tous les regards, n'ayant que cette trouée ronde qui les voyait' ('They were utterly alone, hidden from sight, watched only by that round eye over their heads') (II, 831). Zola emphasises the seclusion of the Deberles' garden; Juliette mentions that 'les arbres empêchent les gens d'à côté d'espionner' ('the trees prevent the neighbours from spying') (II, 834). When Hélène falls from the swing, it is because of Henri's *regard*. Before Henri's avowal of love, their intimacy during the afternoons spent in the garden is expressed above all by their eyes. They rarely exchange words, but their *regard* is not a sign of total communion, silent attachment: 'Et souvent, en parlant, ses yeux rencontraient les yeux d'Hélène. Ni l'un ni l'autre ne détournaient la tête. Ils se regardaient face à face, sérieux une seconde, comme s'ils se fussent vus jusqu'au cœur; puis, ils

souriaient, les paupières lentement abaissées' (II, 882).[17]
A reference to the colour of Hélène's eyes marks their growing
familiarity. This dialogue of looks is echoed when we see them
again in the garden after Hélène's 'chute', before their relationship is severed. *Intimité* is now coloured by sensuous joy, seen in
the difference of emphasis: 'Leurs yeux s'étaient cherchés, ils
avaient appuyé fortement leurs regards l'un sur l'autre' ('Their
eyes had sought each other, and then exchanged a long, meaningful glance') (II, 1052).

A corollary of emphasis on eyes is consciousness of facial
expressions and what they might reveal. When Rambaud's marriage proposal forces Hélène to recognise her suppressed feelings, the Abbé Jouve's 'regard clair et souriant' ('open, smiling
glance') (II, 874) increases her agitation and feelings of guilt:
'elle avait l'effarement de pudeur d'une femme qui sent glisser
son dernier vêtement . . . Et, comme il la regardait toujours, elle
crut qu'il lisait son mensonge sur sa face' (ibid.).[18] Similarly,
Jeanne's tears when Hélène returns from Malignon's 'pink
room' makes her wonder: 'Ça se voyait donc sur son visage?'
('Did it show on her face?') (II, 1038). After Jeanne's outburst in
the garden, her emergence as a barrier is reflected above all in
her eyes, which interpose themselves between those of Hélène
and Henri: 'le docteur trouvait sans cesse entre elle et lui ce
témoin, qui le surveillait de ses grands yeux limpides' ('The
doctor found this observer always between them watching him
with her great limpid eyes') (II, 888). After Henri's avowal of
love, Jeanne's *regard* becomes a sign of her deep jealousy and
increasing despotism ('des regards si noirs', 'ses grands yeux
fixes, d'où sortait une flamme') ('such black looks' 'her great
flashing eyes') (II, 943). Her constantly changing moods of caprice and hostility, her stifling possessiveness, her violent out-
bursts and inert passivity, her cunning use of Rambaud – all are
weapons in a tense comedy in which Jeanne constantly pursues
her opponents with her implacable *regard* and in which victory is
to avert the other's eyes or to see the pain on the other's face.
Jeanne's alienated *regard* surveys her mother when she returns
after yielding to Henri, watching her take off her wet clothes,
then wanting to flee and hide, no longer to see. This is followed
by long, reproachful looks: 'elle ne tourmentait plus sa mère
pour l'accompagner, elle la suivait seulement d'un long regard'
('she had given up begging to be allowed to accompany her

mother: she merely followed her with a long look') (II, 1049). Her opaque, implacable *regard* as she dies ('ses grands yeux vides') ('her large, vacant eyes') (II, 1067, 1071) offers no forgiveness and echoes the fixity of Hélène's eyes during the funeral.

Pressures of feeling mount to a climax in Part IV, with its sustained mood of somnambulism and sense of suspended time. Much of Parts IV and V conveys a strongly oneiric impression: the hallucinatory note, the sense of detachment from external reality, the lack of a sense of time and space, the dramatic intensity of particular sensations and images, the obsessive recurrence of certain images and themes. Part IV, Chapter 2, which preludes Hélène's 'chute', may be taken to epitomise the movement and texture of the whole novel, for it offers a striking synthesis of its dominant imagery and atmosphere. Hélène's dilemma and the tormented ambivalence of her feelings are crystallised in the opposition of images – between the claustrophobic associations of her apartment and the mysterious fascination of the 'pink room' – which are held in tension by her mood of obsessive reverie. The colour symbolism heightens this opposition: the novel's early chapters, and especially its first paragraph, frequently mention that Hélène's bedroom is a 'grande chambre bleue' ('large blue room') (II, 822). As her corrosive frustration wells up by the window, there is hardly a more explicit linking of the suffocation of her bedroom and the temptation to leave it, aggravated by the consciousness of time: 'Pendant des heures, elle restait assise, les mains abandonnées, étouffant dans sa chambre, ayant le besoin de sortir pour respirer, et ne bougeant pas. C'était cette chambre qui la rendait malade; elle la détestait, irritée des deux années qu'elle y avait vécu' (II, 993).[19] The images of squalor with which the 'pink room' is associated, and above all the drumming emphasis on 'ces temps de boue' ('this muddy weather') (II, 990), reveal Zola's vision of Hélène's imminent 'chute' as a nauseous obscenity: 'elle tâchait de s'imaginer la chambre rose au milieu de ces laideurs' ('she tried to imagine the pink room in the midst of this sordid poverty') (ibid.). The 'pink room' is surrounded by poverty: the damp, greasy stairway, the dirty yellow doors on every floor. Hélène's descent down the Passage des Eaux, contrasting with her earlier enjoyment of its shaded seclusion, is clearly portrayed as a slow act of self-abasement. The sense of looking down into a bottomless black hole, of falling, slipping, or being sucked up ('Le passage s'ouvrait sous ses pieds comme un trou noir. Elle n'en voyait pas le fond') ('The passage yawned like a black hole beneath her feet. She could not see the bottom of it') (II, 995) suggest inner collapse heightened by feelings of guilt, fear and underlying shame. Freud writes that in dreams women 'almost always accept the symbolic use of falling as a way of describing a surrender to an erotic temptation'.[20] Hélène hesitates as she holds the handrail to support herself. The shadows, the endless damp walls which seem to close in, and the gigantic shapes of the contorted branches, are menacing omens. The detailed concrete and meteorological notations (the grey sky, the rising mist, the darkness, and especially the insistence on the streams of sticky mud suggesting *enlisement*) could hardly be clearer portents of nemesis: 'elle releva . . . sa robe dont la queue traînait dans *la crotte. La boue* était si épaisse que ses bottines restaient collées sur les marches' ('she picked up her skirt, which was trailing in the dirt. The mud was so thick that her boots stuck to the steps') (II, 995). With the imminence of Hélène's 'chute', the black mud becomes a surging torrent, suggesting mounting desire and the threat of engulfment. As she hurries to warn Juliette, 'de grosses gouttes, coulant des gouttières' ('great drops from the gutters') (II, 1012), fall heavily on her shoulders: 'les ruisseaux de la rue Raynouard débordaient et s'engouffraient' ('the gutters of the Rue Raynouard had overflowed and were pouring down') (ibid.); and she is now forced to hold up her dress as she descends the narrow passage, for the water rises up to her ankles, while she hears a 'chuchotement clair, pareil au murmure des petites rivières qui coulent sous les herbes, au fond des bois' ('a light whispering sound like the murmur of streams flowing under the grass in a deep wood') (ibid.). The highly concrete evocation of the mud of Paris clearly contrasts with the sensations of calm contentment felt in the natural, rich growth of the garden. Images of liquidity ('flot', 'ruissellement', 'dégel') are used to evoke Hélène's passion, and also imply inner dissolution. When she returns to her room after her visit to the kitchen, her numb torpor melts before a fresh flood of passion: 'Cet engourdissement, qui l'avait tenue comme imbécile, se fondait en un flot de vie ardente, dont le ruissellement la brûlait' ('The numbness that had stupefied her dissolved in a flood of ardent life, that streamed fierily through her') (II, 1046). The narration of

Hélène's 'chute' itself is punctuated by the constantly falling rain.

Recurring throughout the chapter is the ambiguous tension between revulsion and fascination: 'Elle trouvait ce mystère d'un goût détestable ... Et pourtant, malgré ses répugnances, elle restait enfiévrée, attirée, les sens occupés du silence et du demi-jour qui devaient régner dans la chambre rose' (II, 992).[21] Indelible images rise up before her with the intensity of an obsession: 'l'idée fixe qui battait dans sa tête levait continuellement les mêmes images' ('the fixed idea that hammered away in her brain kept constantly conjuring up the same images') (II, 993). The emphasis on powerful undercurrents of unconscious desire becomes increasingly strong, suggesting Hélène's powerlessness: 'Sa volonté lui échappait, des pensées inavouables faisaient en elle un travail sourd' ('Her will was failing her; she was secretly tormented by thoughts she could not acknowledge') (II, 999). The anonymous letter is written as if in a dream.

Dominant imagery and themes are concentrated in a series of privileged moments in the description of the 'chute' itself, which occupies several pages. There is a superimpression of significant details in which different threads of the novel are gathered up in a play of associations; and the very simultaneity of these associations emphasises both the intensity of the moment and the theme of ambiguity. The convergence of metaphor is linked to an equal sense of fatality. When Hélène is left alone in the 'pink room' with Henri, the image of an abyss, the emphasis on slow slipping and falling, sapped strength and inevitability, recall the descent of the Passage des Eaux: 'C'était comme un trou noir où elle se sentait glisser elle-même' ('It was like a black hole into which she felt she was slipping') (II, 1020). Inevitability becomes necessity as Hélène yields to Henri in total, dream-like acquiescence: 'Elle avait tout oublié, elle cédait à une force supérieure. Cela lui semblait maintenant naturel et nécessaire' ('She had forgotten everything else, yielding to a superior force. It all seemed to her natural and inevitable now') (II, 1021). The resonances of sensation ('par une journée semblable' ['on a day like this']; the insistence on the silence and heat) evoke sudden, irresistible, dream-like memories of childhood. The interpenetration of sensation and memory, the blending of past and present, converge in a sense of total oblivion, an ineffable, self-contained moment in which the external world, time and space recede, suggesting both sensuous liberation (the memory of the summer day with windows open and the chaffinch flying into the room) and harmonious identity with the unconscious. In this sense of complete absorption, only the memory of her childhood remains. Simultaneous associations of death and voluptuous engulfment ('dans l'anéantissement délicieux de tout son être') ('in the gradual delicious annihilation of her whole being') (ibid.) are evoked by Hélène's memory of a similar winter evening of her childhood when she had nearly died in a small, airless room, also before a large fire.[22]

> Autour d'eux, un désert se déroulait; pas un bruit, pas une voix humaine, l'impression d'une mer noire où soufflait une tempête. Ils étaient hors du monde, à mille lieues des terres. Et cet oubli des liens qui les attachaient aux autres êtres et aux choses était si absolu, qu'il leur semblait naître là, à l'instant même, et devoir mourir là, tout à l'heure, lorsqu'ils se prendraient aux bras l'un de l'autre. (II, 1023)[23]

The intensity of the dream-atmosphere is marked by a sense of floating and suspension, a hallucinatory feeling of detachment from contingent reality. The coherence and unity of the novel are again emphasised, for its privileged moments of intense feeling and sensation are characterised by immobility, silence and isolation, which heightens the impression of a private dream-world.

The description of Hélène's 'chute' ends with intimations of shame: 'Quand Hélène revint, les pieds nus, chercher ses souliers devant le feu qui se mourait, elle pensait que jamais ils ne s'étaient moins aimés que ce jour-là' ('When Hélène came back, in her bare feet, to fetch her shoes in front of the dying fire, she said to herself that they had never loved one another less than that day') (II, 1024). The absence of contact between Hélène and Henri, reinforced by the silence and the enveloping sense of unreality, is again underlined. Henri, significantly, also kisses her cold, naked feet, which thus links him to Hélène's first husband and to Rambaud. The final, conspicuously deflatory note, together with the introduction of the motif of death, leads us into Jeanne's attitudes. There is a modification of perspective as she now comes to occupy a more central position.

VI

Jeanne, used dramatically to exteriorise Hélène's moral dilemma, is closely associated with the motif of *le regard* and must be seen in the context of certain themes which run through the whole of Zola's work. She may be seen as one of a series of watchers or witnesses of sexual scenes, in which anguish and ambiguously portrayed contemplation of nudity is a prominent situation, strongly linked to feelings of shame, guilt, deep unease and sometimes fear.[24] The theme of the *spectacle interdit*, of the obsessively recurring triangular situation involving sexual betrayal, frequently involves children as observers of scenes of eroticism and violence. Jeanne's excited contemplation of Rosalie and Zéphyrin in the sensuous frame of the garden recalls, for example, Nana's sensual curiosity as she spies on Gervaise and Lantier in *L'Assommoir*. *Regard* thus becomes 'transgression', and the theme of the *spectacle interdit* recurs like a leitmotiv in Part IV, Chapter 5: 'Enfin, elle allait donc savoir, elle se poserait sur les dômes et sur les flèches, elle verrait, en sept ou huit coups d'aile, les choses défendues que l'on cache aux enfants' (II, 1070).[25] An added irony in Jeanne's case is that the *spectacle interdit* is itself maleficent: by 'punishing' her mother Jeanne punishes herself for her own transgression. Jeanne's revulsion before the muddy spectacle of Paris might recall scenes from earlier novels in which contemplation gives rise to feelings of revulsion. Connected with this, but less directly, are feelings of self-disgust and self-defilement, especially involving a nauseous sense of one's own naked body (recalling Renée's self-revulsion in *La Curée* before her own reflection in the mirror). Jeanne's shame at her nakedness on her death-bed ('elle se vit nue, elle sanglota de honte') ('she saw herself naked, and sobbed with shame') (II, 1062) is reinforced by the theme of lost innocence, another recurrent theme in Zola (very visible, as we have seen, in *La Curée*, and at the centre of *La Faute de l'abbé Mouret*). The image of childhood recurs at certain key moments: while Hélène is on the swing, for example, and, most significantly, when the upsurge of dream-like memories of childhood during the 'chute' reinforces a sense of nostalgia for the *paradis perdu* of childlike innocence.

The alteration of focus is not sudden. Throughout the novel, Jeanne, delicate, highly strung and neurotically possessive, expresses sexual innocence, curiosity, and growing awareness, before mediating, after Hélène's 'chute', sexual shame and despair, and finally acting as a retributive instrument. Her questions are those of precocious puberty and her *regard* is 'ce regard d'une enfant de douze ans, où luisait trop tôt toute la vie de passion d'une femme' ('that twelve-year-old child's gaze, prematurely ablaze with adult passion') (II, 944). Several times Zola notes, in a sentimental, Dickensian manner, 'la nudité innocente de l'enfant' ('the innocent naked body of the child') (II, 806), 'ses membres innocents et vierges' ('her pure and innocent limbs') (II, 1031). Jeanne's pubertal ignorance and curiosity echo Hélène's own ignorance. The scene in which she excitedly contemplates Rosalie and Zéphyrin in the garden, described in strongly sensuous terms, is briefly reminiscent of *La Faute de l'abbé Mouret*. The *ébats* of Rosalie and Zéphyrin, accompanied by 'l'odeur grasse de la terre que la bêche ne retournait jamais' ('the smell of rich, uncultivated earth') (II, 961) and the penetrating smell of roses and wild growth ('On aurait cru l'enfoncement lointain d'une forêt') (It was like some deep forest glade') (II, 953), seem invigorating and sensuously exciting to her: 'Un flot de santé remontait en elle et l'étouffait' ('A great wave of well-being surged up in her, taking her breath away') (II, 957). It should be noted, however, that their love is only partially identified with a healthy, natural eroticism: they are associated with food, a prominent sex-substitute in Zola; there are taboos limiting their relationship; and they show little concern about when they are to marry. They indicate only the beginnings of a solution to the problem of sexuality in Zola.

With Hélène's 'chute' the emphasis changes as Jeanne becomes victim. Part IV, Chapter 5, in which Jeanne, closely linked to the motif of the bedroom, contemplates Paris from the window, might be analysed as a dream, for it is a dream-landscape that we are offered, shaped by Jeanne's feelings and transparently sexual in its symbolism. But while dreams are usually apparently disconnected, fragmentary and quite illogical, the projection of Jeanne's feelings on to the scene described offers, as Jean Borie points out,[26] the most coherently anthropomorphic of the novel's window-scenes. Borie also makes the pertinent observation that a dream-landscape is most often a representation of the sexual organs.[27] The female sexual connotations of the landscape are plain: the focal centre of the city is the Seine ('coulée géante', 'fente', 'sillon'), with Paris seen as an immense valley and frequently given human features ('Paris, disparu, avait le repos rêveur d'un colosse' ['Paris had vanished, but it lay at rest like a dreamy giant'] [II, 965], 'une haleine si colossale' ['a breath so tremendous'] [II, 1031]). It is thus the body of her mother which Jeanne nostalgically contemplates. It should also be noted that in the apocalyptic vision, the sexual themes merge into the sense of cosmic reverberation which characterises the endings of many of Zola's novels, going beyond purely sexual shame to suggest a whole world collapsing.

There is a coherent sequence of associations connecting the dominant images. As Jeanne contemplates interrogatively 'le vide béant où Paris semblait s'être englouti' ('the gaping void that seemed to have swallowed up Paris') (II, 967), wondering where her mother might be, feelings of anguished loss and rejection are assimilated to increasing sexual nausea, shame and irremediable loss of innocence.[28] She tries to seek out and identify what is hidden and forbidden ('Elle sentit confusément que sa mère était quelque part où les enfants ne vont pas') ('She felt dimly that her mother was somewhere where children might not go') (II, 1028), seen in terms of some profound but unknown wrong ('le mal qu'elle ignorait') ('its unknown evil') (II, 1033). The violence of a fresh storm as it sweeps across the city matches the unmistakably phallic significance of the Panthéon, in which Jeanne momentarily imagines her mother to be: 'celui-là l'étonnait le plus, énorme et planté tout en l'air comme le panache de la ville' ('that was the most amazing of them all, so huge, and stuck up there like a crest on top of the town') (II, 1029). And then, resuming the leitmotiv of Part IV, Chapter 2, with its emphasis on disgust, ugliness and menace, Hélène is identified with the nauseous viscosity of the city mud:

Qu'était-ce donc, ce monument si noir? et cette rue, où courait quelque chose de gros? et tout ce quartier, dont elle avait peur, parce que bien sûr on s'y battait? Elle ne distinguait pas nettement; mais, sans mentir, ça remuait, c'était très laid,[29] les petites filles ne devait pas regarder ... L'inconnu de Paris, avec ses fumées, son grondement continu, sa vie puissante, soufflait jusqu'à elle, par ce temps de dégel, une odeur de misère, d'ordure et de crime, qui faisait tourner sa jeune tête, comme si elle s'était penchée au-dessus d'un de ces puits empestés, exhalant l'asphyxie de leur boue invisible . . . Puis, elle ne savait plus, elle restait effrayée et honteuse, avec la pensée entêtée que sa mère était dans ces vilaines choses, quelque part qu'elle ne devinait point, tout au fond, là-bas. (II, 1029–30)[30]

The words 'inconnu' and 'boue' again stand out. The sexual implications of the supreme convulsion which seems to shake the city as another violent storm erupts ('des rues s'abîmaient, coulant à fond et surnageant, dans des secousses dont la violence semblait annoncer la fin de la cité') ('whole streets were engulfed, sank down and then floated up again, amidst shocks so violent that the end of the city seemed near') (II, 1032), the searing pain which Jeanne experiences, simultaneous with Hélène's 'chute' ('Et, du fond de son être, de son sexe de femme éveillé, une vive douleur jaillit comme un coup reçu de loin') ('And in the depths of her being, in her newly-awakened sexual consciousness, she felt a sharp pang, like a blow aimed from a distance') (II, 1031), and the transformation of the city into a river of mud, clinch the cumulative associations between 'chute' – shame – 'boue' – destruction – nemesis, and make evident the suggestion of lost innocence and (metaphorically) lost virginity: 'Ça la brûlait, ça la prenait comme un mal de tête. Sûrement, tout à l'heure, on lui avait cassé quelque part une chose' ('It was a burning pain within her, it was something that gripped her like a headache. Surely, a few moments ago, something had broken inside her') (II, 1033). Her lost innocence, reflected momentarily in the memory of the visit to the mill, with the fine yellow corn and huge haystacks, seems to cry out under the constantly falling rain: 'le regret de quelque chose d'irrémédiable pleurait en elle. Tout lui semblait fini, elle comprenait qu'elle devenait très vieille' ('her heart ached with regret for something irreparable. She felt as if everything was finished; she realised that she must be growing very old') (ibid.). The themes of sexual loss, shame, guilt and deadened resignation now dominate the tone of the novel. Later, during Hélène's absences, Jeanne sits silently by the fire warming her hands and saying that she has become old. Her shame and terror on her death-bed before Henri's *regard* repeat the point; and the description of her death, Victorian in its sentimentality, gathers up these associations into a clear statement:

> Elle se vit nue, elle sanglota de honte, en ramenant vivement
> le drap. Il semblait qu'elle eût vieilli tout d'un coup de dix ans
> dans son agonie, et que, près de la mort, ses douze années
> fussent assez mûres pour comprendre que cet homme ne
> devait pas la toucher et retrouver sa mère en elle. (II, 1062)[31]

The displacement of point of view as Jeanne assumes a
more dominant role brings into question the problem of Zola's
intentions and the moral framework of the novel. The narrative
is constantly punctuated by rhetorical intrusions and a moralistic vocabulary: 'elle goûtait ainsi un *lâche* bonheur à se dire que
rien n'était défendu' ('she was weakly indulging in the pleasure
of telling herself that nothing was forbidden') (II, 1054); 'cet
abaissement d'elle-même lui donnait la profonde jouissance d'un
besoin contenté' ('this self-abasement gave her a sense of deep
delight, as though some inner need were satisfied') (II, 1045);
'elle portait son secret paisiblement, sans un trouble d'honnêteté, car *rien de mauvais* ne l'agitait' ('she cherished her secret
serenely, without a qualm of conscience, since no thought of evil
disturbed her') (II, 882). After reading *Une Page d'amour*, Gide
wrote in his *Journal:* 'Zola devait avoir de grandes prétentions à
la moralité' ('Zola must have had great pretensions to morality').[32] We have seen that Hélène's moral probity is emphasised
from the beginning. 'Mal' is perhaps the word most often used to
denote moral connotations: 'le mal qu'elle ignorait' ('its
unknown evil') (II, 1033), 'le mal étrange dont elle venait de
souffrir' ('the strange pain she had been enduring') (II, 1034),
'quel coup d'étrange folie, quel mal abominable, aveugle comme
la foudre!' ('what a strange fit of madness; what a terrible disease
had smitten her with the blind swiftness of a thunderbolt!') (II,
1089). The actual term 'chute', which is frequently used, implies
condemnation. Zola intended to portray 'le coup de passion dans
une nature honnête et un peu froide' ('sudden passion in someone of an upright and rather cold disposition'),[33] and the novel's
moral content is indeed deeply puritanical: passion is understood in the original sense of 'la souffrance, les quelques joies
aigües et le déchirement profond; un calvaire' ('suffering, the few
acute joys and deep heartbreak; a calvary').[34] Hélène must suffer
and cannot be condoned; her love must be constrained and

doomed to failure; she must be punished for her act of transgression and her *faute* must be expiated. Zola thus affirms his belief in the importance of marital fidelity and maternal duty. His depiction of Hélène's maternal devotion underlines the prestige of motherhood,[35] while the presentation of Jeanne's mortal illness as the retributive consequence of adultery underlines the primacy of motherhood and the unacceptability of extra-marital sexuality. The point is given further emphasis by the birth of the Deberles' second child, who, it is noted, resembles Jeanne and was conceived at the time of Jeanne's death. This affirmation of motherhood anticipates Zola's later cult of motherhood, which comes to the fore from *Le Docteur Pascal* onwards and achieves its apotheosis in *Fécondité*. The ambiguity of Zola's position is highlighted, however, by the fact that 'he finally puts his heroine in the very situation that he acknowledges leads to incompatibility and potential adultery in his other novels of the loveless marriage'.[36] Although we are intended to approve of the marriage with Rambaud, it is clear that it is a *mariage de raison;* Rambaud's staunch loyalty represents a permanent alternative to passion. Although *Pot-Bouille* is a savage attack on the hollowness of bourgeois marriage and *Une Page d'amour* treats adultery in an ambiguously sympathetic light, neither novel shows that Zola, at this stage in his career, could envisage any alternative to bourgeois marriage.

A study of the thematic imagery, dominant motifs and structural organisation of *Une Page d'amour* thus illuminates some central themes of Zola's work: bourgeois adultery and marriage; the equation between a sense of sexual transgression, disaster and death; a sexuality deeply laden with guilt. The novel gives form to a conflict which was at the heart of his fiction. Zola had declared his intention to produce an anatomy of the birth, development and end of a passion, and insisted on the *general* nature of his enterprise: 'tout le mérite devrait être dans le côté *général* de l'oeuvre' ('the entire merit of the work should lie in its *general* aspect').[37] But there is a gap between intention and achievement, for the vision of sexuality projected through Hélène's consciousness constitutes no dispassionate, clinical analysis of passion, but is marked by deep involvement and reveals important ambiguities of feeling. Flaubert saw immediately that one would be naïve indeed to read *Une Page d'amour* simply as a moral cautionary tale. Despite the novel's lack of overt eroticism, he remarked in a letter to Zola on its strongly erotic character: 'je n'en conseillerais pas la lecture à ma fille, si j'étais mère!!! Malgré mon grand âge, ce roman m'a troublé et *excité*. On a envie d'Hélène d'une façon démesurée et on comprend très bien votre docteur.'[38] The great matriarchal values in Zola are affirmed, but the moralistic content is belied by the degree of our sympathetic identification with Hélène. The novel, despite Zola's conscious intentions, reveals a totally equivocal stance towards both libidinal sexuality and bourgeois marriage. It is the ambivalence characterising the impulses and inner feelings of the heroine which governs the structure and imagery of the novel; and this organic body of metaphor and imagery, built up on partly unconscious patterns of association, constitutes the novel's unity and coherence.

Pot-Bouille: Black Comedy

The declared aim of *Pot-Bouille* was the depiction of the mentality and morals of the Parisian bourgeoisie: 'Montrer la bourgeoisie à nu, après avoir montré le peuple, et la montrer plus abominable, elle qui se dit l'ordre et l'honnêteté.'[1] Paul Alexis, explaining the title of the novel, wrote: 'Aux bourgeois qui disent: nous sommes l'honneur, la morale, la famille, il [Zola] voulait répondre: ce n'est pas vrai, vous êtes le mensonge de tout cela, votre pot-bouille est la marmite où mijotent toutes les pourritures de la famille et tous les relâchements de la morale.'[2] Zola's intentions in this neglected novel are emphatically satirical; but although the book is intended as a comprehensive indictment of the bourgeoisie, it focuses on the theme of sexuality, which is seen as a mechanical, animal activity sustained by habit and propelled by cynicism. The pervading atmosphere, heightened by structural repetition and circularity, is one of furtive secrecy and sour monotony. Although *Pot-Bouille* has some of the outward forms of a bedroom farce, there is no trace of gaiety or *gauloiserie* in its depiction of 'adultères *sans passion sexuelle*' ('adultery *without sexual passion*').[3] What is striking about the novel is the acerbity of its tone, the deeply sombre nature of its indictment. The cumulative vehemence of *Pot-Bouille* clearly distinguishes it from the muted quality of *Une Page d'amour*. It is the starkest and most specific expression in the Rougon-Macquart cycle of the themes adumbrated in *La Fortune des Rougon:* bourgeois hypocrisy and vicious self-interest. *La Curée* had shown moral corruption behind social glitter, *Le Ventre de Paris* the brutality behind sleek, scrupulous *honnêteté, L'Assommoir* the misery of the *faubourgs* behind the public splendour of the Empire. *Pot-Bouille* continues the sexual denunciation of *Nana,* which immediately precedes it in the cycle, but on a different level and in a different register. Sexuality is now seen as an

129

erosive rather than a devouring force; destructive sexuality is viewed within a more sharply satirical framework and is more controlled. The relationship between *Pot-Bouille* and *Nana,* as Henri Guillemin has noted,[4] is similar to that between *Le Ventre de Paris* and *La Curée.* Whereas the satire of *La Curée* is directed against the Second Empire property speculators and the decadent world of the *haute-bourgeoisie, Le Ventre de Paris* shows the complacent *petite-bourgeoisie* to be no more admirable in their brutal egoism, for both milieux share the same uncompromising appetites. Similarly, while *Nana* reveals the frenetic sexual decadence of the upper classes through the mythical prostitute-catalyst, *Pot-Bouille* shows that the respectable bourgeoisie of the 'liberal professions' are no less squalid in their sexual habits, only more dissimulating. *Nana,* however, had concentrated on the particular milieu of the boulevards *noceurs* rather than a whole class, whereas the characters of *Pot-Bouille* form a relatively representative social mixture. The concluding words of *Pot-Bouille,* the brief moral reflections of the cook, Julie, both echo the closing words of *Le Ventre de Paris* (Claude Lantier's contemptuous 'Quels gredins que les honnêtes gens!' ['What swine decent people really are!'] and imply that the *maison Vabre* is entirely representative of its kind: 'celle-ci ou celle-là, toutes les baraques se ressemblent. Au jour d'aujourd'hui, qui a fait l'une a fait l'autre. C'est cochon et compagnie' ('it doesn't matter which hole it is: they're all the same. These days, if you've been in one of 'em you've been in 'em all. They're all pig-sties') (III, 386). Moreover, *Pot-Bouille* was meant to form a deliberate pendant to *L'Assommoir,* and bourgeois applause at what is saw in *L'Assommoir* as working-class 'degeneracy' was to become howls of rage at the unflinching image of its own debasement. Brunetière, reviewing the novel in *La Revue des deux mondes* (15 May 1882), was full of self-congratulation at having anticipated the indignant reaction of bourgeois critics, which he saw as the vindication of his previous denunciations of Zola's work. He sternly reproached all those imprudent bourgeois who had made Zola's reputation.

I

Poetic symbolism and the central presence of an animated concrete entity are fundamental features of Zola's fiction. Houses and buildings constitute the centre of many of his novels.[5] There is the Mourets' house at Plassans, conquered by the Abbé Faujas; the prosperous delicatessen in *Le Ventre de Paris;* the labyrinthine tenement block in *L'Assommoir;* the huge department store in *Au Bonheur des Dames;* the Chouteaus' bleak, isolated house in *La Joie de vivre;* the network of houses in which crimes are commited in *La Bête humaine;* and, as we have seen, Hélène's apartment in *Une Page d'amour.* The apartment block in *Pot-Bouille* (the title of one of the English translations of the novel is *Restless House*) is transformed into an enveloping symbol of the corruption and decadence of the bourgeoisie. The whole house provides the unifying metaphor of the novel. The scene of much of the action, it is inhabited by most of the characters in the book. *Pot-Bouille* is distinctive in that it is a novel without a 'hero'. It is given integrated structure through the use of Octave Mouret as a detached spectator, as well as through its symbolic décor, unity of tone and verbal and dramatic repetition. But Octave hardly constitutes a 'hero'; the central character is, in a sense, the house itself.

When Octave arrives in the rue de Choiseul, he is shown round by Campardon, which permits Zola to establish an equation between material and moral life in the evocation of décor. The brash modernity of the house immediately identifies it as typical of the new bourgeois constructions of the time. Its ostentatious splendour contrasts with the worn façades of the surrounding houses, and the Second Empire vulgarity of its design is heavily pointed, revealing both factitiousness and a suggestion of decadence. A note of cheapness and banality is introduced into the mention of the elaborate window-frames by the added 'taillés à la grosse sur des poncifs' ('roughly chiselled in soft stone') (III, 3). The main entrance, with its ironic 'deux amours' ('two Cupids') is even more richly ornamental. The ornateness of the main entrance implies falseness and deceptive appearances:

Le vestibule et l'escalier étaient d'un luxe violent. En bas, une figure de femme, une sorte de Napolitaine toute dorée, portait sur la tête une amphore, d'où sortaient trois becs de gaz, garnis de globes dépolis. Les panneaux de faux marbre, blancs à bordures roses, montaient régulièrement dans la cage ronde; tandis que la rampe de fonte, à bois d'acajou, imitait le vieil argent, avec des épanouissements de feuilles d'or. Un

tapis rouge, retenu par des tringles de cuivre, couvrait les
marches. (III, 5)[6]

Octave's initial impression is of impenetrable silence and immobility, of an introverted family life whose jealously guarded
privacy implies a cloistered and monotonous existence. He is struck
immediately by the hothouse temperature. The stifling heat,
together with the 'grave silence' of the stairway, suggests claustrophobia: 'C'était une paix morte de salon bourgeois, soigneusement clos, où n'entrait pas un souffle du dehors' ('There
was a deathly calm, the peace of a middle-class drawing-room,
carefully shut in, admitting no sound from without') (III, 6). The
rhetorical exaggeration points to an element of secrecy and dis-
simulation: 'Derrière les belles portes d'acajou luisant, il y avait
comme des abîmes d'honnêteté' ('Behind these fine doors of
gleaming mahogany there seemed to be infinite depths of respectability') (ibid.). As Octave stands contemplating the closed
mahogany doors, introversion is linked to the suggestion of a
hidden life by the references to the 'persiennes éternellement
closes' ('eternally closed shutters') and 'la vie murée' ('walled-in
life') (III, 7) of each apartment. This is reinforced by constant
allusions to the falseness already indicated and further underlined by the grotesque image of the imitation windows painted
on the blank walls of the courtyard.

The motif of hermetic enclosure, of a confined and airless
atmosphere, corresponds to the general furtiveness and the pervasive tone of rancour and suppression. Nearly all of the dramatic action of the novel takes place indoors; the time-scheme too is
relatively compact. Life in the building presents a picture of
close-quartered and criss-crossing relationships, frustrations,
hatreds, petty jealousies and mutual denigration. Enclosing
walls, closed doors and airless rooms create a sense of frustration
and decay. Frustration is an essential experience of most of the
characters. Marie Pichon's dreams of romantic love are dreams
of escape. The frustration of Berthe is quite different but no less
real. The basic components of Mme Vuillaumes's theory of education are rigorous enclosure and total insulation: 'Les portes
fermées, les fenêtres closes, jamais de courants d'air, qui appor-
tent les vilaines choses de la rue' ('Doors and windows shut: no
draughts which bring in nasty things from the street') (III, 66).
These ideas are echoed by Rose Campardon in her confidences

to Octave: 'il fallait écarter d'elle [Angèle] jusqu'aux souffles de la rue' ('she ought to be shielded from the very breath of the streets') (III, 19).

The first chapter ends with the ironic picture of the house going to sleep.

> Lentement, il [Octave] monta à son tour. Un seul bec de gaz brûlait, l'escalier s'endormait dans une chaleur lourde. Il lui sembla plus recueilli, avec ses portes chastes, ses portes de riche acajou, fermées sur des alcôves honnêtes. Pas un soupir ne passait, c'était un silence de gens bien élevés qui retiennent leur souffle. Cependant, un léger bruit se fit entendre, il se pencha et aperçut M. Gourd, en pantoufles et en calotte, éteignant le dernier bec de gaz. Alors, tout s'abîma, la maison tomba à la solennité des ténèbres, comme anéantie dans la distinction et la décence de son sommeil. (III, 20)[7]

The emphasis on the silence and the gradual sinking into sleep, with the progression from verb to verb and the repetition of the same impressions and ideas, gives cumulative weight to the ironic exaggeration of the final sentence, and particularly to the alliterative balance of the last phrase. The comic anthropomorphism increases the note of mock solemnity. The fantasy of the suggestion that the tenants are so modest that they would hold their breath is matched by the fantasy of 's'abîma' and 'comme anéantie', aided by the linking of incongruous adjectives and nouns ('portes chastes').

The image of the sumptuous façade recurs like an obsessive leitmotiv. The morning after the discovery of Berthe in Octave's room sees the reassertion of respectability after the upheavals of the night: 'Ce matin-là, le réveil de la maison fut d'une grande dignité bourgeoise' ('That morning, as the house awoke, it wore a majestic air of middle-class decorum') (III, 294). Dramatic use is made of the décor, of which Zola's recurring descriptions serve as ironic commentary: 'Rien, dans l'escalier, ne gardait la trace des scandales de la nuit, ni les faux marbres qui avaient reflété ce galop d'une femme en chemise, ni la moquette d'où s'était évaporée l'odeur de sa nudité' (ibid.).[8] Verbal fantasy is supported by the odious extension of the décor, Gourd, who is seen sniffing the walls in the early morning as if they would yield up the happenings of the night. The use of the façade as a symbol of bourgeois hypocrisy is illustrated by the sight of the neighbours, who have overheard the gossip of the servants, stopping to gaze up at the house, 'cherchant et fouillant les étages' ('peering hard at the different floors') (ibid.). But the façade allays their suspicions and swiftly disperses them: 'Devant la façade riche . . . le monde se taisait et s'en allait poliment' ('Before the impressive façade . . . the onlookers fell silent and soon passed along politely') (ibid.).

The theme of appearance and reality thus lies at the centre of the novel. It corresponds to the alternating rhythms of noise and silence, *débandade* and suppression, and to the counterpoint between servants and tenants, the doctor and the priest. The driving obsession of Mme Josserand is social ambition; her aim is to ensnare a son-in-law who will enable her to compete with the Duveyriers. Her frequent outpouring of stereotyped maxims sums up her whole code of bourgeois values:

> Dans la vie, il n'y a que les plus honteux qui perdent. L'argent est l'argent: quand on n'en a pas, le plus court est de se coucher. Moi, lorsque j'ai eu vingt sous, j'ai toujours dit que j'en avais quarante; car toute la sagesse est là, il vaut mieux faire envie que pitié . . . On a beau avoir reçu de l'instruction, si l'on n'est pas bien mis, les gens vous méprisent. Ce n'est pas juste, mais c'est ainsi . . . Je porterais plutôt des jupons sales qu'une robe d'indienne. Mangez des pommes de terre, mais ayez un poulet, quand vous avez du monde à dîner . . . Et ceux qui disent le contraire sont des imbéciles! (III, 35)[9]

Mme Josserand and her daughters trudge home through the mud rather than take a cab. Their constant penny-pinching in order to maintain genteel appearances obliges M. Josserand to spend whole nights wrapping periodicals. They often go hungry and starve the servant, Adèle – the only servant they have had who will endure 'cette misère vaniteuse de bourgeois' ('this wretched middle-class vanity') (III, 27). Their assiduous concern for appearances is reflected in the description of the tea-table during the reception: 'Aux deux bouts, un luxe de fleurs, des roses superbes et coûteuses, couvraient la médiocrité du beurre et la poussière ancienne des biscuits' ('At both ends of the table were flowers in profusion; magnificent and costly roses prevented the guests from noticing the stale biscuits and rancid butter') (III, 54). *L'envie de paraître,* with its connexion with the ritual of husband-hunting, is often translated through physical descriptions which impinge on smell and touch. The departure of the irate Auguste in Chapter XVI is sealed by the symbolic 'odeur de beurre rance, de beurre de mauvaise qualité acheté exprès aux Halles' ('smell of rancid butter, of the cheap kind you could buy at the Halles') (III, 331).

With the contrast between appearance and reality given such prominence, irony is vigorously exploited. When Campardon introduces Octave to the house, he emphasises that it is inhabited only by tenants of unimpeachable virtue: 'Tous bourgeois et d'une moralité!' ('All middle-class people, and terribly respectable!') (III, 8). His earnest request that Octave should respect this strict morality helps to establish the façade of bourgeois *honnêteté*. Despite constant assertions of his 'broad-minded' artistic nature, Campardon, like Gourd, acts as the unfailing defender of the house's 'respectability', as if it were a matter of personal pride; and his hypocritical insistence on the paramount need to preserve the bourgeois virtue of the house becomes more ludicrous as his relations with Gasparine become more apparent. Ironies proliferate. Chapter XV, for example, is full of the comedy of hypocrisy and outraged bluster: Bachelard bitterly lamenting his shattered ideals, with the profounder irony that the artificial ingenuousness of Fifi has rebounded upon him; the obvious irony of Bachelard and Duveyrier momentarily breaking off their erotic dramas pompously to defend Auguste in the name of respectability; the ironic twist given to the theme of appearance and reality by the now obsessive bourgeois aspirations of Duveyrier's mistress, Clarisse, who insists on the rigorous maintenance of all the outward forms of bourgeois social life; and the accompanying irony of the progressive ensnarement of Duveyrier in the very domestic atmosphere from which he is trying to escape.

The theme of moral squalor beneath the calm surface of respectability leads to ironic play on noisy self-righteousness and to comic portrayals of smug pomposity: the vigour with which Duveyrier affects to protect the moral fabric of society and the integrity of the family, and his portentous assertions that adultery is very rare among the educated classes; Bachelard's declarations that he finds much 'refreshment' in the innocence of Fifi; Campardon's censorship of morally dubious articles in the newspapers; Mme Juzeur's hypocritical condescension towards the young orphan. To exorcise the lingering scandal of Berthe's adultery, Duveyrier prompts Auguste to effect a reconciliation. Duveyrier (who always takes off his Legion of Honour medal when visiting his mistress) is much preoccupied with allaying the 'moral disfavour' into which the house is falling. Similarly, once the 'illegal situation' between Clémence and Hippolyte becomes public, it is resolved that they must be married; the Abbé Mauduit is naturally employed to inform them of the 'immorality' of their situation, but his arguments are cut short by Hippolyte's announcement that he is already married.

II

The role of the servants is intimately related to the theme of appearance and reality and ironic use of décor. While the bourgeois tenants live in the heated apartments at the front of the house, the servants live in cold, partitioned cubicles under the roof and work in the filthy kitchens overlooking the courtyard. But they are seen in no explicitly political perspective and indeed are not generally presented in a sympathetic light. They act as dramatic counterpoint, occasionally appearing in order to exchange the latest tit-bits concerning the changing state of sexual relations in the house. During the initial guided tour by Campardon, Octave is introduced to the kitchens and finds the servants exchanging raucous gossip from window to window, with the courtyard below: 'C'était comme la déverse d'un égout' ('It was as if a sewer had brimmed over') (III, 9). The sewer comparison, which will become a motif, is immediately contrasted in Octave's mind with 'la majesté bourgeoise du grand escalier' ('the middle-class majesty of the main staircase') (ibid.). The servants reinforce the counterpoint between the pestilential courtyard and the main stairway. The courtyard becomes a symbolic image of the sordid reality of bourgeois domestic life, and the unwholesome smells become the true essence of the house's 'moral filth': 'il ne montait plus, du boyau noir de l'étroite cour, que la puanteur d'évier mal tenu, comme l'exhalaison même des ordures cachées des familles, remuées là par la rancune de la domesticité' (III, 107).[10] The servants clearly know everything: 'Ces filles savaient tout, sans que personne eût parlé' ('Although no one had said a word, these girls knew everything') (III, 269). Servants spy on their masters, neighbours on each other, the *concierge* on everyone. In fact *everyone* knows everything. The themes of omniscience and *le regard*, which are stressed by the marked presence of the author and the prominence of *personnages-témoins*, reinforce the pervasive sense of claustrophobia and also heighten the sense of inner loneliness of the characters, which is felt most strongly in M. Josserand, Marie Pichon and Adèle, and refers us back to the themes of *abandon* and *isolement* in *Une Page d'amour*.

The opposition between the fetid courtyard and the imposing entrance-hall, the *escalier de service* and the main stairway, the contrast between public respectability and private promiscuity, the rigid separation of tenants and servants, dirty kitchens and neat apartments, correspond to a strict compartmentalisation of life and society.[11] Order and hierarchy are the watchwords of the house, well defined and clearly determined relationships the keynote. Zola is concerned not so much with the mechanisms of hypocrisy as with the secrecy which it involves and the constraints and conflicts which it manifests. The bourgeois tenants, far from being victims of each other's deception, are at one in their general collusion and complicity. This brings into question the notion of decadence itself. In *Pot-Bouille* it is identified with a loss of moral consciousness, of any positive standards or values, as all becomes absorbed into a hollow interaction between appearance and reality. As respectable appearances become paramount, awareness of any essential value becomes blurred and lost: 'L'inconscience du crime chez le bourgeois: trait décisif' ('The bourgeoisie's unawareness of moral values: their key trait').[12] And in this perversion of morality, moral guilt is thrust upon the servants; amorality is not only a complicated charade but is viciously brutal.

The servants are thus directly related to the theme of sexual repression within marriage. What is suppressed is a natural sexuality, instinctual needs and desires. *Peuple* and *corps*, the popular and the natural, are closely identified in Zola, and each may be seen to function as a metaphor of the other.[13] Sexual relationships parallel and reflect social relationships. The social repression of the servants becomes the reverse side of bourgeois sexual repression, sexual exploitation the counterpart of social exploitation. Adèle, stupid, superstitious, and exploited by all, takes on

the figure of scapegoat. The height of the novel's sordidness is
the description of her confinement, contrasted with the false
gaiety of the final *soirée*. The agony of Adèle, described with
Naturalist intimacy of physical detail, is an image of bourgeois
indifference: 'Ce n'était donc pas assez de ne jamais manger à sa
faim, d'être le souillon sale et gauche, sur lequel la maison
entière tapait: il fallait que les maîtres lui fissent un enfant!' ('So
it wasn't enough to be starved, and the clumsy, dirty drudge
whom everyone bullied: her masters had to get her pregnant
as well!') (III, 368). Her lonely ordeal in the dark might be seen
as the culmination of the book, as she wraps her child in newspapers and leaves it in the Passage de Choiseul as dawn breaks.
Jean Borie describes thus the vicious circle of Zola's social
vision:

> Si donc le peuple est réduit au corps, c'est qu'il est condamné
> par la bourgeoisie à rester séparé, a rester peuple . . . Nous
> pouvons ainsi formuler cette contradiction: le mal vient du
> peuple, et it est imposé au peuple. La 'générosité' de Zola
> donne l'absolution, mais la vision sociale reste bloquée, et
> le restera nécessairement aussi longtemps que le corps
> demeurera prisonnier dans son enfer.[14]

The presence of the servants also emphasises the sense of
repugnance surrounding sexuality. Trublot's bland account of
the sexual permutations involving the servants is accompanied
by stress on sordid sense-impressions, as Octave waits in the
cold, bare room with its dirty walls and 'insupportable odeur de
fille mal tenue' ('insufferable smell of an unwashed servant-girl')
(III, 264), and listens first to the 'bruits de femmes qui se
déshabillent et se soulagent' ('sounds of women undressing and
relieving themselves') (III, 261), then to robust snores and continual moaning. The texture of the novel is characterised by
impressions of staleness, sourness and claustrophobia. Sense-
impressions contribute to the movement towards total deflation
and debasement. The *ordures* and sewer motifs have strong
associations of nausea. Images of *ordures* are directly related to
ones of mud, which are pervasive in Zola and so prominent in
Une Page d'amour, evoking a sense of sexual revulsion and
ensnarement. This obsessive, horrified vision is expressive of a
fundamental tension, a sense of ultimate disaster, which corres-

ponds to the apocalyptic tendency in Zola's picture of a decomposing world. The central implication is that sexual indulgence is entirely circumscribed by nauseous connotations and destructive consequences. The atmosphere of anxiety and recriminations, of desultory sexual anticipation and dissatisfaction, reaches a peak with the long descriptions of the clandestine meetings between Octave and Berthe and the bribery of Rachel. The early-morning scene in Rachel's room marks the culmination of *depoétisation*, as Octave and Berthe overhear the foul-mouthed talk of the servants, at first describing their various filching triumphs and then reaching a crescendo of sexual gossip which includes cutting comments on both of them: 'Maintenant, leurs amours, si soigneusement cachés, traînaient au milieu des épluchures et des eaux grasses. . . Et une blague ordurière salissait leurs baisers, leurs rendez-vous, tout ce qu'il y avait encore de bon et de délicat dans leurs tendresses' (III, 269).[15] It is clear that *Pot-Bouille* hardly makes salacious reading. The novel reveals a graphic and entirely reductive emphasis on sexual humiliation and squalor. The frank sensuality of Octave, Trublot and Bachelard contrasts with its absence in all those around them. At the same time Zola emphasises the fierce hostility between men and women. Acts of intercourse are often distasteful. When Octave and Marie perfunctorily make love on the kitchen table, she yielding with a mixture of kindness, stupidity and fear, we read: 'Quand il la quitta, il était mécontent, il aurait voulu se coucher et dormir. Sa passion satisfaite avait un arrière-goût gâté, une pointe de chair corrompue, dont sa bouche gardait l'amertume' (III, 281).[16] The note of joylessness is often caricatural. At the end of Chapter XII Octave suddenly shows his usual contemptuous brutality towards women ('le dédain féroce qu'il avait de la femme, sous son air d'adoration câline') ('his ferocious disdain for the female under his gentle air of adoration') (III, 245), and Berthe shows equal antipathy. And the sexual act is savage, violent and totally pleasureless for Berthe: 'Elle, silencieuse, le subit sans bonheur. Quand elle se releva, les poignets cassés, la face contractée par une souffrance, tout son mépris de l'homme était remonté dans le regard noir qu'elle lui jeta' (ibid.).[17]

Images of enclosure and decomposition correspond to the theme of sterility. Images of sterility, of a suppressed and abnormal sexuality, abound: the strict sexual rationing decreed by the frigid Mme Duveyrier, the taboos of Mme Juzeur, the imperious and calculating 'chastity' of the despotic Mme Josserand, the impotence confronted by the hysterical Valérie Vabre, the vaginal constriction of Rose Campardon. Rooms and houses in Zola, as we have already seen, are often symbolic reflections of the bodies of their owners, bearing the firm imprint of their inhabitants. Thus, just as the gaping, engulfing *hôtels* of Nana and Clorinde Balbi, like vast vaginal symbols, provide organic images of their owners, so the closed doors and introverted apartments of *Pot-Bouille* mirror the inviolable bodies of the bourgeois ladies within them.

The theme of sterility is complemented by that of antimalthusianism, and thus looks forward to *Fécondité*. Zola detested the adoption of malthusianism for reasons of *petitbourgeois* economy, and torments the Vuillaumes with the comic regularity with which their commands are 'disobeyed'. The Vuillaumes are, however, representative of the house: all are agreed that three children is madness for *petits employés:* 'et le concierge laissa même entendre que, s'il en poussait un quatrième, le propriétaire leur donnerait congé, car trop de famille dégradait un immeuble' ('and the concierge hinted that, if there was a fourth baby, the landlord would give them notice, as too many children about the house did not look well') (III, 360).

The secret destruction of internal order, and the theme of sterility, carry with them the erosion of the family. There are intimate associations between the idea of family life and the vision of home life, a close identity between *foyer* and *famille*. The erosion of family life is reflected in images of dirt and untidiness, especially the disorder of the kitchen, which is identified with the servants and provides the analogue, at the level of the individual family, of the central sewer image. Traditional family virtues – order, comfort, security, generosity, happiness, harmony – are all negated. We remember the corruption of the family in *La Curée* and, in *La Conquête de Plassans*, the engulfment of family life by repressed sexuality manifested in religious hysteria. Family life in *Pot-Bouille*, with its ingrown acerbities, is a derisory sham based on sordid compromise. Mothers are *entremetteuses*, fathers grotesquely ineffectual. The marginal figure of the hated writer, who enjoys a happy family life, provides a pointed contrast. Money is a dominating preoccupation, and materialism is identified with sterility. Money determines relationships, mercenary

motives govern marriages, adulterous relationships interweave
with money disputes: the unpaid dowry, the quarrels over the
legacy, Berthe's insatiable demands for funds. Octave effectively
buys Berthe's favours by paying her bills and giving her presents. When the contending parties cluster round the dying M.
Vabre, domestic disunity is heightened by malicious innuendo.
The savagery is set off by the problem of the missing will and the
ironic drama of old Vabre's final farewell to his 'grande étude de
statistique' ('immense study in statistics') (III, 209), with the
culminating discovery, after the funeral ceremony, of his 'secret
vice': a passion for gambling. The discovery that his fortune has
dwindled to nothing unleashes vicious recriminations and the
subsequent scramble to seize what remains. No less venal is the
painful charade mounted to extract the dowry money from
Bachelard, with the Abbé Mauduit acting as go-between and
Bachelard led to the bedside of the dying Josserand to be subjected to specially prepared speeches.

III

The stylistic weaknesses of *Pot-Bouille* are clear enough: a
schematic rigidity, shrill overemphasis, didacticism. George
Steiner claims, however, that '*Pot-Bouille* is one of the best novels
of the nineteenth century – great in its comic ferocity and tight-
ness of design'.[18] It is indeed true that as a bitter burlesque of
bourgeois life, *Pot-Bouille* displays an assured and controlled art,
revealing an unfamiliar Zola with no small talent for incisive
satirical comedy.[19] Zola described the novel in his *Ébauche* as 'un
livre férocement gai' ('a ferociously gay book').[20] It is both harsh
and funny; the narrative is full of rich and varied incident,
including episodes of comic-opera extravagance. It has a com-
pelling force, intensity and speed, which combine with repetition, recurring symbolic images and ironic use of décor to create
a sense of the mechanical and the ritualistic. The novel is especially noteworthy for burlesque theatricality in comic elaboration
of theme and situation, strengthened by comic-grotesque caricature, irony, verbal comedy and dramatic counterpoint. To criti-
cise *Pot-Bouille*, like most of the contemporary press, for its poor
documentation and lack of 'realism' is to miss the point that the

essence of the novel is that it *is* a caricature and that it deliberately distorts reality in the creation of satiric fantasy.

The basic conception of bourgeois hypocrisy, husband-hunting, furtive adultery and concern for appearances implies play-acting and masks. Many of the characters do nothing but play roles: Rose is the melancholic *souffrante* waited upon like a queen by her compliant husband and angular cousin; Mme Juzeur is equally a *poseuse*, with her twisted coquettishness. A highly theatrical impression is given by the whole form and rhythm of the book, often evocative of a Feydeau farce; and the dramatic frame of the house itself, with its heavy artificiality, provides an eminently theatrical décor, mere cardboard scenery. The adulterous permutations provide the detachable 'set scenes' upon which the chapters are built, with the crude commentary of the servants as an intermittent chorus. The episodic structure, with its technique of swift sketches which often intersect, produces a kaleidoscopic effect. The well-known contemporary caricaturist, A. Robida, in a drawing in *La Caricature* on 13 May 1882 entitled *'Pot-Bouille* ou tous détraqués mais tous vertueux' (*'Pot-Bouille* or all crazy but all virtuous'), takes the house as a frame and divides it into squared sections in comic-strip style in order to illustrate the multiple facets of bourgeois *détraquement*.[21] Many chapters might be given short, descriptive titles *à la Balzac*: Chapter III might be called 'Un intérieur bourgeois', Chapter IV 'L'éducation dans la famille', Chapter V 'Réception et concert chez les Duveyrier', and so on. 'The whole book', writes Angus Wilson, 'could be most happily presented in the form of a bitter satire on respectable domestic life as a cover for promiscuity, shown on a stage that allowed for six or more compartments in which to play the various intrigues simultaneously.'[22] This comment reveals a rather idiosyncratic conception of theatre. The parallel with theatre cannot be complete, since the novel gives little sense of developing pattern or rising climax of action; nor does *Pot-Bouille* become pure vaudeville, because of its harshness of tone. But the formal characteristics of the novel, which interweaves five or six stories, make the analogy with burlesque or pantomime particularly apt. It is satiric fantasy and the dramatic mode which give *Pot-Bouille* its distinctive style and register.[23]

The most sustained comic scenes, creating a sense of revue-style entertainment, are provided by Chapters III, V, X, XIV and XV. In Chapter III the Josserands give a reception on the occasion of Bachelard's birthday. (It is soon followed in Chapter V by the Duveyriers' reception, underlining the bourgeois hierarchy.) Octave continues to be introduced to the inhabitants of the building. Trublot's cynical commentary heightens the falseness of the scene. The use of Trublot as a crude *raisonneur* highlights the ironic contrast between mask and face; Duveyrier's declarations in Chapter V on the need to give marriage a sound moral basis are thus juxtaposed with Trublot's telling Octave about Duveyrier's 'secret vices'. A note of fantasy is introduced by the caricatural exaggeration of relatives arriving, 'poussant devant eux des troupeaux de demoiselles à marier' ('driving before them flocks of marriageable daughters') (III, 46), all with well-rehearsed roles and prefabricated conversation. The use of military terms to characterise the man-catching process underlines the dominant note of ritual and play-acting. Mme Josserand's glance is 'comme un ordre de combat' ('like a battle order'), and she assumes 'une attitude de général en chef' ('the attitude of a commander-in-chief') as she directs 'le premier engagement' ('the first engagement') (III, 47) from her armchair. Before the reception given by the Duveyriers, Mme Josserand again gives 'orders' and delegates 'roles' in a concerted campaign to ensnare Auguste Vabre, leading off her daughters with her 'air terrible d'homme de guerre qui conduisait ses filles au massacre' ('terrible air of a warrior leading forth his daughters to be massacred') (III, 81). The burlesque is heightened by brief, parenthetical allusions to Trublot disappearing after Adèle, re-emerging, and then disappearing again; and to the sound of Saturnin in the locked bedroom. As the guests continue to flow in, Berthe launches into her usual *morceau, Les Bords de l'Oise* (for two of her main weapons are singing and water-colours). As Octave gazes at the guests he glimpses their masks lowered, momentarily revealing their inner, animal-like ferocity as they laboriously compete in the game of social appearances and the predatory quest for husbands: 'Des mères faisaient visiblement le rêve qu'elles mariaient leurs filles, la bouche fendue, les dents féroces, dans un abandon inconscient; c'était la rage de ce salon, un furieux appétit de gendres, qui dévoraient ces bourgeoises aux sons asthmatiques du piano' (III, 50).[24] But they swallow their mutual hostility while drinking sour tea and eating stale cakes and badly cooked *brioche*. The

gradual decline of Mme Josserand's hopes is marked by significant details: during tea one of the lamps goes out, giving a smell of
rancid oil, and the wick of the other lamp becomes defective,
casting a lugubrious light over the room as the guests melt away;
Mme Josserand is thrown into yet another rage as she surveys
the devastation of the empty table and realises that yet another
campaign has proved abortive.

At the reception given by the Duveyriers, the lady guests are
ranged on rows of chairs before the enormous grand piano, as at
the theatre; and the atmosphere is hot and heavy with 'les pénét-
rantes odeurs des corsages et des épaules nues' ('the pungent
aroma of corsets and naked shoulders') (III, 81). As we flit from
group to group, with Octave usually as the link, conversational
stereotypes interweave with periodic mention of Berthe briefly
succeeding in animating the sickly Auguste in a window-recess.
Hortense gives unobtrusive support while M. Josserand strains
to be agreeable to the obtuse M. Vabre. The burlesque drama of
Berthe successfully luring Auguste into compromising himself at
a climactic point in the concert is comically punctuated by the
vision of a band of mediocre bourgeois – an assorted chorus of
barristers, clerks and simple householders – giving full-throated
resonance to the heroic *Bénédiction des Poignards,* swearing that
they are ready to deliver France. The tone reaches a frenetic
pitch as the chapter closes on the grotesque vision of the Josserands' moment of triumph, as they dance wildly round the
luridly lit room: 'la bougie, au milieu, détachait leurs grandes
ombres, qui cabriolaient le long des murs' ('the candle, in the
middle of the table, flung their huge dancing shadows across the
walls') (III, 97).

The exploitation of narrative speed and a cumulative rhythm,
the fantasy of ironical and bedroom farce elements, the interlinking of different *drames de ménage,* and the rhetoric of the décor,
combine to produce an incantatory and circular effect. The abiding impression is of a wild sexual carousel, an inexhaustibility of
sexual permutations. The movement of the narrative is characterised by considerable momentum. The increasing rapidity of
the narrative also corresponds to the progression of caricatural
fantasy. The flight of Berthe through the corridors in Chapter
XIV, frustrated by locked doors and pursued by the vision of a
murderous husband brandishing a kitchen-knife, thus presents
bedroom farce in an unusual key. The speed of the narrative

intensifies in the whirl of confusion as Berthe finally takes refuge in the flat of the astonished Campardon. The piquant irony of Campardon and Gasparine brought from their adulterous bed to utter words of moral revulsion is underlined by the fantasy of the caricature: Gasparine arriving on the scene, 'les os perçant l'étoffe' ('her bony shoulders sticking through her nightgown'); Campardon with his 'grosse face bouffie et en sueur' ('large face all puffy and sweating') (III, 288). The irony is clinched by the final comment on the episode through the rhetoric of the décor; Berthe is trapped in the disappearing solemnity of the stairway and the respectability of the gilt and stucco: 'Derrière les hautes portes d'acajou, la dignité conjugale des alcôves exhalaient un reproche. Jamais la maison n'avait respiré d'une haleine si vertueuse' ('Behind the high mahogany doors, the conjugal dignity of these hearths seemed full of reproaches. Never had the house appeared more pure and virtuous') (III, 292).

The episodic structure of *Pot-Bouille* means that most of the chapters are built round detachable, self-enclosed scenes. The use of Octave as a philandering, flitting camera maintains a link between these scenes and between the bourgeois homes, combining with narrative speed and the repeated sexual patterns to create both an obsessive and a mechanical impression. Chapter VI offers a good example of the flitting camera technique, with simultaneity of scenes reinforced by the swift rhythm. Octave witnesses Gourd's display of pompous rhetoric as defender of the bourgeois citadel; discovers Trublot in the servants' quarters and listens to their gossip; glimpses the 'monsieur très distingué' ('very distinguished gentleman') on the third floor and his anonymous female visitor; briefly encounters Valérie returning after a night escapade; makes (partially) successful advances to Mme Juzeur; dines with both the Pichons and the Vuillaumes; and finally bumps into Trublot again on his way to the servants' quarters. The chapter merges with increasing speed into pure bedroom farce. There is no real plot, only a series of incidents and sketches. Given these swiftly intercut scenes and the acceleration of the narrative rhythm, which produces the impression of the jerky movement of a silent film, it is important to stress the novel's cinematic elements as well as its dramatic ones.

The cumulative sense of circular monotony is heightened by framing and repetition. The novel leans heavily on verbal repetition and word-motifs. Recurring adjectives are 'grave', 'conven-

able', 'honnête', 'digne', 'close'; recurring nouns include 'solen-
nité', 'silence' and 'honnêteté'. There is repeated ironic play on
the talk of moral anarchy. Verbal repetition is matched by the
repetition of certain scenes and situations. The situation of the
cuckolded Auguste is ironically echoed by that of Bachelard.
Duveyrier's desertion by Clotilde coincides with M. Vabre's
attack of apoplexy. The novel describes variations on the theme
of decadent sexuality, with various interweaving threads: the
domestic disaster of Bachelard; the continuing drama of
Duveyrier and Clarisse; the tribulations of Auguste. The inter-
meshing of intrigues and continuous parallel developments is
well illustrated during the marriage ceremony, which is clearly
overshadowed by the marital disharmony between Théophile
and Valérie: it is a prefiguration of what will happen to Berthe.
Berthe later becomes the harsh, reflected image of her mother;
and this familiar Zolaesque theme of cyclical repetition – we
remember, for example, the return of the Charles's daughter in
La Terre to take over the 'business' of her parents – is strongly
reinforced by the balance between the frequent pregnancies and
deaths in the novel.

Chapter II ends with the snores of Mme Josserand and the
misery of her husband returning to his eternal *bandes* – the image
with which the chapter opened and which also echoes the end of
the first chapter. But the main framing device is the décor.
Recurring symbolic imagery contributes to the pervading sense
of the ritualistic and incantatory. There are constant reassertions
of the calm respectability of the house after flurries of activity.
After the death of old Vabre, for instance, Gourd, in *calotte* and
carpet-slippers, solemnly patrols the corridors with the air of a
beadle: 'L'escalier retrouvait son recueillement de chapelle
bourgeoise; pas un souffle ne sortait des portes d'acajou, toujours
closes sur la profonde honnêteté des appartements' (III, 227).[25]
There is a pointed parallel between the first and last chapters,
with the same emphasis on the silence and outward dignity of
the house and even virtually identical phraseology. Mme Josserand's litany of domestic grudges emphasises the ritualistic
elements in the novel. Soured, hostile relationships forever trace
limited, repetitive patterns.

Circularity complements ritual. This is given crowning
emphasis in the closing chapter, which acts as epilogue. As
Clotilde inaugurates her winter *samedis,* almost all of the charac-

ters in the book flow in as if to take their bow at the end of a pantomime or play. The systematic echoing of the earlier reception is marked by several significant variations of detail: Clotilde is again to present the *Bénédiction des Poignards*, but this time with five tenors ('quelque chose de complet, de magistral') ('something absolutely first-rate') (III, 372); Campardon has recently been decorated; Duveyrier has a new mistress and is to be appointed *président de la chambre* and *officier de la légion d'honneur*; Léon has fallen back into the arms of Mme Dambreville. But the apparent consolidation of a world closing its ranks in complacent self-congratulation is undermined by the juxtaposition between the reception and Adèle's confinement, combined with political discussions which emphasise growing bourgeois fear of socialist revolution. The bourgeois world is rigid as well as empty, giving an impression of both brittleness and vulnerability. With explicit emphasis, Octave is made to feel the repetitive hollowness of the sexual circle and the social ritual: 'Alors, Octave eut une singulière sensation de recommencement . . .: aujourd'hui répétait hier, il n'y avait ni arrêt ni dénouement' ('Then Octave had the strange feeling that it was all beginning anew . . .: today was like yesterday, with neither pause nor stop') (III, 381). He feels that his life has described a full circle as he looks round at the guests in their habitual poses: Bachelard waxing sentimental to Mme Juzeur; Campardon defending God and art; Verdier and Hortense again postponing their marriage; Trublot emerging from the kitchen; the women discussing the merits and demerits of their servants; and the clamour of the chorus beginning anew. The novel closes on the image of the refuse hurled into the stinking courtyard in a malodorous, crescendo-like finale, with the final, vulgar comments of the servants.

Burlesque and ritual are heightened by comic-grotesque caricature, by the frozen, puppet-like quality of the characters. Zola's characters tend to become hardened into symbols or fuse into the crowd. But their lack of sophistication and autonomy, and Zola's weakness with human relationships, do have their advantages. The impression of profound rigidity riven by the world of *Pot-Bouille* is strengthened by repeated emphasis in the characterisation on stereotyped features. Most of the characters are purely emblematic. They are simply given identifying labels, certain fixed traits or significant physical characteristics which encapsulate them. Auguste Vabre is thus given 'son insignifiance et sa migraine de tous les soirs' ('his insignificant appearance and his usual evening headache') (III, 53); the impotent Theophile his constant coughing fits; Rose Campardon her 'tranquille sérénité d'idole' ('the tranquil serenity of an idol') (III, 289); the doctor and priest are stock choric figures, 'le médecin maigre et nerveux, le vicaire gras et affable' ('the thin, nervous doctor and the portly, affable priest') (III, 86); Clotilde eternally plays the piano while Saturnin does nothing but breathe violent threats; Mme Josserand is 'terrible', Gasparine 'sèche et amère' ('cold and bitter'), Adèle 'lourde' ('clumsy'). Caricatural fantasy is frequently the keynote: the Vuillaumes take to their bed under the shock of learning of their daughter's third pregnancy. The Campardons illustrate the progression of caricatural fantasy revealed through the eyes of Octave. On his first introduction to Rose Campardon, Octave finds her plump and complacent, 'très soignée dans toute sa personne' ('paying great attention to her toilette') (III, 18), but apparently deprived of all sexuality by a chronic female indisposition which causes her husband some embarrassment: 'Vous savez, les femmes, il y a toujours quelque chose qui se casse' ('Women, you know, have always got something wrong with them') (III, 11). Campardon is thus condemned to his former attachment to his cousin Gasparine, who is as sour and bony as Mme Campardon is pink and rosy. Chapter IX sees Gasparine beginning to assume the administration of the household and Rose's tearful gratification at the newly created *ménage à trois;* while Chapter XI sees her definitive installation, as Rose preens herself for hours in complacent approval. The ironies of Chapter XIV are anticipated by the elaborate ritual of the preparations for bed and the extraordinary vision of Campardon and the angular Gasparine moaning in their narrow bed while Rose, 'avec son corps douillet, délicat et soigné' ('with her plump, soft body') (III, 276), reclines blissfully in the laced depths of the great conjugal bed and weeps indulgently over Dickens. The description of one of Bachelard's famous and uncontrollable feasts at the Café Anglais has an atmosphere of bloated sensuality and brutish corruption which gives it the harsh, caricatural brutality of a Georg Grosz painting – raw and stark in its emphasis on jaw, mouth and belly: 'Ils avaient la peau tendue, la digestion lente et égoïste de quatre bourgeois qui venaient de s'emplir, à l'écart des ennuis de la famille, . . . et ils se déboutonnaient, ils mettaient leurs ventres sur la table'

(III, 189).[26] The physical descriptions ironically negate the sentiments expressed in dialogue. Duveyrier, 'sa face raide de magistrat tiraillé par de courts frissons sensuels' ('his stiff magistrate's features distorted now and again by little sensual thrills') (ibid.), declares his revulsion from vice and refers to the 'noble mission' of love to reform prostitutes. Bachelard, 'des filets de salive aux deux coins de sa bouche' ('saliva dribbling down from either side of his mouth') (III, 191), drunkenly extols virtue. When they go to Clarisse's bare apartment, the caricatural rigidity and unreal, theatrical impression of the characters as garish marionettes is perfectly evoked by the image of their mounting the stairs in procession, Duveyrier leading the way candle in hand, creating bizarre shadows on the wall: 'En tête, Duveyrier, qui tâchait de comprendre, levait les pieds dans un mouvement mécanique de somnambule; et la bougie, qu'il tenait d'une main tremblante, déroulait sur le mur l'étrange montée des quatre ombres, pareille à une procession de pantins cassés' (III, 193).[27] Thus, the lack of psychological depth of Zola's characters need not be considered a disadvantage if their symbolic function is well integrated into the general structure and texture of the novel.

All the characters are more or less caustic caricatures. Some merge into a Dickensian kind of burlesque fantasy. It is Gourd who, more than any other character, is identified with the stairway and the ironic rhetoric which runs through the book, becoming a grotesque appendage to the framing décor. An emblem of pompous bourgeois hypocrisy, he is reminiscent of Dickens's beadle in his anxiety, as an aspiring *petit bourgeois*, to see his 'authority' respected and his role as servile defender of bourgeois 'virtue' upheld. Highly Dickensian also is the verbal irony with which his troubled moral sensibility is described. Hence his absurd threats to the woman who comes once a month to spend a night with her husband: 'Et il semblait que ce cabinet habité par un ouvrier fût le cloaque de la maison, un mauvais lieu dont la surveillance révoltait ses délicatesses et troublait ses nuits' (III, 100).[28] His preoccupation with the morality of the house is intensified, with an increasing note of fantasy, as he vigilantly patrols the stairway and is even seen making night-rounds, which heightens the general atmosphere of furtiveness. The most memorable example of ironic rhetoric and fantasy is the comic hyperbole of Gourd's indignation at the enormous belly of the pregnant boot-stitcher, together with the hyperbole of the description itself: 'Et son ventre avait grossi sans mesure, hors de toute proportion' ('And her belly had begun to swell beyond all bounds, beyond all reasonable proportion') (III, 254). This fantastic magnification is highly characteristic of Zola, reminding us of other examples of comic exaggeration or enlargement: the enormous buttocks of La Mouquette in *Germinal*, the monster goose in *L'Assommoir*, the prodigious flatulence of Jésus-Christ in *La Terre*. As Zola dwells on Gourd's exasperated disgust at this all too palpable moral affront to the bourgeois apartment block, the mock-pompous tone nicely balances the hyperbole:

> Le ventre, maintenant, lui semblait jeter son ombre sur la propreté froide de la cour, et jusque sur les faux marbres et les zincs dorés du vestibule. C'était lui qui s'enflait, qui emplissait l'immeuble d'une chose déshonnête, dont les murs gardaient un malaise. A mesure qu'il avait poussé, il s'était produit comme une perturbation dans la moralité des étages. (ibid.)[29]

Bachelard, whose noisy grossness makes him a vulgar music-hall figure, has the garish, caricatural features of the *noceur:* his false teeth, whose crude whiteness shows up his ravaged features, the glowing red nose emphasised by a thatch of white hair, 'et, par moments, ses paupières [qui] retombaient d'elles-mêmes sur ses yeux pâles et brouillés' ('while now and again his eyelids dropped involuntarily over his pale, rheumy eyes') (III, 39). Made even more marionette-like by the insistence on his red nose and chronic half-drunkenness, he embodies the degradation of the world in which he lives. The despotic Mme Josserand is nothing if not a caricature. She is as much surrounded by verbal comedy as Gourd, the rhetorical irony springing from her physical appearance: 'Sa face carrée, aux joues tombantes, au nez trop fort, exprimait une fureur tragique de reine qui se contient pour ne pas tomber à des mots de poissarde' ('Her square face, with its big nose and flabby cheeks, expressed all the tragic fury of a queen trying not to talk like a fishwife') (III, 23–4). A 'terrible' figure in her nightdress, like a colossal Ceres 'aux triples mamelles et drapée de blanc' ('triple-breasted and robed in white') (III, 232), she stands dominating the unrelenting domestic warfare. After Berthe has returned to her parents,

Auguste has to face the formidable 'gorge courroucée' ('angry bosom', (III, 328) of Mme Josserand, which seems constantly on the verge of bursting out of her corset. In the violent altercation on the themes of money and adultery, her anger reaches a pitch of intense ferocity as she unleashes her amassed bitterness against Auguste for not having added to the expected lustre of her *salon*. During the whole scene she occasionally taps her bodice to adjust her fearsome bosom: 'elle donnait, sur son corsage vert, de grandes tapes qui lui rejetaient la gorge sous les bras' ('she gave her green bodice great slaps which thrust her bosom up under her arms') (III, 333).

IV

Sex is dominant in *Pot Bouille*, but the portrayal of the hypocrisies, guilts and perversions of bourgeois sexual life are seen as part of a more general social malaise. The treatment of both politics and religion evokes a crumbling world. Zola wrote in his working notes: 'Pour avoir le rôle social de la bourgeoisie, mêler mon drame aux événements historiques, à une période de l'Empire' ('To evoke the social role of the bourgeoisie, intersperse my narrative with real historical events and link it to a particular phase of the Empire').[30] The political element is schematic and summary, giving a roughly accurate indication of prevailing attitudes. The elections of 1863 and the Roman question are the two main debating-points used to illuminate bourgeois positions. Recurring themes are bourgeois egoism and fear of a new '93. Some characters are republican, but they are essentially conservative and self-interested, only serving to bolster the existing social order: 'la bourgeoisie jouissant et ne voulant rien changer. Ils votent par intérêt pour maintenir leur situation. Haine des idées nouvelles, peur du peuple, volonté d'arrêter la révolution à leur propre avènement. Quand ils se croient menacés, tous se liguent.[31] The important point, however, is that their progress from wanting to 'teach the Emperor a lesson' to shrinking back at working-class strength reinforces the image of a social class in decomposition.

There are three main political discussions. The double theme of the Roman question and the elections is introduced during the concert-party at the Duveyriers'. The previous day had seen a

stormy sitting in the Senate over the Roman question. Familiar
positions are schematically presented, with the Abbé Mauduit
and Dr Juillerat (intransigent Catholic cleric and dogmatic
atheistic socialist) as the two poles. Juillerat is in favour of handing over Rome to the King of Italy, while Mauduit 'prévoyait les
plus sombres catastrophes, si la France ne versait pas jusqu'à la
dernière goutte de son sang, pour le pouvoir temporel des papes'
('foresaw the direst catastrophes if France did not shed the last
drop of her blood in defence of the temporal power of the Pope')
(III, 86). Léon Josserand, secretary of a left-wing deputy, is a
'doctrinaire' republican. Théophile Vabre 'rêvait le bonheur
universel par l'organisation d'une république humanitaire'
('dreamed of universal happiness achieved by the formation of a
humanitarian republic') (ibid.). When the talk turns to the
important elections of the following year, Duveyrier alone rallies
to the Empire in the face of Juillerat's hostility. He comes from
an Orleanist family, but since he owes everything to the Empire
he upholds it as the guarantor of order and stability. It is a time
of bourgeois animosity towards the Empire, caused mainly by
anxiety over an unpopular foreign policy, Juillerat condemning
the Mexican adventure and Mauduit the recognition of the
kingdom of Italy. Despite Duveyrier's evocation of another '93,
Théophile and Léon declare that they will vote against the
Emperor, 'car il avait besoin d'une leçon' ('for he had to be
taught a lesson') (ibid.) The discussion of politics in Chapter XI
is stimulated by the news that Thiers is to stand in the Rue de
Choiseul constituency in the forthcoming elections. Campardon,
the total opportunist, declares that, although formerly a Jacobin
and atheist like Juillerat, he would never vote for Thiers:
'décidément passé aux prêtres' ('wholly on the side of the
Church') (III, 219), Campardon is now vigorously anti-
republican. But all the 'liberals' present (Josserand, Octave,
Trublot) affirm their support for Thiers. They still agree on the
need to inflict a 'lesson' on the Empire, but begin to show
apprehension about 'le cauchemar du spectre rouge' ('the
spectre of the Scarlet Woman') (III, 220). The final political
discussion is that which punctuates the final *soirée*. Established
positions are systematically repeated (there is more talk of
Thiers and renewed attacks on the Mexican expedition) and
allusions are made to various contemporary developments
(Campardon is enraged by Renan's recently published *Vie de*

Jésus and Mauduit refers to anti-Church feeling, especially in Parliament). The main emphasis, however, is on the effect produced by the decisive electoral success of the opposition: 'Ce triomphe de la bourgeoisie frondeuse les inquiétait sourdement, malgré leur joie apparente' ('This triumph of the liberal bourgeoisie secretly alarmed them, despite their apparent satisfaction') (III, 373). They now begin to rally round the Empire in order to defend their social position, Duveyrier mouthing his usual warnings against the dangers of anarchy and portentously identifying himself with the authoritarian Rouher. Self-satisfaction has turned into anxiety, for the assembled bourgeois company is shaken, increasingly afraid of social disruption and growing working-class strength: 'Ils voyaient des ouvriers, noirs de poudre et de sang, entrer chez eux, violer leur bonne et boire leur vin. Sans doute l'empereur méritait une leçon; seulement, ils commençaient à regretter de lui en avoir donné une aussi forte' (III, 374).[32]

If the political element gives weight to the cumulative impression of a social class in decomposition, it is further reinforced by the role of religion and the correlated opposition between Juillerat and Mauduit. The fact that Campardon is an ecclesiastical architect provides the link between the apartment house and the Church. There are also certain verbal links: 'l'escalier retrouvait son recueillement de chapelle bourgeoise' ('the staircase once more became as peaceful as a middle-class chapel') (III, 227). Religion is a ritualistic means of keeping up appearances or of furthering one's prestige or *intérêt*. The Voltairean M. Vabre is buried *en bon chrétien*. Campardon is 'converted' when he becomes diocesan architect, for the title *architecte du gouvernement* permits him to find work in high society. Lip-service is universally paid to the Church as the necessary bulwark of the family, the government and the social order. Duveyrier asserts that 'la religion moralise le mariage' ('religion makes marriage moral') (III, 95). Saint-Roch is thus an eminently bourgeois church; with the ornate tranquillity of a heated bourgeois drawing-room, it glitters with red marble and gold-plate. Mauduit, although less of a stereotype than Juillerat, is a mere appendage to the bourgeoisie, presiding over bourgeois decadence while maintaining its outward appearances, 'en maître de cérémonie jetant sur cette bourgeoisie gâtée le manteau de la religion'('as a sort of master of ceremonies covering this corrupt bourgeoisie with the cloak of religion') (III, 96). The image of an unctuous master of ceremonies is a recurring one. The ironic juxtaposition in Chapter VIII between the religious ceremony and the drama of suspected adultery points the consecration of bourgeois corruption by the Abbé: the confrontation between Théophile and Octave is punctuated by the benedictory phrases of the choir and priest, who subsequently smothers the scandal. This is echoed by his blessing the 'family union' of Rose Campardon and Gasparine, and clinched when he acts as go-between in the attempt to extract a dowry from Bachelard. The Abbé's despair is relieved only by aesthetic satisfaction in his church, ironically punctuated by the mock-sexual tone of the description of the plaster Virgin which he shows to Octave.

The religious problem complements the political element in its progressive emphasis on fear of imminent collapse. Juillerat constantly brings into question the continued existence of the Church, and hence of Mauduit's own role. Zola explicitly indicates that the Abbé possesses '[une] foi ardente et sincère' ('[an] ardent and sincere faith') (ibid.); but Mauduit becomes increasingly aware of the hollowness of his position, and this reaches a climax in the crisis of despair, self-revulsion and guilt he experiences after an animated discussion with Juillerat. Should he continue in his role or let the rotten edifice of bourgeois society crumble, carrying with it the Church itself? The whole of Chapter XVII leads up to Mauduit's stark vision of the bankruptcy of religion.

The image of a crumbling world is also mirrored in the careers of the hapless Duveyrier, staggering from frustration to despair, and the impoverished Josserand, sinking from despair into death. Emphasis on progressive rottenness and decline is matched by the explicitness of the recurring phrases with which it is indicated: M. Josserand 'sentait un monde crouler sous lui' ('felt as if the whole world was giving way under his feet') (III, 336); Mauduit 'jetait une fois encore le manteau de la religion sur cette bourgeoisie gâtée, en maître de cérémonie qui drapait le chancre, pour retarder la décomposition finale' (III, 382).[33] Portentous intimations of impending apocalypse look forward to the engulfing disasters of *L'Argent* and *La Débâcle* and to the nemesis of the post-*Rougon-Macquart* works. But the main *raisonneur* is the disabused Juillerat, whose estimate of the bourgeoisie as a dead and retrogressive force in society is discursively expressed. His constant attacks on the bourgeoisie contribute to their anxiety: 'Il renouvelait ses attaques contre la bourgeoisie, lui promettait un joli coup de balai, pour l'heure où le peuple viendrait jouir à son tour; et les autres l'interrompaient violemment, criaient que la bourgeoisie était la vertu, le travail, l'épargne de la nation' (III, 374).[34] In an important passage during the 'debate' between Mauduit and Juillerat in Chapter XVII, Zola evokes a broad vision of both the imminent destruction of the bourgeoisie as a class and the sexual patterns described in the book:

'Dicu les abandonne', reprit le premier.
'Non', dit le second, 'ne mettez donc pas Dieu là-dedans. Elles sont mal portantes ou mal élevées, voilà tout.'
Et, sans attendre, il gâta ce point de vue, il accusa violemment l'Empire: sous une république, certes, les choses iraient beaucoup mieux. Mais, au milieu de ses fuites d'homme médiocre, revenaient des observations justes de vieux praticien, qui connaissaient à fond les dessous de son quartier. Il se lâchait sur les femmes, les unes qu'une éducation de poupée corrompait ou abêtissait, les autres dont une névrose héréditaire pervertissait les sentiments et les passions, toutes tombant salement, sottement, sans envie comme sans plaisir; d'ailleurs, il ne se montrait pas plus tendre pour les hommes, des gaillards qui achevaient de gâcher l'existence, derrière l'hypocrisie de leur belle tenue; et, dans son emportement de jacobin, sonnait le glas entêté d'une classe, la décomposition et l'écroulement de la bourgeoisie, dont les étais pourris craquaient d'eux-mêmes. (III, 362–3)[35]

There can be no doubt about the seriousness of Zola's moral and didactic intentions in *Pot-Bouille*. At one point during the Duverdy case, the latter's counsel argued that the use of his client in the novel was defamatory because the book was an obscenity.[36] Zola promptly protested the earnestness of his moral intentions in an indignant letter to A. de Cyon, editor of *Le Gaulois,* in which *Pot-Bouille* was appearing: 'Pas une page, pas une ligne de *Pot-Bouille* n'a été ecrite par moi, sans que ma volonté fût d'y mettre une intention morale. C'est sans doute une oeuvre cruelle, mais c'est plus encore une oeuvre morale, au sens vrai et philosophique du mot.'[37] Zola was clearly concerned to defend himself, particularly given the circumstance of a legal case, but his assertions are consistent with the moral 'lessons' which he attempted systematically to indicate in his novel. But as in *Nana*, the denunciatory fervour goes far beyond the strict perspectives of rational 'sociological' examination. The novel is less interesting as sociological *reportage* than as sexual denunciation; it moves immediately beyond the purely representational and documentary towards a heightened satiric fantasy. Zola's despairing sense of horror at the sterile expenditure of sexual energy corresponds to the savage joy in exposure, the violent urge to degrade and defile, the shrillness and stridency of the tone, the intransigent 'persévérance dans l'immonde' ('perseverance in squalor').[38] To see rampant sexual decadence as announcing the destruction of the bourgeoisie and total collapse on every level is hardly justifiable in purely rational terms – it is indicative, rather, of continuing unease and conflict concerning sexuality. Sexuality is equated in *Pot-Bouille* with destruction, failure, nausea and corruption; nearly every character is contaminated, corrupt, ineffectual or abject. The novel embodies a sombre vision of the basic hostility between men and women, for Zola portrays sexual alienation, repression and sterility only within the context of marriage. Bachelard and Trublot, who are both bachelors, survive, and neither is conspicuously repressed. Octave and Mme Hedouin also escape contamination and prosper; but there is a strong suggestion, supported by Octave's femininity and Mme Hédouin's masculinity, that their marriage will be a *mariage blanc,* a purely commercial association. Some ambiguity is thus attached to the theme of sterility, since it is seen as a source of strength in Octave and his eventual wife. It is only, as it were, when Octave is away from the building, and with Mme Hédouin, that he prospers and fulfils his role as social climber.

It is important to note, finally, that despite the mordant tone of *Pot-Bouille* and the general stress on bourgeois degeneration, Zola's portrayal of the bourgeoisie is not wholly negative. Sympathy is expressed for certain characters, most notably M. Josserand, who has a sense of professional integrity and is not contemptible like Duveyrier. Zola clearly approves of Mme Hédouin, who is a model of industry and integrity; her virtue and perfect health contrast with the adulteries and maladies of the bourgeois ladies of the Rue de Choiseul. And Octave himself, although an opportunist and a *jouisseur,* is in a sense the least degenerate person in the book. The key to his success is his detachment. While repression leads to destruction and is surrounded by images of disintegration, Octave, like the Abbé Faujas and Eugène Rougon finding strength in continence, always retains control over his own appetites, evincing an exploitative, utilitarian sexuality. Like Maupassant's Bel-ami, he uses sex to advance his career and conquer Paris. He wins the respect of Mme Hédouin with his business flair and his ambitious ideas on the expansion and improvement of her shop. His rapidly achieved professional success contrasts with the static, ingrown nature of the bourgeois community portrayed in the novel; his energetic and determined efforts to build a career set him apart from the failures and frustrations of the bourgeois world Zola describes with such vehemence. This contrast is emphasised at the final reception, at which it is noted that Mme Hédouins's expanding drapery store is now squeezing Auguste Vabre's small shop out of business; *Au Bonheur des Dames* will see the full consolidation of Octave's success.

L'Argent: Energy and Order

Although the vocabulary and imagery of 'la curée' are sporadically visible throughout *L'Argent*, evoking the ruthless aggression that characterises the cut-throat world of the Bourse, there are several significant differences between the later novel and its distant precursor. First, the themes of *L'Argent*, unlike those of *La Curée*, display a concern with cosmic forces and broad social issues. Zola's earlier novels are more directly satirical in their approach; his subjects become more and more general, and less topical, as the Second Empire receded into the past. The mythic dimension of *L'Argent*, which corresponds to the novel's strong allegorising tendency, contrasts with the more polemical treatment of contemporary material embodied in *La Curée*. Secondly, the problems of leadership and responsibility become overt themes in *L'Argent*, whereas in *La Curée* they are merely latent. *L'Argent* is palpably about the valuation to be made of the character and conduct of its protagonist, Saccard; and this valuation brings into question the crucial role of Mme Caroline and the mythic themes of redemption and hope. Thirdly, although *L'Argent* is artistically unremarkable and rather ponderous, the social background does not dominate the characters as in *La Curée;* the characters stand out more clearly and their symbolic and quasi-allegorical function, which corresponds to the novel's mythic framework, assumes heightened importance. Fourthly, *L'Argent* constitutes a much more optimistic statement than *La Curée:* 'Je voudrais, dans ce roman, ne pas conclure au dégoût de la vie (pessimisme). La vie telle qu'elle est, mais acceptée, malgré tout, pour l'amour d'elle-même, dans sa force. Ce que je voudrais, en somme, qu'il sortît de toute ma série des Rougon-Macquart.'[1] This increased note of optimism corresponds to Zola's general preoccupation with creative energy and to the marked differences between Saccard I and Saccard II. The pur-

158

pose of this chapter is to examine these differences, to place them in the context of the novel's antithetical structure, and to relate them to the theme of leadership which, as we have seen in Part I of this study, runs through *Les Rougon-Macquart* and helps to define Zola's treatment of the bourgeoisie.

I

The fact that *L'Argent* is centrally concerned with the themes of leadership, energy and order is underlined by the correlations which Zola seeks to establish between the fortunes of his protagonist and their historical background. Zola's creative readjustment of the historical background to the novel enabled him to develop the novel's narrative framework and structural cohesion; but this fictional transposition of political fact is above all directed towards the enrichment of the novel's symbolic meaning. The imperative which Zola clearly formulated in his preparatory notes was to establish a parallelism between the bankruptcy of Saccard's personal empire and the liquidation of the Imperial regime itself. This parallelism is established with a methodical schematism which virtually amounts to didacticism. Two quotations from the working notes are particularly revealing:

Mêler l'affaire d'argent à la politique de la fin de l'empire, faire que la guerre et la débâcle soit [*sic*] au bout. En étudiant l'état du marché financier bien montrer où en est l'esprit public, la démoralisation, les caisses vides (?) [*sic*], les classes en désarroi, tout prêt à l'écroulement. L'ennemi n'a plus qu'à entrer et prendre nos provinces. *Donc une peinture de société de décadence pendant tout le livre.* Les personnages choisis pour cela. *Il faut qu'un entende dans tout le livre le craquement d'une société, le prochain effondrement.* [Zola's italics][2]

je ne crois pas qu'il sera [*sic*] très difficile de transporter l'affaire de l'union vers '67. Il y avait déjà eu l'écroulement du Crédit mobilier. D'autre part, il ne me faut qu'un engouement du public, un coup de folie dans la spéculation, laissant le marché exsangue. C'est la dernière flambée de l'empire, une fin d'empire, une danse sur le volcan classique: la guerre de '70 est là, et on se rue une dernière fois à la jouissance, à la

satisfaction de tous les appétits. Il faut une très grande prospérité, et que cette prospérité soit fictive.[3]

These quotations reveal Zola's apocalyptic vision of the Second
Empire as a period of factitious splendour and unregenerate
decadence, dissipating its vital energies to the point of self-
destruction. The political references in the novel indicate the
decline of France and the ascendancy of Prussia, thus referring
back to the ending of *Nana* and anticipating the *débâcle* at Sedan
which Zola treats in the penultimate novel of the cycle.

Zola's attempt to establish correlations between the development of Saccard's finance company, prevailing political conditions and the tonality of the period is particularly apparent in his
exploitation for symbolic purposes of the 1867 World Fair. There
is a remarkable passage at the end of Chapter V in which the
comparison with the World Fair is introduced:

> . . . de grandes affiches jaunes, collées dans tout Paris, annon-
> çant la prochaine exploitation des mines d'argent du Carmel,
> achevaient de troubler les têtes, y allumaient un commence-
> ment de griserie, cette passion qui devait croître et emporter
> toute raison. Le terrain était préparé, le terreau impérial, fait
> de débris en fermentation, chauffé des appétits exaspérés,
> extrêmement favorable à une de ces poussées folles de la
> spéculation, qui, toutes les dix à quinze années, obstruent et
> empoisonnent la Bourse, ne laissant après elles que des ruines
> et du sang. Déjà, les sociétés véreuses naissaient comme des
> champignons, les grandes compagnies poussaient aux aven-
> tures financières, une fièvre intense du jeu se déclarait, au
> milieu de la prospérité bruyante du règne, tout un éclat de
> plaisir et de luxe, dont la prochaine Exposition promettait
> d'être la splendeur finale, la menteuse apothéose de féerie. Et,
> dans le vertige qui frappait la foule, parmi la bousculade des
> autres belles affaires s'offrant sur le trottoir, l'Universelle enfin
> se mettait en marche, en puissante machine destinée à tout
> affoler, à tout broyer, et que des mains violentes chauffaient
> sans mesure, jusqu'à l'explosion. (V, 170–1)[4]

In many ways this passage epitomises the symbolic meaning of
the novel. Zola establishes a close connexion between the spectacular growth of Saccard's company and the propitious condi-

tions offered by the final years of the Empire ('Le terrain était préparé . . .'). The phrase 'la menteuse apothéose de féerie', stressed by being thrown to the end of the sentence, points to the falseness of the 'prospérité bruyante' and euphoric atmosphere of the World Fair. The hollow prosperity of the age (recalling the theme of factitiousness in *La Curée*) is mirrored in the false financial position of the Banque Universelle, whose success belies artificially inflated share prices, the falsification of accounts and a huge concealed liability. The vision of disaster contained in the final phrase ('jusqu'à l'explosion') is prefigured by the words 'débris' and 'ruines'. And the image of a powerful machine, reinforced by the earlier reference to 'raison' eclipsed by 'passion' and images of madness and fever ('un commencement de griserie', 'appétits exaspérés', 'ces poussées folles', 'une fièvre intense', 'tout un éclat', 'le vertige'), suggests reckless misman-agement.

The image of a dangerous, mishandled machine not only recalls the frenetic activity of the big store in *Au Bonheur des Dames* and the runaway train in *La Bête humaine*, but recurs throughout the novel like a leitmotiv. Mme Caroline is impressed by Sac-card's boundless energy: '. . . se dépensant du matin au soir pour assurer le bon fonctionnement de cette grosse mécanique neuve, dont les rouages grinçaient, près d'éclater' (V, 164). Hamelin dreams of transforming the Universelle into a Catholic bank, that is, into 'toute une vaste machine destinée à écraser, à balayer du globe la banque juive' ('a vast machine which would crush the Jewish bankers and sweep them off the face of the earth') (V, 259). During the climactic struggle for mastery bet-ween Saccard and Gundermann, we read that 'dans sa victoire [i.e. that of Saccard], le moindre gravier devait culbuter sa vaste machine' ('despite his victory, the smallest bit of gravel would upset his vast machine') (V, 314). The machine image usually evokes the dangers of recklessness and the need for moderation. Mme Caroline's recurring apprehension of catastrophe is evoked by a comparison between the Universelle and a locomotive travelling at breakneck speed. Her fear is of self-destruction incurred by manic excess:

Ce qui surtout l'angoissait, c'était ce terrible train, ce galop continu dont on menait l'Universelle, pareille à une machine, bourrée de charbon, lancée sur des rails diaboliques, jusqu'à ce que tout crevât et sautât, sous un dernier choc. Elle n'était point une naïve, une nigaude que l'on pût tromper; même ignorante de la technique des opérations de banque, elle comprenait parfaitement les raisons de ce surmenage, de cet enfièvrement, destiné à griser la foule, à l'entraîner dans cette épidémique folie de la danse des millions. (V, 216)[6]

The machine image is reinforced by images of fever, madness and excess ('surchauffe', 'surmenage'). Hamelin, when he returns to France, is aghast at 'le surchauffement mensonger de toute la machine' ('the deceptive overheating of the whole machine') (V, 243). Later, when Mme Caroline pleads with Saccard to allow their shares to regain their true value, he refuses, and so they are finally quoted at over three thousand francs, 'au milieu d'une agitation de foule démente' ('amid the uproar of an insane multitude') (V, 294). Saccard himself recognises that 'Quand on chauffe trop une machine, il arrive qu'elle éclate' ('When a machine is overheated it bursts') (V, 335), while Mme Caroline reflects near the end of the novel: 'N'était-ce donc pas lui qui, de ses mains sans scrupules, avait chauffé l'énorme machine follement, jusqu'à la faire sauter en morceaux et à blesser tous ceux qu'elle emportait avec elle?' (V, 382).[7]

The direct links between Saccard's personal fortunes and their historical background receive particular stress throughout Chapter VIII, which describes the opening of the World Fair. Two weeks after the opening of the Fair Saccard inaugurates the sumptuous new *hôtel* built to house his company. Both the flamboyant splendours of the Fair and the increasing expansion of the bank seem to reflect the euphoria and confidence of the age. They are both described in terms which suggest misguided values, wild abandon and a dangerous lack of restraint.

Par les soirées claires, de l'énorme cité en fête, attablée dans les restaurants exotiques, changée en foire colossale où le plaisir se vendait librement sous les étoiles, montait le suprême coup de démence, la folie joyeuse et vorace des grandes capitales menacées de destruction. Et Saccard, avec son flair de coupeur de bourses, avait tellement bien senti chez tous cet accès, ce besoin de jeter au vent son argent, de vider ses poches et son corps, qu'il venait de doubler les fonds destinés à la publicité, en excitant Jantrou au plus assourdissant des tapages. (V, 230–1)[8]

The suggestion that Saccard's company forms a microcosm of the nation is reinforced by the fact that the range of anonymous shareholders seems to represent the whole of society:

> Puis, ce fut enfin l'effrayante cohue des petits, la foule piétinante qui suit les grosses armées, la passion descendue du salon à l'office, du bourgeois à l'ouvrier et au paysan, et qui jetait, dans ce galop fou des millions, de pauvres souscripteurs n'ayant qu'une action, trois, quatre, dix actions, des concierges près de se retirer, des vieilles demoiselles vivant avec un chat, des retraités de province dont le budget est de dix sous par jour, des prêtres de campagne dénudés par l'aumône, toute la masse hâve et affamée des rentiers infimes, qu'une catastrophe de Bourse balaye comme une épidémie et couche d'un coup dans la fosse commune. (V, 253)[9]

The apprehension of disaster contained in the last phrase is echoed by the intimation of nemesis brought by the news of the catastrophic Mexican adventure. Similarly, Saccard's exhibiting of Mme de Jeumont, a mistress of the Emperor, at the Foreign Ministry ball ('ce fut la minute culminante de son existence') ('it was the supreme moment of Saccard's existence') (V, 258), is symbolically juxtaposed at the end of the chapter with the sinister presence of Bismarck. Later, after the crash and Mme Caroline's review of the disaster, the financial *débâcle* is placed in a larger context of impending doom. The concluding paragraph of Chapter XI describes Mme Caroline looking up at the Bourse, which she sees outlined against the dark red glow of the evening sky, 'une nuée d'un rouge sombre, qu'on aurait crue faite des flammes et des poussières d'une ville prise d'assaut' ('a dark red cloud which might almost have been formed by the flames and dust of a stormed city') (V, 360–1). This doom-laden image matches her sense of foreboding and plainly prefigures the *semaine sanglante* and the destructive flames of the Commune, which will be described in *La Débâcle:* 'derrière cette fumée rousse de l'horizon, dans les lointains troubles de la ville, il y avait comme un grand craquement sourd, la fin prochaine d'un monde' (V, 361).[10]

II

The developing political situation in *L'Argent* (the growing menace of Prussia) symbolically interlocks with the financial drama (the rivalry between Saccard and Gundermann) in so far as Gundermann is identified with Prussia. A Jew of Prussian origin, Gundermann is a German nationalist, and his nationalist feelings are reinforced by motives of revenge which have their origin in the historical background. News of the Sadowa treaty is leaked to Saccard by Rougon's minion, Huret; and this advance information is immediately exploited by Saccard, who makes a 'killing' on the stock market at the considerable expense of his rival. The rivalry between Saccard and Gundermann is reinforced by an anti-Semitism which characterised Eugène Bontoux, the President of the Union Générale (1878–82) and one of the historical prototypes on which Zola based the character of Saccard. The Union Générale was supported by Catholic money and it annually contributed funds to the Vatican; after the collapse of the company, Bontoux attempted to portray himself as the victim of a Jewish conspiracy. The antithesis between the two rivals is further accentuated by Saccard's stereotyped view of the Jews as mere parasites – a view which contrasts with his own conception of the creativity of money: 'Est-ce qu'on a jamais vu un juif faisant oeuvre de ses dix doigts? est-ce qu'il y a des juifs paysons, des juifs ouvriers? Non, le travail déshonore, leur religion le défend presque, n'exalte que l'exploitation du travail d'autru' (V, 91).

The conflict between Saccard and Gundermann goes beyond mere questions of personal rivalry and racial hatred, however. It enlivens documentary description with personal drama; but Zola's depiction of the mechanisms of Bourse activity, focused by the epic duel between Saccard and Gundermann, may be seen in a quasi-allegorical as well as a documentary and investigative perspective – for the essence of their duel is the defeat of 'passion' (Saccard) by 'logic' (Gundermann). The essential coherence of the novel is indeed best brought out by an allegorical reading. Although, through his account of the remarkable rise and dramatic fall of a banking company, Zola attempts to grasp the mechanisms of the social life of contemporary France and to present the Bourse as a paradigmatic representation of the capitalist system itself, the documentary and sociological intentions of the novel do not constitute its primary source of interest. Ultimately, it is more interesting to study the personal vision and values that emerge from *L'Argent* than to elucidate Zola's adroit use of his sources or the significance of the novel as a statement about capitalism. For it may be argued that the novel is less deeply concerned with exploring the structure of capitalism than with depicting the interplay of vital forces. In other words, it is as valid to assert that *L'Argent* embodies a vision of mental structures as to say that it is an exploration of social structures.

Zola's description of the power struggle between Saccard and Gundermann, which constitutes the central antithesis of the novel, is transposed, then, into an allegorical drama. What Zola does is set up a pattern of conflict between two different kinds of vital forces: 'Ils ne pouvaient s'entendre, l'un passionné et jouisseur, l'autre sobre et de froide logique' ('They could not get on together – the one passionate and fond of the pleasures of life, the other sober and coldly logical') (V, 22). His characters thus tend to become archetypes. Saccard, the modern tycoon, is reckless, bold and passionate:

> . . . il avait toujours été l'homme d'imagination, voyant trop grand, transformant en poèmes ses trafics louches d'aventurier; et, cette fois, avec cette affaire réellement colossale et prospère, il en arrivait à des rêves extravagants de conquête, à une idée si folle, si énorme, qu'il ne se la formulait même pas nettement à lui-même. (V, 314)[12]

Obsessed to the point of madness, he is able to conceive of his schemes only in terms of hyperbole: 'Saccard ne s'échauffait que par l'outrance de ses conceptions' ('Only the extravagance of his ideas could excite Saccard') (V, 78). Gundermann, on the other hand, is cold, methodical and prudent. His vast fortune has been created by shrewdness, single-minded application and 'l'heureux concours . . . des événements' ('the help . . . of events') (V, 90).

> Il n'était point un spéculateur, un capitaine d'aventures, manoeuvrant les millions des autres, rêvant, à l'exemple de Saccard, des combats héroïques où il vaincrait, où il gagnerait pour lui un colossal butin, grâce à l'aide de l'or mercenaire, engagé sous ses ordres; il était, comme il le disait avec bonhomie, un simple marchand d'argent, le plus habile, le plus zélé qui pût être. (V, 94–5)[13]

While Saccard is a *jouisseur*, Gundermann, who nourishes himself exclusively on milk, has a dessicated quality:

> Saccard, qui, dans ses terribles appétits, faisait cependant la
> part de l'amour désintéressée de l'argent, pour la puissance
> qu'il donne, se sentait pris d'une sorte de terreur sacrée, à voir
> se dresser cette figure, non plus de l'avare qui thésaurise, mais
> de l'ouvrier impeccable, sans besoin de chair, devenu comme
> abstrait dans sa vieillesse souffreteuse, qui continuait à édifier
> obstinément sa tour de millions . . . (V, 96)[14]

Gundermann's strategy towards the Banque Universelle, to wait
patiently for it to exhaust its own resources, is based on his
mathematical confidence in the self-destructiveness of excess and
an artificially high quotation: 'La logique seule régnait, la vérité
était, en spéculation comme ailleurs, une force toute-puissante'
('Logic was the sole ruler; truth, in speculation as in all other
things, was an omnipotent force') (V, 202).

Saccard's passion and intemperance do indeed lead fatally,
and as if by logical necessity, to disaster. In his cell at the Conciergerie he reveals to Mme Caroline, in a sort of lucid involun-
tary confession, that his vitality, the essence of his personality, is
self-consuming and that Gundermann, who seems to be a kind of
impersonal force, was the ineluctable victor:

> Moi, je suis trop passionné, c'est évident. La raison de ma
> défaite n'est pas ailleurs, voilà pourquoi je me suis si souvent
> cassé les reins. Et il faut ajouter que, si ma passion me tue,
> c'est aussi ma passion qui me fait vivre. Oui, elle m'emporte,
> elle me grandit, me pousse très haut, et puis elle m'abat, elle
> détruit d'un coup toute mon oeuvre. Jouir n'est peut-être que se
> dévorer . . . (V, 384)[15]

He argues that his crime is excess rather than deception.

The heightened mythic and allegorical quality of *L'Argent*,
combined with Zola's desire to provide a global perspective on
the financial world, corresponds to the transparently symbolic
and representative function of his characters, of whom nearly all
are presented in a very formal, Balzacian manner. The minor
characters who circulate round Saccard largely represent the
various types of fauna – speculators, brokers, financiers, jobbers
– that compose the financial world. The gallery of types includes

small speculators who dream of overnight wealth, naive and innocent investors, the unscrupulous large-scale speculator (Daigremont), prudent and reckless types of speculator, and the parasite who trades in the shares of bankrupt companies (Busch, aided by the sinister La Méchain). In addition, there is the treacherous female who exploits sex for information (Sandorff); the declining aristocracy, proudly keeping up appearances despite their vanished fortune (the de Beauvilliers); an embodiment of charity (Princess d'Orviedo); and the tubercular socialist dreamer (Sigismond).

A primary function of Zola's minor characters is to reinforce the theme of the destructiveness of immoderation. Although Zola includes prudent types among his characters, we are struck by the prevalence of obsessional and passionate characters. Busch is obsessed with money: 'sa cupidité assassine . . . mettait dans la conquête de l'argent l'unique raison de vivre' ('his murderous greed . . . converted money-making into the sole motive of life') (V, 41); Sandorff, with her 'visage de passion à la bouche saignante' ('passionate face, with blood-red lips') (V, 29), is obsessed with gambling; Sédille and La Méchain are similarly obsessed; Jordan, the journalist, is 'enragé de littérature' ('obsessed with the idea of being a writer') (V, 26); Sigismond is a passionate idealist. Princess d'Orviedo, with her 'imagination déréglée qui lui faisait jeter ses millions en bonnes oeuvres d'un luxe colossal et inutile' ('disorderly imagination which induced her to throw away her millions in good works of colossal and useless luxury') (V, 110), is a further striking case of immoderation. The undisciplined, obsessive generosity of Princess d'Orviedo is coupled with the theme of waste associated with Saccard. This seems to be exemplified by the 'sagesse' with which Mme Caroline attempts to administer her charitable enterprise and by her critique of its excesses: 'à quoi bon toute cette charité grandiose, si l'on ne pouvait, dans ce milieu large et salubre, redresser un être mal venu, faire d'un enfant perverti un homme bien portant, ayant la droite raison de la santé?' (V, 375).[16] Mme Caroline's doubts about aristocratic charity are reinforced by its patent value as psychological compensation.

Passion suggests disorder. The passionate characters in *L'Argent* are thus portrayed as the victims of their untrammelled appetites. The way in which a passion for money sours and degrades personal relationships is clearly seen in the Maugendres, whose increasing obsession with gambling kills their generosity and prevents them from helping their poverty-stricken daughter. The characteristic Zola themes of the subversive power of sexuality and the perils of dissipation are illustrated in Flory and Jantrou. Flory, initially a reliable worker, is brought to ruin by the demands of his mistress, Mlle Chuchu. It is the dissolute Jantrou, however, who is most obviously the victim of his passions: 'des disparitions brusques, des bordées, d'où il revenait anéanti, les yeux troubles, sans qu'on pût savoir qui, des filles ou de l'alcool, le ravageait davantage' (V, 192).[17] It is Jantrou who encourages Sandorff to go over to Gundermann's side; and the alliance between the publicity agent and the Fatal Woman leads to the personal collapse of both of them. Significantly, it is the well-balanced Jordan, with his contempt for money, who recounts their *déchéance*:

> Peut-être n'a-t-elle roulé jusqu'à lui que par les lois mêmes de la chute, toujours de plus en plus bas. Il y a, dans la passion du jeu, un ferment désorganisateur que j'ai observé souvent, qui ronge et pourrit tout, qui fait de la créature de race la mieux élevée et la plus fière une loque humaine, le déchet balayé au ruisseau . . . (V, 350)[18]

Zola also illustrates clearly that Saccard's indulgence of his own sexual appetites (which contrasts with the self-control of Faujas, Eugène Rougon and Octave Mouret) is detrimental to him in so far as his mistress, Baroness Sandorff, eventually betrays him, and the violent confrontation with Delcambre (following a scene which is as sexually explicit as any in Zola) has disastrous results for Saccard as his duel with Gundermann reaches its climax.

III

The allegorical meaning and the marked ambiguities of *L'Argent* correspond to a series of antithetical patterns. The novel dramatises a tension between energy and order, and its thematic structure is determined by a set of contrasts and conflicts: Zola's characterisation is partly determined by antithetical construction; his attitude towards liberal capitalism is equivocal, for money is seen to be both creative and destructive, causing ruin in one area but prosperity in another; the novel's mythical framework is based on the antithesis between Catastrophe and Hope; the character of Saccard is fundamentally ambiguous; the movement of Mme Caroline's thoughts as she struggles with her feelings towards Saccard is dialectical – the novel moves indeed towards an attempted resolution of the antitheses which inform Mme Caroline's moral perplexities.

The central antithesis between Saccard and Gundermann is mirrored in the opposition between the exuberant bull, Pillerault, 'un joueur qui érigeait en principe le casse-cou' ('a gambler who made recklessness a principle') (V, 12), and the gloomy bear, Mazaud. Saccard's exuberance contrasts with Hamelin's prudence, the former's cynicism with the latter's naïveté. Hamelin's credulity is correspondingly set against his sister's knowledge and experience of the world. Saccard's creativity and dynamism contrast with the indolence and egoism of his legitimate son, the parasitic Maxime, 'si correct dans son égoïste jouissance de la vie, si joliment désabusé des liens humains, même de ceux que crée le plaisir' ('so demurely egotistic in his enjoyment of life, so disengaged from all human ties, even from those which a life of pleasure creates') (V, 218). Maxime himself is juxtaposed with Saccard's illegitimate son, Victor: they respectively illustrate idle luxury and squalid poverty. Mme Caroline's visit to see Victor in the Cité de Naples, a slum area behind the Butte Montmartre, is immediately followed by her visit to Maxime, who lives in solitary opulence. Mme Caroline's reflections on this contrast underscore the reality of huge social inequalities:

> Tant de saletés ignobles, la faim et l'ordure inévitable, d'un côté, et de l'autre une telle recherche de l'exquis, l'abondance, la vie belle! L'argent serait-il donc l'éducation, la santé, l'intelligence? Et, si la même boue humaine restait dessous, toute la civilisation n'était-elle pas dans cette supériorité de sentir bon et de bien vivre? (V, 154)[19]

This question is related to the antithesis between the restoration of moral and, by extension, social health (Mme Caroline's ideal realised in Madeleine) and the persistence of depravity (Victor's subversion of Mme Caroline's ideal). The juxtaposition between Maxime and Victor, which is intended to represent the unequal distribution of wealth within society, may perhaps be compared with another, less obvious juxtaposition: that between Princess d'Orviedo (the philanthropical aristocrat) and Sigismond Busch (the modern socialist). The idealistic Sigismond is contrasted with his rapacious elder brother, who, ironically, permits Sigismond to indulge his taste for political theory by looking after his physical needs. Sigismond is entirely ignorant of his brother's squalid business affairs: 'il vivait plus haut, dans un songe souverain de justice' ('he lived in a loftier region, in a sovereign dream of justice') (V, 42). The limits of the power of money are shown in the contrast between Mme Conin, who, despite her discreet sexual liberality, refuses Saccard's monetary advances, and the expensive courtesan, Mme de Jeumont, whom Saccard 'purchases' as an act of self-display. The principal juxtaposition of females, however, is that between the treacherous and shallow Sandorff and the sincere, devoted Caroline. Contrasts between characters are matched by contrasts within characters. Busch is savage and pitiless in his business dealings, yet remains totally devoted to his tubercular brother; it is in the last chapter, following the death of Sigismond, that Mme Caroline realises that Busch is capable of deep human feelings.

Whereas in *La Curée* money is seen in its entirely destructive aspects (people are reduced to the level of merchandise, materialist greed debases human relationships), in *L'Argent* Zola's treatment of the economic organisation of society is deeply marked by ambiguity. *L'Argent* was intended to be both an anatomy of the Bourse and a study of the role of money in society; the world of the Bourse was meant to be a paradigmatic representation of the capitalist system itself. Within the metaphoric structure of *La Curée*, the fluid quality of money reinforces the themes of dissolution and dissipation; in *L'Argent*, however, water imagery reflects a vision of money as a vital, fecundating force. Saccard declares: 'rien n'était possible sans l'argent, l'argent liquide qui coule, qui pénètre partout, ni les applications de la science, ni la paix finale, universelle. . .' ('nothing would be possible – neither the applications of science nor final, universal peace – without money, liquid money which flows and penetrates everywhere. . .') (V, 125–6). In his working notes, Zola is anxious to stress the beneficial aspects of speculation in as much as it signifies social and material progress. In this sense, the novel partially constitutes a defence of speculation:

. . . le bien que fait l'argent, la spéculation elle-même. Donc un tableau de chemins de fer, des mines, du pays transfiguré, amélioré. Le bien-être. Grandes idées réalisées, grandes inventions mises en oeuvre, le progrès, la vie décuplée. Cette idée que la spéculation mauvaise est à la spéculation nécessaire, ce que la débauche, la luxure est à l'amour: sans l'amour pas d'enfant, sans la spéculation, pas d'affaires.[20]

The same antithesis and the same sexual analogy are present in the Mirecourt section of the documentation[21] in which Zola is at pains to distinguish between speculative investment and mere profiteering: '*Très important*. Il y a une grande spéculation, honnête, utile, organisatrice, logique et sincère. Elle fait de la vie, tandis que l'autre – l'agio – comme la débauche, fait de la mort.' [Zola's italics][22]

Zola's vision of the creative potential of money is magnified by its association with the magical qualities of science, figured in the grandiose engineering projects of Hamelin. Zola, as we have seen in Part I of this study, entirely approves of the bourgeois as technocrat. Capitalism and science, in alliance, are seen as capable of infinite social improvement and renovation. The self-belief of Saccard and the dreams of Hamelin correspond to their vision of a new Eden in the Middle East, a vision which, reinforced by an epic tonality and comparisons with Napoleonic conquest, acquires mythic undertones that transcend Catholic religious fervour or personal ambition. Saccard reflects: 'Puisque la civilisation était allée de l'est à l'ouest, pourquoi donc ne reviendrait-elle pas vers l'est, retournant au premier jardin de l'humanité. . .? Ce serait une nouvelle jeunesse, il galvanisait le paradis terrestre, le refaisait habitable par la vapeur et l'électricité. . .' (V, 78).[23] This myth of fecundity and eternal regeneration, of a *paradis perdu* regained through human creativity, looks forward to the utopia described in *Travail*, with its concluding images of limitless material improvement; the new society in the Middle East, as well as the collectivist dreams of Sigismond, anticipates Luc Froment's 'cité idéale', while the pattern of manager/technician (Saccard and Hamelin) looks forward to the partnership between Luc and Jordan.

The structure of capitalism is seen as dualistic, however, in as much as destruction is inseparable from creativity. As Mme Caroline painfully recognises, and as Saccard clearly explains, 'on ne remue pas le monde sans écraser les pieds de quelques passants' ('one can't move the world without crushing the feet of a few passers-by') (V, 116). The reverse side of positive speculation is an image of money as a source of corruption, egoism, greed, exploitation and misery: money is the origin of all injustice, and destructive of personal relationships: '[il est] le grand coupable, l'entremetteur de toutes les cruautés et de toutes les saletés humaines' ('[it is] the great culprit, the agent of all human cruelties and abominations') (V, 219). The essence of this dualistic vision, as in *Au Bonheur des dames*, is a Darwinian conception of the struggle for life as the governing principle of society; the weak are crushed by the strong, dupes are the victims of exploiters.

The doubts and dilemmas arising from these anarchic tendencies, and from the unequal distribution of wealth in society, form a major theme in the novel. In a letter to J. Van Santen Kolff, dated 9 July 1890, Zola referred to the unavoidable need to accommodate socialist ideas in a novel dealing with the role of money in society: 'Non seulement j'ai voulu étudier le rôle actuel de l'argent, mais j'ai désiré indiquer ce qu'a été jadis la fortune, ce qu'elle sera peut-être demain. De là toute une partie historique et toute une partie socialiste.'[24] The socialist viewpoint is represented by the dreamy and idealistic Sigismond, who makes three significant appearances in the novel (Chapters I, IX and XI) in order that Zola might give an extended synthetic exposition of collectivist ideas: rational economic planning by the state following the collapse of capitalism, the abolition of money and its replacement with credit vouchers proportional to individual effort, the compensation of private owners, the requirement that every one should work, the retention of a form of competition and individualism within the new socialist system in order to encourage efficiency, the rejection of violence and the safeguarding of individual liberty. Despite Sigismond's formative meeting with Karl Marx, the fact that he is in continual correspondence with him, and that the second exchange between Sigismond and Saccard takes place after the former has spent a night reading *Das Kapital* (received the day before), Sigismond's arguments and terminology represent a synthesis of notes Zola took on two texts, Schaeffle's *La Quintessence du socialisme* (Brussels, 1886) and Georges Renard's 'Le Socialisme actuel en France' (*La Revue socialiste*, 1887–8).[25] These two writers were utopian, not Marxist. This reflects Zola's own quite natural ignorance of Marx. Marxist critics have made the obvious points that there is only an indirect correspondence between the ideas of Sigismond and the theories of historical materialism, and that Sigismond does not even refer to some social issues considered crucial by Marx.[26] Sympathy for Sigismond and his ideas is undoubtedly felt; and it is significant that, in his preparatory notes, Zola ascribed to the free-thinking Mme Caroline 'des tendances socialistes' ('socialist tendencies').[27] But, despite this sympathy, the central emphasis in the portrayal of Sigismond is on the utopian nature of his vision, 'sa chimère de justice et d'amour' ('his dream of justice and love') (V, 396). The motifs which define his character are his childlike naïveté, his absent-mindedness, his detachment from reality, his lack of practical engagement in life. His role in the novel is undermined by the artificiality of the three interludes concerning him; his detachment from the world is ironically underscored by the fact that his physical needs, albeit meagre, are tended by his predatory brother; and his feverish and moribund state, and his final death, suggest that, like other revolutionary figures in Zola, he is an ineffectual visionary whose dreams have little meaningful connexion with present reality.

Zola's stress on the impracticality of Sigismond, and the consequent suggestion that no immediate solution to social problems is to be found in socialism, highlights all the more the positive qualities of Saccard, to whom we are thus obliged to return. It is the bourgeois Saccard rather than the collectivist Sigismond who ultimately reflects the social optimism Zola wished his novel to express. The narrative importance of Saccard is greater in *L'Argent* than in *La Curée*; whereas concentration on Renée diminishes our interest in Saccard I, Mme Caroline constantly directs our attention towards Saccard II. The crux of *L'Argent* clearly lies in Zola's conception of his protagonist, who differs from his distant twin in several significant respects. He is ambiguous in ways in which the Saccard of *La Curée* is not. Saccard I, although he incarnates the commercial expansion of the age, epitomises dissolution, waste, impermanence and sterility; he is surrounded by images of destruction and ruin. Saccard II, although his passion destroys him, has a number of important redeeming features and emerges as a much more positive figure than Saccard I. The marked contrasts and ambiguities within Saccard correspond to the ambiguities that define Zola's conception of the role of money in society. A messianic figure *and* a failed leader, he is a symbolic agent of both creativity and destruction.

Saccard sharply distinguishes his own motivation from that of other people. When Maxime contemptuosly refuses his offer of company shares, Saccard reacts angrily: 'Saccard eut un geste de colère, trouvant la réponse d'un irrespect et d'un esprit déplorables, prêt à lui crier que l'affaire était réellement superbe, qu'il le jugeait trop bête, s'il le croyait un simple voleur, comme les autres' (V, 130).[28] Saccard's self-conception is that of a new Napoleon. Excited by Hamelin's dream of Catholic hegemony in the Middle East, his imagination is inflamed by thoughts of the Crusades and of Napoleon. Saccard is not motivated by altruism or social idealism, but by the excitement of megalomaniac dreams. Deep megalomania is similarly revealed by Saccard's agreement to administer Princess d'Orviedo's charitable institution, L'Oeuvre du Travail. He is not seduced by the idea of personal gain, but derives gratification from both the grandiose scale of the Princess's charitable works and the prospect of their efficient organisation:

Seulement, dans ce gaspillage, au milieu des devis énormes, elle était abominablement volée; une nuée d'entrepreneurs vivaient d'elle, sans compter les pertes dues à la mauvaise surveillance; on dilapidait le bien des pauvres. Et ce fut Saccard qui lui ouvrit les yeux, en la priant de le laisser tirer les comptes au clair, absolument désintéressé d'ailleurs, pour l'unique plaisir de régler cette folle danse de millions qui l'enthousiasmait. (V, 55)

. . . au bout, il y avait le rêve de sa vie entière, la conquête de Paris. Etre le roi de la charité, le Dieu adoré de la multitude des pauvres, devenir unique et populaire, occuper de lui le monde, cela dépassait son ambition. Quels prodiges ne réaliserait-il pas, s'il employait à être bon ses facultés d'homme d'affaires, sa ruse, son obstination, son manque complet de préjugés! Et il aurait la force irrésistible qui gagne les batailles, l'argent, l'argent à pleins coffres, l'argent qui fait tant de mal souvent et qui ferait tant de bien, le jour où l'on mettrait à donner son orgueil et son plaisir! (V, 56)[29]

Saccard's vision of popular acclaim and his disinterested motives
were entirely absent from Zola's characterisation of him in *La
Curée*. Whereas in *La Curée* Zola stresses Saccard's venality and
corruption, in *L'Argent*, although his cynicism is still strong, he is
invested with a heroic and grandiose quality. This corresponds
to a marked strain of lyricism in the presentation of his personality.

Saccard's status as a domineering and messianic figure is reinforced by frequent comparisons, both explicit and implicit, with
a king, a despot, a god, a conqueror and a hero. The grandiose
nature of his self-conception is reflected in images and allusions
which have both an epic flavour and mythical connotations. The
opening of the new premises of the Universelle, which follows
upon the opening of the World Fair, marks a heightening of
Saccard's aura of authority:

> Maintenant, le matin, Saccard, dans son luxueux cabinet
> Louis XIV, était obligé de défendre sa porte, lorsqu'il voulait
> travailler; car c'était un assaut, le défilé d'une cour venant
> comme au lever d'un roi, des courtisans, des gens d'affaires,
> des solliciteurs, une adoration et une mendicité effrénées
> autour de la toute-puissance. (V, 234)[30]

Images of power and military conquest combine, as this passage
reveals, with frequent allusions to the faith and hero-worship of
which Saccard is the object. There is an intensification of such
language during the chapter which describes the climax of the
power struggle with Gundermann: 'dans l'aveuglement de sa
fièvre, il croyait encore marcher à la conquête, avec tout son
peuple d'actionnaires derrière lui, ce peuple des humbles et du
beau monde, engoué, fanatisé, les jolies femmes mêlées aux ser-
vantes, en un même élan de foi' (V, 326).[31] The tone of the
description becomes epic, as Saccard seems transfiguré into a
figure of myth, and elegiac, as Zola extols his heroism and courage in defeat: 'A cette minute, il fut vraiment superbe, toute sa
mince personne bravait la destinée. . .' ('At that moment, he was
truly magnificent, his whole slight body defying destiny. . .')
(V, 330).

The themes of blindness and betrayal reinforce Saccard's
status as a failed and frustrated leader. Zola is clearly concerned

that his protagonist should not appear a misguided fool, but rather a potential genius who gets carried away. His blindness and his total commitment lead to the prodigal folly which provokes the inflation of share prices to quite unrealistic levels. As the climax of the contest with Gundermann approaches, he remains totally confident of final victory. However, he is blind to the significance of the movement against him and blind to the fact of betrayal. Eventual realisation of his betrayal brings with it a comparison with Napoleon at Waterloo vainly awaiting Grouchy and his troops: 'Comme à Waterloo, Grouchy n'arrivait pas, et c'était la trahison qui achevait la déroute' ('As at Waterloo, Grouchy failed to arrive, and it was treason that completed the rout') (V, 328). Zola stresses Saccard's betrayal – at first by Baroness Sandorff, then by the cunning Daigremont and the company members who sell at the last moment. It is Sandorff who, prompted by Daigremont, gives Gundermann the information which enables him to unleash all his forces against the Universelle. After the crash, the general disloyalty of the bank's administrators becomes apparent.

It is important to note that Saccard is sharply distinguished from his corrupt acolytes, whose motives are straightforwardly opportunistic and mercenary. Just as he is not a misguided fool, so he is not merely a cynical profiteer. He is not interested in the sheer accumulation of wealth like Gundermann; he is a spendthrift, not a hoarder. Although unprincipled, he is not merely rapacious; his satisfaction lies in the contentment of his own drive. After the crash, he reveals that he had poured all his private gains back into the company. Saccard is thus contrasted in his lack of *mesquinerie* with his more corrupt followers. Moreover, the efficaciousness – albeit flawed – of the financial manipulator and the skilled technician, both of whom are bourgeois, is contrasted with the relative insignifance of the now ineffectual aristocracy, who play a 'window-dressing' role like the wasteful Princess d'Orviedo and the selfish Marquis de Bohain, or, like the impoverished de Beauvilliers, attempt to cling on to an illustrious past.

Saccard's messianism is complemented by his benevolent and humane impulses which contrast with the cold ruthlessness of his character as displayed in *La Curée*. He helps and supports the Jordans in a number of ways, and even after the crash Jordan expresses gratitude for Saccard's generosity towards them; he is 'moved' (V, 126) that Countess de Beauvilliers should place her faith in him and agree to invest her meagre savings (including her daughter's dowry) in company shares; he is also moved that Dejoie should trust him, and promises him a job on the newspaper. And despite the *débâcle*, the company shareholders retain blind faith in Saccard: 'Malgré les fautes commises, tous gardaient en lui une foi aveugle' ('In spite of the mistakes that had been made, they all retained a blind faith in him') (V, 337).

The themes of megalomania and benevolence are closely related to the theme of creativity. Zola's conception of Saccard reveals a deep preoccupation with creative energy. This preoccupation is reflected in Saccard's early involvement with L'Oeuvre du Travail. Zola stresses Saccard's keen sense of his own talents and his determination to use those talents fruitfully and creatively: 'cette colossale idylle du bien fait à coups de millions avait attendri sa vieille âme de corsaire' ('this colossal idyll of good accomplished by dint of millions had moved his old corsair heart') (V, 46). Similarly, Hamelin and Saccard are complementary in so far as Hamelin needs a person of dynamic energy and experience to realise his grandiose and imaginative ideas. Hamelin's naïveté and lack of practical sense contrast with the organisational ability and financial genius of Saccard, who undertakes to promote Hamelin's vast schemes for the regeneration of an entire society in the Middle East.

Saccard's theorising on the role and potentiality of commerce is another facet of his character which is not present in *La Curée* and which increases his stature in *L'Argent*. It is precisely as a creator of opportunities that Saccard justifies himself when Mme Caroline expresses early anxieties about the operations of his new company. His inspirational abilities thus correspond to the creative potential of money:

> Il était bâti pour faire de la vie et non pour panser les blessures que la vie a faites. Enfin, il allait se retrouver sur son chantier, en plein dans la bataille des intérêts, dans cette course au bonheur qui a été la marche même de l'humanité, de siècle en siècle, vers plus de joie et plus de lumière. (V, 81)[32]

When Mme Caroline, fearing illicit practices, expresses further anxieties about Saccard's conduct of affairs, he reacts indignantly: 'Apportez-moi de bonnes idées, et je me charge de tirer d'elles tout le bénéfice désirable, en courant le moins de risques possible. Je crois qu'un homme pratique ne peut pas dire mieux' (V, 113).[33] His response to her grave declaration that she would not wish the company to resort to illegal measures and that she would prefer bonds to shares is an impassioned – almost lyrical – defence of speculation. He argues that speculation is a fecundating and vital force and a necessary agent of social progress: 'Sans lui [le jeu], les grands mouvements de capitaux, les grands travaux civilisateurs qui en résultent sont radicalement impossibles. . .' ('But for speculation, the great movements of capital and the great civilising works that result from them would be utterly impossible') (V, 115). Saccard argues that money is the agent of perpetual social renewal, that temerity and a taste for risks are essential, and that his principal intention in the creation of the bank is to promote the dreams of Hamelin, which are dreams of social improvement. At the same time, he states the impossibility of accomplishing anything without some social disruption: 'Ah! dame! je ne réponds pas de la casse, on ne remue pas le monde, sans écraser les pieds de quelques passants' ('Ah! I won't say there will be no damage done – one can't move the world, you know, without crushing the feet of a few passers-by') (V, 116). With unassailable logic, he justifies speculation by equating it with the life-instinct, and develops a thesis of necessary excess by comparing speculation with copulation:

> Oui, la spéculation. Pourquoi ce mot vous fait-il peur? . . .Mais la spéculation, c'est l'appât même de la vie, c'est l'éternel désir qui force à lutter et à vivre. . .
> . . .Voyons, pensez-vous que sans . . . comment dirai-je? sans la luxure, on ferait beaucoup d'enfants?. . . Sur cent enfants qu'on manque de faire, il arrive qu'on en fabrique un à peine. C'est l'excès qui amène le nécessaire, n'est-ce pas? (V, 135)[34]

By implicitly suggesting that society is like nature Saccard develops a quasi-Darwinian vision of social development. He argues that he merely identifies with the way life works:

> Avec la rémunération légitime et médiocre du travail, le sage équilibre des transactions quotidiennes, c'est un désert d'une platitude extrême que l'existence, un marais où toutes les

forces dorment et croupissent; tandis que, violemment, faites flamber un rêve à l'horizon, promettez qu'avec un sou on en gagnera cent, offrez à tous ces endormis de se mettre à la chasse de l'impossible, des millions conquis en deux heures, au milieu des plus effroyables casse-cou; et la course commence, les énergies sont décuplées, la bousculade est telle, que, tout en suant uniquement pour leur plaisir, les gens arrivent parfois à faire des enfants, je veux dire des choses vivantes, grandes et belles . . . Ah! dame! il y a beaucoup de saletés inutiles, mais certainement le monde finirait sans elles. (V, 135–6)[35]

Mme Caroline's reaction to Saccard's eloquent protestations is ambivalent: she is attracted by his vitality but remains unconvinced by his Darwinian theories:

Elle le regardait, et, dans son amour de la vie, de tout ce qui était fort et actif, elle finissait par le trouver beau, séduisant de verve et de foi. Aussi, sans se rendre à ses théories qui révoltaient la droiture de sa claire intelligence, feignit-elle d'être vaincue. (V, 116)[36]

IV

The thematic centre of *L'Argent*, as I have already indicated, is the ambivalence of Zola's protagonist. The reader's response to him is not channelled along a single path of unambiguous moral judgment. The novel expresses a problematic of creation and destruction through the perpetual oscillation of Mme Caroline's attitudes towards Saccard. 'Etait-ce un coquin, était-ce un héros?' ('Was he a knave? Was he a hero?') (V, 384) – this question of Mme Caroline's (in free indirect speech) epitomises her perplexity. The relationship between Mme Caroline and Saccard is another facet of *L'Argent* which sharply distinguishes the later novel from the earlier one.

When Mme Caroline becomes Saccard's mistress, 'dans une sorte de paralysie de sa volonté' ('in a sort of paralysis of the will') (V, 67), their relationship is immediately defined by a statement of the hopes and expectations which Saccard must fulfil: 'l'ignorant encore, elle voulait le croire serviable, d'une intelligence supérieure, capable de réaliser les grandes entreprises de son frère, avec l'honnêteté moyenne de tout le monde' (ibid.).[37] Mme Caroline herself clearly states that her support and solidarity are conditional upon his fulfilment of certain promises: 'je vous assure que je suis prête à avoir de la vraie amitié pour vous, si vous êtes l'homme actif que je crois, et si vous faites toutes les grandes choses que vous dites. . .' (V, 81)[38] Judgment of Saccard and his behaviour is thus immediately posed as a problem. Mme Caroline's solidarity with Saccard is directly linked to their resolve to realise Hamelin's plans to wrench the Middle East from centuries of stagnation and transform it into a thriving industrial society. She sees money as a powerful humanitarian instrument; speculation, allied with science, is a galvanising force:

> Et c'était bien cela qu'elle voyait se dresser de nouveau, la marche en avant, irrésistible, la poussée, sociale qui se rue au plus de bonheur possible, le besoin d'agir, d'aller devant soi, sans savoir au juste où l'on va, mais d'aller plus à l'aise, dans des conditions meilleures; et le globe bouleversé par la fourmilière qui refait sa maison, et le continuel travail, de nouvelles jouissances conquises, le pouvoir de l'homme décuplé, la terre lui appartenant chaque jour davantage. L'argent, aidant la science, faisait le progrès. (V, 77)[39]

In the early days of their association Saccard has an inspirational and invigorating effect upon her: 'si Mme Caroline retournait à cette joie naturelle, inhérente à sa santé même, cela provenait du courage que leur apportait Saccard, avec sa flamme active des grandes affairs' (V, 74).[40] But authorial commentary, signalling her blindness to the dangerous extravagance of his conceptions, prefigures her own later doubts: 'Mme Caroline, d'un bon sens si solide, très réfractaire d'habitude aux imaginations trop chaudes, se laissait pourtant aller à cet enthousiasme, n'en voyait plus nettement l'outrance' (V, 75).[41]

Chapters V and VII both centre on Mme Caroline's uncertainty about Saccard's moral worth, and both describe a similar pattern: agonised doubts about Saccard are followed by final affirmation of his positive features. She is pursued by two images of him. On the one hand, there is the evidence of his disreputable past, associated with Victor and reinforced by Maxime's frankly cynical view of his father's reliability; on the other hand, there are his charitable actions and the worship of admirers: 'Aussi arriva-t-elle à ne plus vouloir le juger, en se disant, pour mettre en paix sa conscience de femme savante, ayant trop lu et trop réfléchi, qu'il y avait chez lui, comme chez tous les hommes, du pire et du meilleur' (V, 162).[42] Her acceptance of her sexual relationship with Saccard is reinforced by admiration of his energy and of his socially creative role: 'Si elle était maintenant à Saccard, sans l'avoir voulu, sans être certaine qu'elle l'estimait, elle se relevait de cette déchéance en ne le jugeant pas indigne d'elle, séduite par ses qualités d'homme d'action, par son énergie à vaincre, le croyant bon et utile aux autres' (V, 163).[43]

The sexual theme in *L'Argent* is related to the novel's main issues in as much as Mme Caroline's discovery of the secret meetings between Saccard and Sandorff again brings into question her attitudes towards Saccard and revives her doubts about his moral worth: 'sa jalousie lui ouvrait de nouveau les yeux et les oreilles' ('her jealousy again opened her eyes and ears') (V, 215). In Chapter VII her perplexity before the ambivalence of Saccard is linked more specifically than in Chapter V to her similar perplexity before the ambivalence of money. The pattern of doubt and affirmation is repeated, and again it is Maxime's revelations about Saccard's murky past, and his assertion of his father's ruthlessness and immorality, which provoke Mme Caroline into a violent reaction against money and bitter recriminations over her attachment to Saccard: 'Elle voyait Saccard à nu, cette âme dévastée d'un homme d'argent, compliquée et trouble dans sa décomposition. Il était en effet sans liens ni barrières, allant à ses appétits avec l'instinct déchaîné de l'homme qui ne connaît d'autre borne que son impuissance' (V, 221).[44] Her horrified vision of the chaotic and destructive character of capitalism produces a deep crisis of loyalty. However, a gay and optimistic letter from her brother restores her spirits and reverses her attitudes:

> Si, là-bas, son frère s'égayait, chantait victoire, au milieu des chantiers qui s'organisaient, des constructions qui sortaient du sol, c'était qu'à Paris l'argent pleuvait, pourrissait tout, dans la rage du jeu. L'argent, empoisonneur et destructeur, devenait le ferment de toute végétation sociale, servait de terreau nécessaire aux grands travaux dont l'exécution rap-

procherait les peuples et pacifierait la terre. Elle avait maudit l'argent, elle tombait maintenant devant lui dans une admiration effrayée . . . (V, 224–5)[45]

Her reflections on money merge into reflections on life itself, ending with fresh hope in the self-renewing powers of life, the simple joy of living: 'Vivre, cela devait suffire, pour que la vie lui apportât sans cesse la guérison des blessures que la vie lui faisait' ('To live, that must suffice, in order that life might continually bring her the cure for the wounds which life inflicted') (V, 226). Her thoughts are concluded by a final authorial statement of love springing from admiration of creative energy: 'C'était l'amour triomphant, ce Saccard, ce bandit du trottoir financier, aimé si absolument par cette adorable femme, parce qu'elle le voyait, actif et brave, créer un monde, faire de la vie' (V, 228).[46]

The role of Mme Caroline is clearly crucial for an understanding of the novel. Zola's deliberations in the *Ébauche* on the possibility of an important female role reveal that he came to consider this role to be of central importance in his general conception of the novel: 'C'est évidemment dans cette femme que gît le noeud, le pivot du roman' ('It is clearly this woman who represents the crux, the pivot of the novel').[47] The function of Mme Caroline is partly structural, for she is intended to establish links between different characters, episodes and themes. But more importantly, the conception of her character emerged from Zola's emphatic desire that his novel should express an optimistic view of life and should not ignore the social benefits derived from money. His thoughts ran thus:

Il me faudrait un autre coin, si je veux montrer l'honnêteté, la santé, la beauté, par l'argent. Cela aussi pourrait me donner aussi [*sic*] ce que je voudrais, l'amour de la vie quand même: malgré le pessimisme, tout croule, mais l'invincible espoir en la vie, qui est sans cesse en travail.[48]

In order to articulate this optimism Zola resolved to create a mature woman; Mme Caroline is thus intended to illustrate the positive values in the novel and, indeed, to serve as a vehicle for his own convictions: 'Me mettre tout entier là-dedans' ('Put the whole of myself into this character').[49] The ideal figure of Mme Caroline becomes transfigured into an almost mythical creation.

Her own self-estimate reflects the mythic significance Zola intended her to assume:

> 'J'ai pensé souvent que mon cas est, en petit, celui de l'huma-
> nité qui vit, certes, dans une misère affreuse, mais que ragail-
> lardit la jeunesse de chaque génération. A la suite de chacune
> des crises qui m'abattent, c'est comme une jeunesse nouvelle,
> un printemps dont les promesses de sève me réchauffent et me
> relèvent le coeur . . . Voyez-vous, j'ai beaucoup trop lu pour
> une femme, je ne sais plus du tout où je vais, pas plus, d'ail-
> leurs, que ce vaste monde ne le sait lui-même. Seulement, c'est
> malgré moi, il me semble que je vais, que nous allons tous à
> quelque chose de très bien et de parfaitement gai. (V, 74)[50]

Mme Caroline, 'avec son vaste savoir, sa tolérance universelle' ('with her vast knowledge and universal tolerance') (V, 385), thus incarnates an indomitable joy in life despite the misfortunes she has experienced. The inextinguishable fund of hope she retains connotes a mature and balanced acceptance of the vicis-situdes of life springing from her extensive knowledge and experi-ence; a tolerance unmarked by naïveté; a blithe optimism and faith in progress; a natural prudence and integrity; a generosity of spirit and outlook. Intelligent, scrupulous and liberal-minded, she is one of Zola's series of Ideal Women who are characterised by charity, hope, stoicism and self-abnegation.

As we have already seen, Saccard is viewed fairly consistently in terms of Mme Caroline's judgements of him. After the crash she comes to occupy the centre of the stage. There is an antithet-ical opposition between the novel's final two chapters, which are largely concerned with Mme Caroline's assessment of the catas-trophe and the definition, through her eyes, of conflicting attitudes towards it. Chapter XI concludes with her violent sense of hatred and resentment, while the following chapter describes the dissolution of her feelings of anger and the reaffir-mation of her hope in the future.

Her feelings are split between compassion for her brother, whose life's work has been seriously jeopardised, and loyalty to Saccard, to whom she still feels tightly bound. The violent con-frontation in Chapter XI between Saccard and Hamelin opposes the latter's prudence to the former's exuberance. Hamelin denounces Saccard as being irresponsibly reckless and almost wilfully destructive: 'Il attaqua le jeu avec une violence extrême, l'Universelle succombait à la folie du jeu, une crise d'absolue démence . . . Le vrai matériel d'une banque est son crédit, elle agonise, dès que son crédit chancelle. Seulement, il y avait là une question de mesure' (V, 333).[51] Saccard, however, recognises no guilt ('L'argent lui avait manqué, voilà tout') ('Money had been lacking, that was all') (V, 335) and remains obstinately convinced that he will be able to begin his ventures anew. Mme Caroline systematically reviews the situation after the crash, registering the series of personal disasters incurred by the catastrophe: Countess de Beauvilliers and her daughter, thrust into deeper poverty; Dejoie, as if shrunken, can no longer provide a dowry for his daughter, who has, moreover, decamped with a neighbour; the Maugendres, who will now be looked after by the impoverished Jordans; the honest Sédille, the wealthy silk manufacturer; Mazaud, the broker, who has committed suicide; Massias; and the innumerable anonymous victims who had perhaps invested their life's savings in the company. To the victims are opposed those who have made a profit: the treacherous Daigremont and the Marquis de Bohain, Huret and Kolb, Delarocque, Jacoby and Nathansohn. Mme Caroline's panoramic reflections and her harrowing, apocalyptic vision culminate as she walks through the streets, shaken, after visiting Mazaud's establishment. Her judgment of Saccard is violently reiterated: 'Elle ne pouvait plus se taire, le mettre à part comme s'il n'existait pas, pour s'éviter de le juger et de le condamner. Lui seul était coupable, cela sortait de chacun de ces désastres accumulés, dont l'effrayant amas la terrifiait' (V, 360).[52]

In the final chapter, it is after Mme Caroline overhears the three little girls praying ardently that Saccard be rewarded for his kindness that she is possessed by fresh doubts about her feelings and that an awareness of the ambiguity of human conduct reasserts itself: 'Un trouble profond l'avait saisie, elle retrouvait cette preuve qu'il n'y a point d'homme condamnable, qui, au milieu de tout le mal qu'il a pu faire, n'ait encore fait beaucoup de bien' (V, 377).[53] It is shortly after this episode that, encouraged by her brother, she visits Saccard in his cell at the Conciergerie and symbolically forgives him for his crimes. Through Mme Caroline Zola sets up an equivalence between love and money in order to reinforce the rhetorical generalisations about the processes of life and nature which envelop the novel's final pages. Mme Caroline's reflections on capitalism are inseparable from her judgment of Saccard. The assimilation of the sentimental to the social themes in the character of Mme Caroline points both to the dualistic nature of Zola's vision and to the theme of fertility: 'sans la spéculation, il n'y aurait pas de grandes entreprises vivantes et fécondes, pas plus qu'il n'y aurait d'enfants, sans la luxure. Il faut cet excès de la passion, toute cette vie bassement dépensée et perdue, à la continuation même de la vie' (V, 225).[54] The burden of the sexual analogy is that both love and money may involve suffering as well as joy – but their negative and destructive aspects must be accepted because they form an integral part of the eternally self-renewing processes of life itself. It is from this optimistic view of the continuance of life, grounded in life's fundamental ambiguity, that Mme Caroline draws sustenance and hope. Her financial/sexual involvement with Saccard, which is both exhilarating and agonising, thus leads to her ultimate affirmation of hope in the future and enables her to gain renewed moral strength and deepened insight into basic cosmic truths. She affirms her optimism with a resonance which prefigures the rhetoric of Zola's last novels.

The ambiguity of Saccard's character is thus placed under the sign of hope; and within the mythic idiom that Zola creates, the myth of hope is paralleled by a myth of redemption. For alongside the affirmation of hope is the desire to redeem. Mme Caroline loves and finally forgives Saccard because of his dynamism. Zola wrote in his *Ébauche*:

> . . . Elle se serait mise chez lui, comme intendante; elle aurait couché et il tromperait avec la femme achetée. Plus tard, elle est prise dans le désastre et c'est elle qui finirait le livre avec l'espoir. Cela suffirait, cela me donnerait même cette originalité: ce gueux de Saccard aimé par une nature foncièrement honnête, et aimé pour des raisons d'activité, de bravoure, de continuel espoir . . . Pour qu'elle l'aime, il faut qu'elle ait trouvé en lui la paillette d'or, le filon d'or que je suivrai d'un bout à l'autre du livre.[55]

Referring to Mme Caroline's role as Saccard's *intendante*, Zola writes: 'et cela l'amusait certainement, elle la savante, la philosophe, de n'être plus qu'une bonne femme de ménage, la gouvernante d'un prodigue, qu'elle se mettait à aimer, *comme on aime les enfants mauvais sujets*' (V, 65). (My italics.)[56]

The significance of Mme Caroline as a character is not circumscribed, however, by the ultimate approbation of Saccard which Zola articulates through her as his delegate in the novel. An important conclusion we may draw from *L'Argent* – a conclusion strengthened by a reading of the novel in the light of the development of Zola's principal male protagonists outlined in Part I of this study – is that Zola is working towards a kind of synthesis of the qualities of Saccard and the values of Mme Caroline. Within the allegorical framework of the novel, Mme Caroline (like Denise Baudu in *Au Bonheur des Dames*) represents the principle of order. In this respect, the key word associated with her is 'equilibrium'. We are told that 'elle devait surtout à ses voyages, à son long séjour parmi des civilisations lointaines, une grande tolérance, un bel équilibre de sagesse' (V, 60).[57] Her two primary virtues are identified when Zola refers to 'son grand bon sens, sa nature droite' ('her great good sense, her upright nature') (V, 112). First, an important aspect of her symbolic function in relation to Saccard, mirrored in her role as *intendante*, is to exercise a moderating influence; as Saccard's *intendante* she organises his house and restrains his domestic extravagance. The reader is told that Saccard secretly 'envies' 'cette taille haute, cette carrure saine' ('her tall figure, her healthy breadth of shoulders') (V, 58). Mme Caroline thus represents the bourgeois ethic of moderation, the desirability of curbing Saccard's excesses and controlling his anarchic tendencies. Her rationality and sense of discipline counterpoint both the utopian dreams of Sigismond and the wild fantasies of Saccard. According to this interpretation, she embodies the values of organisation, stability and control. Secondly, Mme Caroline embodies a moral conscience, and her anxiety in the face of Saccard's uncontrolled behaviour springs from instinctively humane impulses. What she would wish to transmit to Saccard – like Denise Baudu enticing Octave Mouret to reorganise the store in *Au Bonheur des Dames* on more humanitarian lines – is a sense of social responsibility. The theme of responsibility is focused by their contrasting postures towards Victor, who, apart from being Saccard's son, symbolises social injustice and the harmful effects of a poor environment: while Mme Caroline displays a sincere concern for his welfare, Saccard virtually abrogates all paternal responsibility and remains essentially indifferent to him, claiming later that he never had any spare moments to devote to the boy. Saccard's prodigality clearly leads to a neglect of the parental duties which Zola considered so important. Zola, with his strong sense of social obligation, implies that the corollary of leadership is responsibility. The word 'inconscience' recurs several times in the novel's final chapters, implying Saccard's blind self-belief, the fact that he has no conception of moderation or control, and his lack of moral scruple:

> ... elle emporta dans son oreille ces voix angéliques appelant les bénédictions du ciel sur l'homme *d'inconscience* et de catastrophe, dont les mains folles venaient de ruiner un monde. (V, 377–8)

> Mme Caroline le regardait, saisie de son *inconscience* qui en arrivait à une véritable grandeur. (V, 382)

> Lui, cette force *inconsciente* et agissante, elle le subissait de nouveau, comme une des violences de la nature, sans doute nécessaires. (V, 388)[58]

We are thus constantly drawn back to a description of Saccard and of valuations of him. Mme Caroline reflects that, although the Universelle has spread ruin and devastation in France, it has created infinite prosperity in the Middle East: 'Il [Saccard] avait raison: l'argent, jusqu'à ce jour, était le fumier dans lequel poussait l'humanité de demain' ('He was right: money had hitherto been the dung-heap in which the humanity of the future had grown') (V, 398); and we learn, as Mme Caroline is about to depart for Rome to begin a new life with her brother, that Saccard is now in Holland, 'lancé de nouveau dans une affaire colossale' ('again immersed in some colossal enterprise') (ibid.).

The assimilation in *L'Argent* of naturalistic narrative to an allegorical meaning results in a strong discursive element and some stilted dialogues. But although the novel's marked discursiveness and strong didactic strain mean that it is of limited artistic merit, it remains a valuable text for any attempt to determine the development of Zola's vision of society and his conception of the bourgeoisie. It illustrates both the ambivalence and the heterogeneity of Zola's bourgeois world; but it is most useful as an expression of the theme of leadership. It is the bourgeois Saccard rather than the socialist Sigismond or the ineffectual aristocracy who offers the possibility of social progress. The central, integrating theme of *L'Argent* may be defined as the problematic nature of human vitality embodied in the character and conduct of Saccard. The novel dramatises the catastrophic effects that ensue from a radical dissociation of human energies from moral responsibility and proper constraint. Prodigality and uncontrolled energy lead to disaster; the novel describes, after all, a case of disastrous mismanagement. Zola's development of the themes of leadership and organisation means that Saccard, as a failed leader, joins similar messianic characters in the *Rougon-Macquart*, Etienne Lantier in *Germinal* and Lazare Chanteau in *La Joie de vivre*, while on the other hand he prefigures Luc Froment in *Travail*. The close relationship between Saccard's passion for money-making and the themes of philanthropy and creative energy suggests that his energies, which are largely wasted, might be harnessed for the general benefit of society. The ideal expressed in *L'Argent* (a balance between energy and order, a reconciliation of dynamism with the demands of moral and social equilibrium) is fully realised in the stable and harmonious society created by Luc Froment in *Travail*.

Conclusion

It is difficult to make a simple statement about Zola's conception of the bourgeoisie, since his bourgeois world is not monolithic but a very heterogeneous social group. Moreover, bourgeois values transcend purely class distinctions.[1] It is possible, however, to discern an underlying unity in Zola's treatment of the bourgeoisie.

A striking feature of his depiction of the bourgeoisie is its ambivalence. Parasitic, unregenerate, sterile bourgeois are opposed by bourgeois figures characterised by active, dynamic and creative qualities. Zola attacks bourgeois dissipation and predatory greed (notably in *La Curée*, arguably the most representative of the novels which preceded *L'Assommoir*), *petit-bourgeois* egoism and social conservatism, the attachment of the *bourgeoisie mondaine* to a world of superficial and ephemeral appearances (as portrayed in the undervalued *Une Page d'amour*), and bourgeois hypocrisy (particularly in *Pot-Bouille*, Zola's most sharply satirical anatomy of bourgeois values). But he also sees in the bourgeoisie a source of energy and potential social leadership (this is especially visible in *Au Bonheur des Dames* and *L'Argent*). This opposition within the bourgeois spectrum of positive and negative elements corresponds, in the context of the evolving mythical structures of Zola's fiction, to a pattern of degeneration and regeneration, sterility and fertility.

Zola's treatment of the bourgeoisie is informed by a preoccupation with creative energy and the organisation of vital forces. The governing pattern of his work might be defined as a concern with social purpose, social order and responsible social leadership. Zola's bourgeois world is marked by the motifs of waste, profligacy and dissipated energy, and, on the other hand, by the motifs of egoism and sterility. What emerges as an underlying theme is a preoccupation with organisation, that is, control over

189

and constructive exploitation of creative energy. Much of Zola's fiction shows the pernicious consequences of misdirected human energies; and what his fiction develops towards is the creatively channelled human energies, the patriarchal and rationally ordered society, of the utopia described in *Travail*, which provides a virtually systematic *dénouement* to the history of the bourgeoisie as outlined in *Les Rougon-Macquart*. The essence of Luc Froment's ideal community lies in the principles of social equilibrium and natural harmony; and Zola's final vision of the ideal society corresponds to class collaboration and a rearranged bourgeois hierarchy. *Travail* describes a radical reform of institutions and managerial personnel rather than a proletarian revolution; the rearrangement of the bourgeois hierarchy corresponds, in other words, to the advocacy of bourgeois reformism and the creation of a bourgeois patriarchy. The importance of *Travail* in the context of this study is that the regeneration of society it describes is not effected by the workers but by a reforming bourgeois whose antecedents may be traced back to the beginning of *Les Rougon-Macquart*; Luc Froment may clearly be related back to the messianic figures in *Les Rougon-Macquart*, to the problematics of leadership and responsibility that emerge from *Au Bonheur des Dames*, *Germinal* and *L'Argent*, the preoccupation with power and controlled energy manifest in Eugène Rougon, Faujas and Octave Mouret, and the discreetly indicated *embourgeoisement* of the peasant/farmer Jean Macquart. Throughout his work Zola places no hope in the people as an agent of social change; the masses are seen as guided by their instincts and by irresponsible or inadequate leaders. The crucial point, in other words, is that the inception and success of the new society described in *Travail* is dependent, not on mass working-class action, but on the providential intervention of a bourgeois messiah. It is this messiah who, through the liberation and organisation of human energies, creates a marriage of social idealism and personal fulfilment. The opposition between 'good' and 'bad' bourgeois thus becomes very striking in *Travail*, which (unlike *Germinal*) is concerned with conflicts within the bourgeoisie rather than with the class struggle itself.

A vital corollary of Zola's scepticism about the workers' capacity for self-determination, and of his fascination with energy and power, is thus the fact that, although he displays a desire for humane forms of social organisation, his humanitarian messianism is deeply paternalistic. The bourgeoisie as an exploitative, property-owning class is consigned to extinction in his utopian works; parasitic/ *petit-bourgeois* and non-working bourgeois are similarly condemned. But although *Travail* describes the liberation of the workers, the abolition of economic privilege and the collapse of the old bourgeois order, the principles of bourgeois leadership and authority are both retained and affirmed. Zola sees the ideal bourgeois as a leader and an organiser: his ideal bourgeois is a kind of inspired technocrat seeking to organise and to rationalise rather than to bring about violent revolutionary change. The propertied bourgeoisie of the capitalist variety is eclipsed by a new class of managerial leaders, a kind of ruling élite. Hope is placed in a form of élitist interventionism rather than mass political action. Zola's social outlook might thus be described as conservative in the sense that he makes it clear that society is held together by hierarchy and authority. Moreover, his utopian society – like the social criticism voiced in *Les Rougon-Macquart* – is grounded in the traditional bourgeois values of work, moderation and order, as well as in his faith in the natural forces of fecundity, scientific progress and a liberal education.

Zola's portrayal of the bourgeoisie is also marked by a complex preoccupation with sexuality and by vigorous anticlericalism. Several points emerge from Zola's treatment of bourgeois sexuality: first, in his satirical portrayal of the decaying society of the Second Empire in such novels as *La Curée* and *Pot-Bouille*, social corruption is reflected in sexual promiscuity and sterility. Secondly, bourgeois education, cupidity, pretentiousness and idleness are seen as conducive to adultery. Thirdly, sexual hypocrisy is a prominent bourgeois trait, and Zola's fiction does much to subvert the moral pretence of the bourgeoisie. Fourthly, Zola's critique of bourgeois sexual morality is itself grounded in a rather stern and puritanical morality which might be termed 'bourgeois'; throughout most of his career, he believed in the stabilising influence of marriage and the family, and Luc Froment, although he does not believe in the bourgeois institution of marriage, does believe in fidelity and responsible parenthood. Fifth, his delineation of the ideal feminine type reflects his approval of the bourgeois values of work, moderation and order. Sixth, the sexual and social themes of Zola's fiction are linked through the themes of creativity and social purpose. For Zola, the only legitimate end of sexuality is procreation; adultery (that is, pleasure pursued with no social purpose) and the (mainly but not exclusively) bourgeois practice of birth-control are condemned, while total abstinence is also wrong. One of the themes of *Fécondité* is a polemical anti-malthusianism, and one of its theses is that procreation will increase the national resources. Finally, the paternalistic social vision of Zola's final works is mirrored in his view that the role of women is to be good wives and mothers. Zola's approval of certain bourgeois values does not include approval of the established forms of bourgeois religion, first, because he sees Catholicism as both socially reactionary and ineffectual, as well as a facet of bourgeois hypocrisy and the bourgeois world of appearances, and secondly, because the Christian themes of renunciation and chastity are incompatible with his myth of fecundity.

It is quite misleading to say, as one critic has done, that 'à mesure qu'il prend conscience des problèmes sociaux, Zola tend à peindre la bourgeoisie sous des couleurs plus sombres, en même temps qu'à idéaliser le prolétariat' ('as his awareness of social problems increases, Zola tends to paint the bourgeoisie in darker colours, while at the same time idealising the proletariat').[2] Similarly, Juillerat's apocalyptic words on the collapse of the bourgeoisie in *Pot-Bouille* have to be qualified and placed in perspective. Despite Zola's reputation as a *bête noire* of the bourgeoisie (reflected in the reactions to his work of critics like Brunetière and Faguet), and in spite of his radicalist *parti pris* against the Second Empire and the humanitarian eloquence of *L'Assommoir* and *Germinal*, his treatment of the bourgeoisie is far from being entirely satirical or straightforwardly antagonistic. Although he exposed the abuses of his society, he was highly sceptical of those trying to save society by violent revolution. Zola's conception of the bourgeoisie evolves from aggressive anti-bourgeois polemic to an expression of faith in the bourgeoisie as the main force for change in the reorganised society elaborated in his utopian works. Thus the apparent paradox emerges that the nineteenth-century writer who aroused the greatest hostility and fear among bourgeois readers and critics was himself, in some significant respects, profoundly bourgeois.

Notes

INTRODUCTION

1. *Emile Zola: An Introductory Study of his Novels,* revised edition (London: Secker and Warburg, 1964), pp. 44–5.
2. 'The family whose history I will relate will represent the great democratic revolution of our age; from the people, this family will penetrate into the educated classes and will achieve the highest offices, displaying both infamy and talent. This assault on the heights of society by those who in the last century were regarded as people of no account is one of the great developments of our age. My work will, for this very reason, be a study of the contemporary bourgeoisie.' (Notes de travail, B.N. MS. *Nouv. acq. fr.* 10303, fol. 76 ['Premier plan remis à Lacroix', 1869].)
3. *The Age of Capital, 1848–1875* (London: Abacus, 1977), p. 391.
4. Ibid., p. 283.
5. Ibid.
6. Ibid., p. 286.
7. Ibid., p. 288.
8. F.W.J. Hemmings, *The Life and Times of Emile Zola* (London: Paul Elek, 1977), p. 9.
9. See Jean Borie, *Zola et les mythes ou de la nausée au salut* (Paris: Seuil, 1971), pp. 15–40; and Sandy Petrey, 'Obscenity and Revolution', *Diacritics*, III (Fall 1973), 22–6.
10. See Ferdinand Brunetière, *Le Roman naturaliste* (Paris: Calmann Lévy, 1882); and Emile Faguet, *Zola* (Paris: Eyméoud, 1903).
11. Ira N. Shor, 'The Novel in History: Lukács and Zola', *Clio*, II (1972), 19–41 (p. 20).

PART I   THE BOURGEOIS WORLD

WASTE AND PARASITISM

1. Notes de travail, B.N. MS. *Nouv. acq. fr.* 10345, fol. 3 ('Notes générales sur la marche de l'oeuvre').
2. Michel Butor has shown that, throughout the Rougon-Macquart cycle, the symbol of blood is equated with the themes of common hereditary guilt and usurpation: see 'Emile Zola, roman expérimental, et la flamme bleue', *Critique*, 239 (1967), 407–37.

3. 'With another goodnight kiss, they fell asleep. And, on the ceiling, the blob of light became round like a terrified eye, wide open and staring fixedly at these pale, sleeping bourgeois, sweating in their dreams with criminal fear and seeing blood raining down in their bedroom, the large drops changing into gold coins on the floor.'

4. 'Thus it was that this grotesque figure, this pale, paunchy, flabby bourgeois became, in a single night, a formidable gentleman whom no one dared to laugh at any more. For he now had blood on his hands.'

5. 'He thought that he saw for an instant, as in the middle of a flash of lightning, the future of the Rougon-Macquart, a pack of unleashed and sated appetites, in a blaze of gold and blood.'

6. '*An unleashing of appetites*. . . Aristide's appetite for money; Sidonie's appetite for well-being; Renée's appetite of luxury and sensual pleasure; Maxime's growing appetite without moral restraint.' (Notes de travail, B.N. MS. *Nouv. acq. fr.* 10282, fol. 221.)

7. 'The greedy throng made its way into surroundings of luxury, light and warmth, like a sensuous bath in which the musky scent of the ladies' gowns mingled with a faint aroma of game picked out with shreds of lemon.'

8. See Philippe Bonnefis, 'Le bestiaire d'Emile Zola', *Europe*, 468–9 (1968), 97–109.

9. 'According to popular opinion, the tradition of the Rougon-Macquart family was to devour each other; and the onlookers, instead of separating them, would rather have incited them to bite each other.'

10. 'I have produced only wolves . . . a whole family, a whole litter of wolves . . . each of them has taken a bite; their lips are still covered in blood.'

11. 'The smallness of this hand, hovering pitilessly over a gigantic prey, ended by becoming disquieting; and as, without effort, it tore asunder the entrails of the enormous city, it seemed to assume a strange reflex of steel in the blue of the twilight.'

12. 'The *coup d'état* helped them to realise this dream of good things which had been tormenting them for forty years. And what guzzling, what indigestion over it all when the good things came!'

13. '[*Le Ventre de Paris*] complements *La Curée*, it is the scramble for the spoils of the middle classes, the sensual enjoyment of rich food and quiet, undisturbed digestion. . . In reality, the same degeneration, the same moral and social decomposition.' (Notes de travail, B.N. MS. *Nouv. acq. fr.* 10338, fols 49–50.)

14. Notes de travail, B.N. MS. *Nouv. acq. fr.* 10345, fol. 15 ('Différences entre Balzac et moi').

15. 'Blinded, drowned, his ears ringing, his stomach crushed by everything he had seen, guessing at the presence of new and never-ending mountains of food, he prayed for mercy and was gripped by a terrible desire thus to die of hunger, in the midst of Paris gorged with food, at the moment of this dazzling awakening of the Halles.'

16. 'The giant Halles, strong and overflowing with food, had hastened the crisis. They seemed to him like a satiated and digesting beast, a well-stuffed Paris nurturing its fatness, passively supporting the Empire. They surrounded him with huge breasts, monstrous hips, round faces, like never-ending arguments against a body as thin as a martyr and a face yellow with discontent. The Halles were the shopkeepers' belly, the belly of the ordinary, respectable people, ballooning with well-being, shining in the

sun, finding that everything happened for the best and that never before had people of peaceable habit been so wonderfully plump.'

17. 'The shop was filled with a crowd of Lisas, showing off their broad shoulders, the strength of their arms, their rounded breasts so hard and passionless that they aroused no more lustful thoughts than a belly would.'

18. 'Lisa's thick-set profile, with its soft curves and swelling bosom, was like the effigy of a fattened queen in the midst of all this bacon and raw meat.'

19. Angus Wilson, *Emile Zola: An Introductory Study of his Novels*, revised edition (London: Secker and Warburg, 1964), p. 45.

20. 'I'm grateful to the Government when my business is doing well, when I can eat my meals in peace, and when I can sleep without being woken up by gunfire. . . It was a terrible mess, wasn't it, in 1848? Uncle Gradelle – a good man – showed us his books for that period. He lost more than six thousand francs. . . And now that we have the Empire, everything's going well, trade is good. . .

    Of course I take advantage of favourable circumstances and of course I support a Government which helps trade. If it does criminal things, I don't want to know about it. I do know that *I* don't commit any crimes. . .'

21. 'total, egoistic enclosure, rejection of the outside world, great heat, great importance of food, digestion and sleep, serenity of life, absolute respect for the family as a value, complete renunciation of "normal" sexual pleasures.' (*Zola et les mythes, ou de la nausée au salut* [Paris: Seuil, 1971], p. 149.)

22. 'The bed was especially remarkable, with its four mattresses, its many blankets, its eiderdown, its soft, belly-like shape in the clammy depths of the alcove. It was a bed built for sleep.'

23. The themes of waste, dissipation and parasitism also inform Zola's treatment of the working classes (especially in *L'Assommoir*, where Lantier is the wastrel-parasite *par excellence*, literally eating Gervaise out of house and home), but they are not treated in the context of the themes of leadership and social responsibility.

24. 'It seemed as if some wind of sensuality had come in from the street and was sweeping a whole vanished epoch out of the proud mansion, carrying away the Muffats' past, a century of honour and religious faith which had fallen asleep beneath the lofty ceilings.'

25. On the house as a symbol of the body, see Sigmund Freud, *The Interpretation of Dreams*, edited and translated by James Strachey (New York: Avon Books, 1967), p. 381ff.

26. 'The house seemed to have been built over an abyss in which men – their possessions, their bodies, their very names – were swallowed up without leaving a trace of dust behind them.'

27. 'In the midst of the disintegration of the household and the servants' frenzied orgy of waste, there was still a mass of riches stopping up the holes and overflowing the ruins.'

LEADERSHIP

1. For an excellent anatomy of Zola's revolutionaries, see Aimé Guedj, 'Les révolutionnaires de Zola', *Les Cahiers naturalistes*, 36 (1968), 123–37 (p. 135).

2. 'When it came to the means of destroying the old order he was vaguer, jumbling up his odd bits of reading, and not hesitating, with such an ignorant audience, to embark on explanations he could not follow himself.'

3. Pluchart is portrayed as a self-serving political careerist: 'Depuis cinq ans, il n'avait plus donné un coup de lime, et il se soignait, se peignait surtout avec correction, vaniteux de ses succès de tribune; mais il gardait des raideurs de membres, les ongles de ses mains larges ne repoussaient pas, mangés par le fer. Très actif, il servait son ambition, en battant la province sans relâche, pour le placement de ses idées' ('He had not touched a file for five years now, and he took great care of his appearance, especially his hair, and was very proud of his success as an orator; but he was still awkward in his movements, and the nails on his broad fingers had not grown for they had been eaten away by iron. He served his own ambition very actively, constantly travelling up and down the country to promote his ideas') (III, 1344).

4. 'Les révolutionnaires de Zola', p. 135.

5. The same conclusions are reached in the post-*Rougon-Macquart* works: see my section on 'Utopia'.

6. See Henri Mitterand, *Zola journaliste. De l'affaire Manet à l'affaire Dreyfus* (Paris: Armand Colin, 1962), pp. 133–60.

7. The articles in *Une Campagne* which are directed against politics either directly or incidentally are: 'Un homme très fort' (20 Sept. 1880); 'Les trente-six républiques' (27 Sept. 1880); 'Le parti de l'indignation' (4 Oct. 1880); 'L'encre et le sang' (11 Oct. 1880); 'Bêtise' (20 Dec. 1880); 'Emile de Girardin' (8 May 1881); 'Souveraineté des lettres' (30 May 1881); 'Le suffrage universel' (8 Aug. 1881); 'Esclaves ivres' (29 Aug. 1881); 'La démocratie' (5 Sept. 1881); 'Adieux' (22 Sept. 1881).

8. 'For ten years now we have been floundering about absurdly . . . We are dying of politics, of that turbulent, tiresome kind of politics which the gang of mediocrities, thirsting for publicity and good jobs, has every interest in maintaining, so that they might fish in troubled waters. I can see only one means of salvation: do away with these mediocrities in order to put an end to their racket.' (*Oeuvres complètes*, XIV, 440 ['Un homme très fort'].)

9. 'La République et la littérature', *Revue bleue*, 25 April 1879; reprinted in *Oeuvres complètes*, X, 1380.

10. *Oeuvres complètes*, XIV, 443 ('Les trente-six républiques').

11. Henri Mitterand, commenting on Zola's energetic campaign of self-advertisement during the period 1876–81, writes: 'Le goût de la "puissance", chez Zola, comme chez son personnage Eugène Rougon: voilà la raison profonde de cette campagne de cinq ans – une des plus persévérantes et des plus spectaculaires batailles littéraires qu'un écrivain ait jamais conduites' ('Zola's taste for "power", which is reflected in his character Eugène Rougon, is the basic reason for this five-year campaign – one of the most persistent and spectacular literary battles ever waged by a writer'). (*Zola journaliste*, p. 210.) Various critics have commented on the temperamental affinity between Zola and Eugène Rougon. Paul Alexis, Zola's friend and devoted follower, writes: 'Eugène Rougon, ce chaste qui échappe à la femme et qui aime le pouvoir intellectuellement, moins pour les avantages que le pouvoir procure que comme une manifestation de sa propre force, Eugène Rougon, c'est pour moi Emile Zola ministre' ('The

chaste Eugène Rougon, who eludes the grasp of women and loves power intellectually, less for the advantages it provides than as a manifestation of his own strength, is for me an image of Emile Zola as a minister'). (Quoted by Armand Lanoux, *Bonjour, Monsieur Zola* [Paris: Le Livre de poche, 1972], p. 214.)

12. See 'Le suffrage universel', *Oeuvres complètes*, XIV, 632–7.
13. But for many stimulating remarks on the themes of power and leadership in the context of individual/crowd relationships and in the perspective of the structural analysis of myth, see Naomi Schor, *Zola's Crowds* (Baltimore: The Johns Hopkins University Press, 1978). See also Chantal Bertrand-Jennings, 'Le conquérant zolien: de l'arriviste au héros mythique', *Romantisme*, 23 (1979), 43–53.
14. 'Being superior to the common herd, in whom he saw either fools or rascals, and bullying them all along, had developed, in contrast to his thickset frame, an extraordinarily vigorous quick-wittedness. He believed only in himself; while others had arguments he had convictions, and subordinated everything to the incessant aggrandisement of his own personality. Though utterly devoid of vices, he nevertheless indulged in secret orgies of supreme power.'
15. 'Involuntarily, the young woman had glanced down at Rougon's large hands. . . But he had drawn himself very erect and might have been cracking stones in his fists. Clorinde watched him with admiration.'
16. Quoted by Jean-Luc Steinmetz, 'Interscriptions (Mallarmé-Zola)', *Revue des sciences humaines*, 160 (1975), 597–617 (p. 609).
17. It is interesting to note the recurrence in Zola's *contes* and early fiction of the theme of the admiration of a strong and powerful male figure by a smaller or weaker man (see 'Le Grand Michu', 'Aventures du grand Sidoine et du petit Médéric', 'Le Forgeron', *La Confession de Claude*, *Le Voeu d'une morte* and *Madeleine Férat*). This theme – often linked to that of betrayal – may be given a wider meaning than the purely sexual sense given to it by John Lapp (*Zola before the 'Rougon-Macquart'* [University of Toronto Press, 1964]) and Jean Borie (*Zola et les mythes*).
18. 'this struggle of appetites, this pressure of one against another, was the very thing which made the machine run smoothly, which whipped up sales and ignited that blaze of success which astounded Paris.'
19. Vallagnosc anticipates Lazare Chanteau, the protagonist of *La Joie de vivre* (1884), a dilettante whose morbid inactivity is also portrayed as the consequence of Schopenhauerian pessimism compounded by advanced hypochondria and an obsession with death, and whose career consists in a series of disastrous projects ranging from the composition of symphonies to marine engineering. The contrast between the inertia of Lazare and the energy of Octave Mouret and Saccard II is accentuated by the hope placed in Lazare by Pauline Quenu and the local villagers.
20. 'Really, people would have to be deformed, they must have something wrong with their brains and limbs, to refuse to get on with the job at a time when there was such wide scope for work, when the whole century was plunging towards the future.'
21. 'Was it humane or right, this appalling consumption of flesh every year by the big shops? She would plead the cause of the cogs in the machinery, not from sentimental reasons, but from arguments based on the employers'

own interests. When one wants a sound machine one uses good metal; if the metal breaks or is broken there is a halt in the work, repeated expense in getting it going again, and a considerable wastage of energy.'

22. 'He did not sit on a distant throne in some unknown temple; he was not one of those shareholders who pay managers to fleece the miners and whom the miners never saw; he was an employer, he had other things to lose besides his money – his intelligence, his health, and his life.

23. A bourgeois figure who is similar in some ways to Deneulin is the hard-working farmer Hourdequin in *La Terre*. The perennial conservatism of the peasants is contrasted with the progressive outlook of Hourdequin, who attempts to employ modern agricultural methods but meets with the unyielding hostility of the peasants (who are as selfish and rapacious as the most greedy bourgeois).

24. *Le Voltaire*, Dec. 1879; quoted by Mitterand, *Zola journaliste*, p. 214.

25. For a full account of Zola's attitude to the Commune, see Paul Lidsky, *Les Ecrivains contre la Commune* (Paris: François Maspéro, 1970), *passim*; Mitterand, *Zola journaliste*, pp. 139–52 ('Zola et la Commune'); and Roger Ripoll, 'Zola et les Communards', *Europe*, 468–9 (1968), 16–26.

26. 'there were also the reports of the abominations of the Commune, which incensed him by outraging his respect for property and his need for order. He had remained typical of the very heart of the nation, the sensible peasant, longing for peace so as to get back to work, earn some money and regain strength.'

UTOPIA

1. *The House of Fiction*, Leon Edel (ed.) (London: Hart-Davis, 1957), p. 234.

2. Studies of *Travail* I have found particularly useful are Frederick Ivor Case, *La Cité idéale dans 'Travail' d'Emile Zola* (University of Toronto Press, 1974) and Bernard Chartreux, 'Après *Germinal*', in *'Germinal'. Project sur un roman*, ed. Daniel Lindenberg, Jean-Pierre Vincent, Michel Deutsch and Jacques Blanc (Paris: Christian Bourgois, 1975), pp. 39–50.

3. *'La Terre' d'Emile Zola. Etude historique et critique* (Paris: Les Belles Lettres, 1952), p. 383ff.

4. All parenthesised page references to *Travail* are to vol. VIII of the *Oeuvres complètes*, Mitterand (ed.).

5. 'Love alone could create harmony in the city he dreamed of. The adorable Josine was now truly his; and his union with the disinherited was thereby sealed. Apostle that he was of a new creed, he felt that he needed a woman to help him to redeem mankind.'

6. 'Nothing is founded without a child; a child is living work, the broadening and propagation of life, the assurance that tomorrow will duly follow today. The couple alone brings life and will alone save poor men from iniquity and wretchedness.' There are numerous symbolic childbirths in Zola, and it must be remembered that the birth of Pascal's child, echoed by that of the child of Pierre and Marie in *Paris*, provides the symbolic transition from *Les Rougon-Macquart* to *Les Trois Villes*.

7. 'It would suffice to reorganise work in order to reorganise the whole of society, of which work would be the one civic obligation, the vital rule. . . A town, a commune, would become an immense hive in which there would

not be a single idler and in which each citizen would contribute his share towards the general sum of labour necessary for the town to live.'

8. 'Authority, property, religion and the family must all be defended. The whole of Beauclair ended by joining this faction, the injured tradesmen drew their customers together, and the middle class joined in as well, since the new ideas terrified them.'

9. 'They absorbed a tremendous wastage of strength and wealth with the relative honesty of tradespeople who practised robbery according to established usage, glowing with satisfaction every evening at having profited from the needs of others. They were useless cogwheels in the social machine, which was now getting out of order; they made it grate, and consumed much of its remaining energy.'

10. 'In three generations the reserve of creative power which had required so many centuries of wretchedness and effort to accumulate had been gluttonously consumed. Amidst the eager satisfaction of sensual appetites, the nerves of the race had become unstrung, refinement had led to destructive degeneracy. Gorged too quickly, unhinged by material prosperity, the race had collapsed amidst all the folly born of wealth.'

11. Zola's relegation of the proletariat to a subsidiary role in the transformation of society was strongly criticised by Jean Jaurès in a lecture on *Travail* (published in *L'Aurore* on 16 May 1901) and in articles in *La Petite République* on 23 and 25 April 1901.

12. 'Morfain, dwelling in his rocky cave, and for whom nothing existed apart from the difficulties and the glory of his calling, seemed to Luc like the direct descendant of those primitive toilers, whose far-off characteristics still survived in him, silent and resigned as he was, giving all the strength of his muscles without ever a murmur, just as his predecessors had done at the dawn of human society.'

13. In *Paris* (1898) Zola brings his protagonist, Pierre Froment, into direct confrontation with the maze of conflicting ideologies of the age. Catholicism is condemned, but Zola stresses that the answers to contemporary problems offered by political parties and ideologies are of no use. He depicts in *Paris* the fragmentation and antagonisms of rival socialist groups – from the authoritarian collectivism of Mège (a transposition of Jules Guesde) to the fanatical anarchism of Salvat and Jansen (behind whom we see the anarchist bomb-outrages and trials of 1892–4). Pierre explosively condemns both the destructiveness of anarchism and the impotent confusion of socialist sects.

14. 'The matter on which Bonnaire grew muddled was the practical method to employ in order to establish, by laws, this socialisation, and particularly the working of it when it was put into practice; for such complicated machinery would need direction and control, a harsh and vexatory system of state policing.'

15. 'It was perhaps that revolutionary violence was quite repugnant to him personally, since he had placed his scientific faith in ceaseless evolution, which has all eternity before it to achieve its ends.'

16. 'It is excellent to conclude the series with this hope in eternal nature, eternal life: hope that there will be born someone who will begin the experiment anew, who will create a new world out of this old, decrepit one.' (Notes de travail, B.N. MS. *Nouv. acq. fr.* 10290, fol. 229.)

17. 'He had often considered the frightful problem of the shame and torture of the wage system; he had fully sounded its atrocious iniquity, the horrible sore which is eating away present-day society, and he had spent hours of generous enthusiasm in dreaming of a remedy, but forever encountering the iron wall of existing reality.'

18. The stones and abuse hurled at Luc by the inhabitants of Beauclair as he returns to La Crècherie after his acquittal recall the rejection of Etienne Lantier by the Montsou miners after the shooting incident and the failure of the strike.

19. 'He was alone, he wished to act alone, he set all his faith in action. He was the man who dares, and that would be sufficient, his mission would be fulfilled.' Zola's unsocialistic portrayal of social reform as dependent on individual initiative rather than working-class solidarity was stressed by Jaurès in his article in *La Petite République* (see note 11).

20. 'Luc was everywhere at once, encouraging the men in the workshops, promoting brotherliness between one and all at the community-house, and watching over the management of the co-operative stores. He was constantly to be seen in the sunlit avenues of the new town, amidst the women and the children, with whom he liked to laugh and play, as if he were the young father of the little nation now springing up around him. Thanks to his genius and creative fruitfulness, things arose and grew methodically; it was as if seeds fell from his hands wherever he went.'

21. 'He was the Founder, the Creator, the Father; and all these joyous people, all who sat at the tables celebrating work and the fruitfulness of summer, were his people, his friends, his kinsfolk, his ever-spreading, brotherly and prosperous family. An acclamation greeted the ardently loving wishes which he offered up for his city, ascended into the evening air, and rolled from table to table even to the most distant avenues. All had risen to their feet, in their turn holding their glasses aloft and drinking the health of Luc and Josine, the heroes, the patriarchs of work – she, the redeemed one, glorified as spouse and as mother, and he the saviour, who, to save her, had saved the whole wretched world of the wage-earners from iniquity and suffering.'

22. Jordan's conviction that progress and truth are only possible through the irresistible march of science allies him with Bertheroy, the apologist of science in *Paris*. According to Bertheroy, science, contrasted with the impotence and obscurantism of the Church, will guarantee social justice; believing that he is the true revolutionary, he, like Jordan, is dismissive of all forms of political action.

23. For a useful analysis of the thematic similarities and differences between *Germinal* and *Travail*, see Henri Mitterand, 'L'évangile social de *Travail*: un anti-*Germinal*', *Mosaic*, V (Spring 1972), 179–87.

24. See A.A. Greaves, 'Emile Zola and the Danger of Optimism', *Pacific Coast Philology* (Northridge, California), IV (April 1969), 37–40.

SEX

1. *The House of Fiction*, p. 276.
2. *Oeuvres complètes*, XIV, 531–7 (from *Une Campagne*).

3. 'the three winters devoted to man-hunting, the various youths into whose arms she was hurled, the failure of this offer of her body in the authorised prostitution accepted in middle-class drawing-rooms. Then she spoke of all that mothers taught their dowryless daughters: a whole series of lessons in polite prostitution – the touch of fingers while dancing, the relinquishing of hands behind a door, the indecency of innocence speculating on the appetites of the foolish; then, finally, the husband ensnared behind a curtain, falling into the trap in the heat of his sexual excitement.'

4. 'It was the collision of two individuals quite different from each other both in temperament and education – a husband morose, meticulous and devoid of passion, and a wife reared in the hothouse of specious Parisian luxury, vivacious, and determined to get all she could out of life, though for herself alone, like a selfish spoilt child.'

5. 'She, . . . with the indifference of a girl reared in a hothouse, seemed to take no pleasure in their guilty passion, except for the secret outings, the presents, the forbidden pleasures and the hours of luxury spent in cabs, theatres and restaurants. All her early eduction increased her lust for money, for clothes, for squandering. . .'

6. Fraser Harrison, in his study of Victorian sexuality, writes: 'Ill-educated, inexperienced and over-protected, the average daughter of middle-class parents was, in effect, maintained in a state of suspended infantilism.' (*The Dark Angel: Aspects of Victorian Sexuality* [London: Sheldon Press, 1977], p. 38.)

7. Notes de travail, B.N. MS. *Nouv. acq. fr.* 10319, fol. 274.

8. See Borie, *Zola et les mythes*, pp. 15–40; and Sandy Petrey, 'Obscenity and Revolution', *Diacritics*, III (Fall 1973), 22–6.

9. Ferdinand Brunetière, 'A propos de *Pot-Bouille*', *Revue des deux mondes* (15 May 1882).

10. Although Zola's intention in *Une Page d'amour* was to underline the unacceptability of extra-marital sexuality, his treatment of adultery is highly ambiguous: see my chapter on this novel.

11. *Oeuvres complètes*, XIV, 538–42 (from *Une Campagne*).

12. Notes de travail, B.N. MS. *Nouv. acq. fr.* 10313, fol. 229.

13. *Oeuvres complètes*, XIV, 1375 (letter to Louis Ulbach, 6 Nov. 1871).

14. But Zola criticises excessive maternal indulgence in Mme Faujas, whose devotion to her son is blind and dog-like, and in Mme Chanteau, who merely exacerbates her son's neurosis.

15. 'Jesus is destructive of all order, all labour, all life. He repudiated woman and all wordly things, eternal nature, the eternal fecundity of all creatures and things. Then, Catholicism came to build on his teaching its terrible edifice of terror and oppression.' (*Oeuvres complètes*, VII, 1442–3 [*Paris*].)

16. 'In the period following the Industrial Revolution, . . . there is a certain justification in calling Christianity a bourgeois ideology, because the bourgeoisie used the Christian tradition and its personnel in its struggle against the new industrial working class, which in most European countries could no longer be regarded as "inhabiting" the Christian universe.' (Peter L. Berger and Thomas Luckmann, *The Social Construction of Reality: A Treatise on the Sociology of Knowledge* [Harmondsworth: Penguin Books, 1971], p. 141.)

17. 'He accepted . . . the invitations to La Guerdache without any illusions

about the virtues of the bourgeoisie; in a way, he lunched and dined there from a spirit of duty, in order to hide under the cloak of religion the sores he knew to be there.'

PART II   FOUR PERSPECTIVES

La Curée: SPECULATION AND DISSIPATION

1. '. . .For three years I had been collecting documentation, and what dominated, what I was constantly confronted with, was scurrilous facts, incredibly shameful and wild adventures, stolen money and bought women. This note of gold and flesh, this note of flowing millions and the mounting noise of orgies, rang so loudly and insistently that I resolved to evoke it. I wrote *La Curée*. Should I remain silent? Could I leave in darkness the spectacular debaucheries which show up the Second Empire in a suspect light, as a place of ill repute? The story I want to write would then have remained obscure.

    It is essential for me to point out, since I have been misunderstood, and since I cannot otherwise make myself clear, that *La Curée* is the unwholesome plant which has sprouted out of the dung heap of the Empire; it is the incest grown on the compost of millions. My aim, in this new *Phèdre*, has been to show the terrible social breakdown that occurs when all standards of morality are eroded and family bonds no longer exist. My Renée is the Parisienne driven crazy and into crime by luxury and extravagant living; my Maxime is the product of an effete society, the hermaphrodite, passive flesh which accepts the ultimate degradation; my Aristide is the speculator born out of the disruption of Paris, the impudent self-made man who gambles on the Stock Exchange with everything that comes to hand, women, children, honour, cobblestones, conscience. And I have attempted, with these three social monstrosities, to give some idea of the terrible quagmire into which France was sinking.' (*Oeuvres complètes*, XIV, 1375 [letter dated 6 Nov. 1871].)
2. From the preface Zola wrote for the first edition of *La Curée* (dated 15 Nov. 1871 and reproduced by Henri Mitterand in *Les Rougon-Macquart*, I, 1582–3).
3. Bourgeois corruption and venality, rapid social transformation, *arrivisme*, conquest of the city, monomania, and a preoccupation with energy and vital forces are eminently Balzacian themes. There is an obvious similarity between Saccard's excited contemplation of the city from the Buttes Montmartre and Rastignac's gesture at the end of *Le Père Goriot*. Prompted by the appearance of a new edition of the *Oeuvres complètes* by Michel Lévy, Zola had written enthusiastic articles on Balzac in *Le Gaulois* on 8 Feb., 17 March, 2 June and 13 July 1870. A reverential piece in *Le Rappel* on 13 May 1870, in which Zola presented his predecessor as a merciless social critic, clearly revealed Zola's conscious desire to treat his themes with the *Comédie humaine* as a model: see *Oeuvres complètes*, X, 927–8; see also Henri Mitterand, *Zola journaliste. De l'affaire Manet à l'affaire Dreyfus* (Paris: Armand Colin, 1962), pp. 110–13.
4. *The Gates of Horn: A Study of Five French Realists* (New York: OUP, 1963), p. 350.

5. 'Should I give the names and tear off the masks in order to prove that I am a historian, not a scandal-monger? It would be futile, surely. The names are still on everyone's lips.' (*Oeuvres complètes*, XIV, 1375: see note 1.)

6. Zola wrote two articles on *haussmannisation*, one for *La Tribune* (18 Oct. 1868), the other for *La Cloche* (8 June 1872). The former is reprinted in Martin Kanes (ed.), *L'Atelier de Zola*. *Textes de journaux 1865–1870* (Geneva: Droz, 1963), pp. 173–6. See also Mitterand, *Zola journaliste*, pp. 92–7, 115–17; Michel Claverie, 'La fête impériale', *Les Cahiers naturalistes*, 45 (1973), 31–49.

7. For suggestive discussions of the relationship between these two themes, see Roland Bourneuf, 'Retour et variation des formes dans *La Curée*', *RHLF*, LXIX (1969), 993–1008; Sandy Petrey, 'Stylistics and Society in *La Curée*', *Modern Language Notes*, LXXXIX (1974), 626–40.

8. 'Her story illustrates well some of the ambiguities of the *Rougon-Macquart*: the bourgeois world is at once valorised by the nostalgic dream of family decency and sheltered happiness (in this case the house on the Ile Saint-Louis where, long ago, the purity of the child was matched by the stern probity of the father) and denounced as the setting for the mortal struggle of appetites.' (*Zola et les mythes, ou de la nausée au salut* [Paris: Seuil, 1971], p. 26)

9. Notes de travail, B.N. MS. *Nouv. acq. fr.* 10282, fol. 218.

10. 'The race of the Rougons became refined in him, grew delicate and vicious. Born of too young a mother, constituting a strange, jumbled, and, so to say, scattered mixture of his father's furious appetites and his mother's self-abandonment and weakness, he was a defective offspring in whom the parental shortcomings were fulfilled and aggravated. This family lived too fast; it was dying out already in the person of this frail creature, whose sex must have remained in suspense; he represented, not a greedy eagerness for gain and enjoyment like Saccard, but a mean nature devouring ready-made fortunes, a strange hermaphrodite making its entrance at the right moment in a society that was growing rotten.'

11. Parody of classical tragedy was much in vogue in an age which saw the triumph of Offenbach's *La Belle Hélène*. Zola attacked Offenbach, who was immensely popular during the Second Empire, in a number of newspaper articles, seeing in his success a symptom of moral decay: see *L'Evénement illustré* (6 June and 1 July 1868); *L'Avenir national* (18 March 1873); *Le Voltaire* (13 August 1878). The first of these articles is reprinted in Kanes (ed.), *L'Atelier de Zola*, pp. 80–2.

12. Notes de travail, B.N. MS. *Nouv. acq. fr.* 10282, fol. 298. For a detailed study of the theme of Phèdre in *La Curée*, see Auguste Dezalay, 'La "nouvelle *Phèdre*" de Zola ou les mésaventures d'un personnage tragique', *Travaux de linguistique et de littérature*, IX (1971), 121–34.

13. 'Everything was becoming unhinged in her head. Ristori was no longer anything but a great buffoon who pulled up her peplum and stuck out her tongue at the audience like Blanche Muller in the third act of *La Belle Hélène*, Théramène danced the can-can, and Hippolyte ate bread and jam, and stuffed his fingers up his nose.'

14. 'This scrap of nature, that seemed like a newly-painted piece of scenery, lay bathed in a faint shadow, in a pale blue vapour which succeeded in lending to the background an exquisite charm, an air of entrancing artificiality.'

15. 'A new grotto was shown; . . . it was situated seemingly in the centre of the earth, in a nether, fiery region, a fissure of the hell of antiquity, a crevice in a mine of molten metals inhabited by Plutus. . . And the eyes of the spectators grew accustomed with delight to this yawning cavity opening on to the inflamed bowels of the earth, to this heap of gold on which lay sprawling the riches of a world.'

16. 'I should like to have a nun in love with me. Eh? that might be amusing. . . Have you ever dreamt of loving a man of whom you would not be able even to think without committing a crime?'

17. 'Renée was the man, the passionate, active will. Maxime submitted. Smooth-limbed, slim and graceful as a Roman stripling, fair-haired and pretty, stricken in his virility since childhood, this epicene being became a great girl in Renée's inquisitive arms.'

18. For a discussion of *La Curée* in the context of Decadence, see Sara Via, 'Une Phèdre décadente chez les naturalistes', *Revue des sciences humaines*, 153 (1974), 29–38. See also A.E. Carter, *The Idea of Decadence in French Literature, 1830–1900* (University of Toronto Press, 1958), pp. 71–9; George Ross Ridge, *The Hero in French Decadent Literature* (Athens, Georgia: University of Georgia Press, 1961), pp. 74–80; and John C. Lapp, 'The Watcher Betrayed and the Fatal Woman: Some Recurring Patterns in Zola', *PMLA*, LXXIV (1959), 276–84.

19. 'All the woman in her vanished; she became a mere man of business, a commission-agent bustling about Paris at all hours, carrying in her fabulous basket the most equivocal articles, selling everything, dreaming of milliards.'

20. '. . .The Paris of that period offered a most fascinating study to a man like Aristide Saccard. . . In Eugène Rougon's happy phrase, Paris had sat down to dinner, and was contemplating bawdiness at dessert. Politics terrified it, like a dangerous drug. Men's enervated minds turned towards pleasure and speculation. . . And underneath the turmoil there ran a subdued quiver, a nascent sound of five-franc pieces, of women's rippling laughter, and the yet faint clatter of plate and murmur of kisses. . . It was as if one were passing in front of one of those little houses whose closely-drawn curtains reveal nothing beyond the shadows of women, whence no sound issues but that of the gold on the marble chimney-pieces. The Empire was on the point of turning Paris into the bawdy-house of Europe. The handful of adventurers who had succeeded in purloining a throne required a reign of adventures, of shady transactions, of sold consciences, of bought women, of rampant and universal drunkenness. And in the city where the blood of December was yet hardly washed away, there sprang up, timidly as yet, that mad desire for dissipation that was destined to drag down the country to the limbo of decayed and dishonoured nations.'

21. The city seen as a place of perdition, as opposed to the purity and rejuvenating powers of nature, is, of course, a traditional literary theme; the theme of Paris as *la ville maudite* or *la ville-enfer* is a Romantic cliché. A central theme of *La Confession de Claude* is the polarity between Paris, associated with debauchery and vice, and the idyllic life of Provence, associated with purity and innocence; similarly, Florent Quenu (*Le Ventre de Paris*) and Hélène Grandjean (*Une Page d'amour*) are both out of place in the city; in *Son Excellence Eugène Rougon* Zola notes that the Charbonnels, in

their damp, dark hotel, long to return to their sunny garden at Plassans; in
Nana the brief bucolic idyll at La Mignotte provides a momentary respite
from the corruptions of the city; and the opposition between the city and
the country will become a central theme of *Fécondité*.

22. 'she seemed to hear a mysterious appeal; it seemed to her that Paris
    flaring in its winter's night was being lighted up for her, and making
    ready for her the unknown gratification that her glutted senses yearned
    for.'

23. For a detailed examination of the Café Riche episode, see Roland Bour-
    neuf (1969), note 7 above.

24. 'The wide pavement, swept by the street-walkers' skirts, and ringing with
    peculiar familiarity under the men's boots, the grey asphalt, over which it
    seemed to her that the gallop of pleasure and facile love was passing, awoke
    her slumbering desires.'

25. 'Renée left the window-rail with regret. An intoxication and langour rose
    up from the vaguer depths of the boulevard. In the enfeebled rumbling of
    the carriages, in the obliteration of the bright lights, there was a coaxing
    summons to voluptuousness and sleep. The whispers that sped by, the
    groups assembled in shadowy corners, turned the pavement into the pas-
    sage of some great inn at the hour when the travellers repair to their casual
    beds.'

26. '. . .only in the darkness of the boulevard could she find consolation. What
    lingered on the surface of the deserted road of the noise and vice of the
    evening made excuses for her. . . The shamefulness that had lingered there,
    momentary lusts, whispered offerings, prepaid weddings of a night, was
    evaporating, was floating in a heavy mist dissipated by the breath of
    morning. Leaning out into the darkness, she inhaled this quivering silence,
    that alcove fragrance, as an encouragement that reached her from below,
    as an assurance of shame shared and accepted by an approving city.'

27. '. . .a pair of soft tinted tights . . . reached from her feet to her breasts,
    leaving her arms and shoulders bare, and over these tights a simple muslin
    blouse, short, and trimmed with two flounces so as to hide the hips a little.
    A wreath of wild flowers in her hair; gold bangles on her wrists and ankles.
    And nothing more. She was naked.'

28. The mirror motif is also expressive of ostentation and narcissism: Saccard's
    mansion has 'des glaces si larges et si claires qu'elles semblaient, comme
    les glaces des grands magasins modernes, mises là pour étaler au dehors le
    faste intérieur' (sheets of plate glass so wide and so clear that they seemed
    like the window-fronts of a big modern shop, arranged so as to display to
    the outer world the wealth within') (I, 332); the narcissistic Maxime car-
    ries with him a little mirror, while the third *tableau* of the *bal travesti* repres-
    ents the punishment of Narcissus-Maxime, who is seen looking into the
    clear mirror of a stream.

29. 'Renée climbed the staircase, and at each step her image rose in the glass;
    she wondered, with the feeling of doubt common to the most popular
    actresses, whether she was really delicious, as people told her.'

30. 'she derived profound enjoyment from this equivocal furniture which she
    felt about her; from that limpid, cynical mirror whose pure surface, barely
    wrinkled by those filthy scrawls, had helped in the adjusting of so many
    false chignons.'

31. 'She knew now. These were they who had stripped her naked. Saccard had unhooked her bodice, and Maxime had let down her skirt. Then between them they had at last torn off her shift.'

32. 'Renée, as she looked at the two apparitions emerging from the light shade of the mirror, stepped back, saw that Saccard had thrown her like a stake, a speculation, and that Maxime had happened to be there to pick up that louis fallen from the gambler's pocket. She had always been an asset in her husband's wallet. . .'

33. '. . .the bath exhaled the scent of her body, the water in which she had soaked herself filled the room with a sick woman's feverishness; the table with its soap-dishes and cosmetics, the furniture with its bed-like fullness spoke to her rudely of her flesh, of her armours, of all the filth that she longed to forget. She returned to the middle of the room, with crimson face, not knowing where to fly from this alcove perfume, this luxury which bared itself with a harlot's shamelessness, this pink display. The room was naked as herself; the pink bath, the pink skin of the hangings, the pink marble of the two tables assumed an aspect of life, coiled themselves up, surrounded her with such an orgy of living lusts that she closed her eyes, lowering her forehead, crushed beneath the lace of the walls and ceiling which overwhelmed her.'

34. Renée herself thinks in terms of objects: she loves Maxime 'de cette tendresse qu'elle avait pour ses dentelles' ('as she might love her lace') (I, 533); 'Alors l'incestueuse s'habituait à sa faute, comme à une robe de gala, dont les roideurs l'auraient d'abord gênée' ('Then the incestuous woman grew accustomed to her sin as to a gala-dress whose stiffness had at first inconvenienced her') (I, 510).

35. *Zola et les mythes*, p. 26.

36. See especially Gaston Bachelard, *La Psychanalyse du feu* (Paris: Gallimard, 1938) and *L'Eau et les rêves* (Paris: Corti, 1942).

37. 'Saccard was insatiable, he felt his greed grow at the sight of the flood of gold that glided through his fingers. It seemed to him as though a sea of twenty-franc pieces extended about him, swelling from a lake to an ocean, filling the vast horizon with a sound of strange waves, a metallic music that tickled his heart; and he grew adventurous, plunging more boldly every day, diving and coming up again, now on his back, then on his belly, swimming through this immensity in fair weather and foul, and relying on his strength and skill to prevent him from ever sinking to the bottom.'

38. 'Her life unrolled before her. She witnessed her long bewilderment, that racket of gold and flesh that had mounted within her, that had first come up to her knees, then to her belly, then to her lips; and now she felt its flood passing over her head, beating on her skull with quick blows.'

39. 'In this burning atmosphere, in this bath of flames, she almost ceased to suffer; her pain became as a light dream, a vague oppression, whose very uncertainty ended by becoming voluptuous. Thus she lulled till the evening the remorse of yesterday, in the red glow of the firelight, in front of a terrible fire, that made the furniture crack around her, and that at moments deprived her of the consciousness of her existence.'

40. See Philippe Bonnefis, 'Fluctuations de l'image, en régime naturaliste', *Revue des sciences humaines*, 154 (1974), 283–300; Philippe Hamon, 'A propos de l'impressionnisme chez Zola', *Les Cahiers naturalistes*, 34 (1967), 139–48;

J. H. Matthews, 'L'impressionnisme chez Zola: *Le Ventre de Paris*', *Le Français moderne*, XXIX (1961), 199–205; Joy Newton, 'Emile Zola impressionniste', *Les Cahiers naturalistes*, 33 (1967), 39–52; 34 (1967), 124–38, and 'Emile Zola and the French Impressionist Novel', *L'Espirit créateur*, XIII (1973), 320–8. Zola's impressionism has also been touched on by Martin Turnell in his analysis of Zola's style in *The Art of French Fiction* (London: Hamish Hamilton, 1959), pp. 180–92.

41. *The House of Fiction*, Leon Edel (ed.) (London: Hart-Davis, 1957), p. 249.
42. Introduction to the Garnier-Flammarion edition of *La Curée* (Paris, 1970), 17–31 (p. 21). Philippe Hamon comments: 'Le personnage ne crée plus l'action romanesque, mais la description: les traditionnels éléments du roman, l'élément statique (la description) et l'élément dynamique (le personnage) semblent s'inverser' ('The characters no longer create the plot of the novel, but description: the traditional elements of the novel, the static element (description) and the dynamic element (the characters) seem inverted'). ('A propos de l'impressionnisme de Zola', p. 142.)
43. 'Saccard left the Hôtel-de-Ville and, being in command of considerable funds to work with, launched furiously into speculation, while Renée, in mad intoxication, filled Paris with the clatter of her equipages, the sparkle of her diamonds, the vertigo of her riotous existence.'
44. 'A singular apartment, this first floor in the Rue de Rivoli. The doors were slamming to and fro all day long. The servants talked aloud; its new and dazzling luxury was continually traversed by a flood of vast, floating skirts, by processions of tradespeople, by the uproar of Renée's friends, Maxime's school friends and Saccard's callers.'
45. 'Sometimes the husband and wife, those two feverish devotees of money and of pleasure, would penetrate the icy mists of the Ile Saint-Louis. They felt as though they were entering a city of the dead.'
46. 'The whirlwind of contemporary life, which had set slamming the doors of the first floor in the Rue de Rivoli, had become, in the mansion, a genuine hurricane which threatened to carry away the partitions.'
47. 'In the midst of these princely rooms, along the gilded balustrades, over the fine velvet carpets, in this fairy parvenu palace, there trailed the aroma of Mabille, there danced the jauntiness of the popular quadrilles, the whole period passed with its mad, stupid laugh, its eternal hunger and its eternal thirst. It was the disorderly house of fashionable pleasure, of the unblushing pleasure that widens the windows so that the passers-by may enjoy the confidence of the alcoves. Husband and wife lived there freely, under their servants' eyes. They divided the house into two, encamped there, not appearing as though at home, but rather as if they had been dropped, at the end of a tumultuous and bewildering journey, into some palatial hotel where they had merely taken the time to undo their trunks in order to hasten more speedily towards the delights of a fresh city.'
48. 'Meanwhile the fortune of the Saccards seemed to be at its zenith. It blazed in the midst of Paris like a colossal bonfire. This was the moment when the eager division of the hounds' fee filled a corner of the forest with the yelping of the pack, the cracking of whips, the flaring of torches. The appetites let loose were satisfied at last, in the shamelessness of triumph, amid the sound of crumbling districts and of fortunes built up in six months. The town had become a sheer orgy of gold and women. Vice, coming from on

high, flowed through the gutters, spread out over the ornamental waters, shot up in the fountains of the public gardens to fall down again upon the roofs in a fine, penetrating rain. And at night-time, when one crossed the bridges, it seemed as though the Seine drew along with it, through the sleeping city, the refuse of the town, crumbs fallen from the tables, bows of lace left on couches, false hair forgotten in cabs, banknotes slipped out of bodices, all that the brutality of desire and the immediate satisfaction of an instinct fling into the street bruised and sullied. Then, amid the feverish sleep of Paris, and even better than during its breathless quest in broad daylight, one felt the unsettling of the brain, the golden and voluptuous nightmare of a city madly enamoured of its gold and its flesh. The violins sounded till midnight; then the windows became dark, and shadows descended upon the city. It was like a colossal alcove in which the last candle had been blown out, the last remnant of shame extinguished. There was nothing left in the depths of the darkness save a great rattle of furious and wearied love; while the Tuileries, at the waterside, stretched out their arms into the night, as though for a huge embrace.'

49. 'A thousand lively coruscations sprang up, quick flashes played among the wheels, sparks flew from the horses' harness. On the ground, on the trees, were broad reflections of trotting glass. This glitter of wheels and harness, this blaze of varnished panels glowing with the red gleam of the setting sun, the bright notes of colour cast by the dazzling liveries perched up full against the sky, and by the rich costumes projecting beyond the carriage doors, were carried along amid a hollow, sustained rumbling sound, timed by the trot of the horses.'

50. 'She remembered how he sprang over obstacles, rolling over in the mud, not taking the time to wipe himself, so that he might attain his aim in good time, not even stopping for enjoyment by the wayside, munching his gold pieces while he ran.'

51. '. . .She could see the eagerness of the feet, the whirling of glazed shoes and white ankles. At intervals it seemed to her as though a gust of wind was about to carry off the dresses. Those bare shoulders, those bare arms, those bare heads that flew and reeled past, caught up, thrown off and caught up again at the end of the gallery, where the waltz of the band grew madder, where the red hangings swooned amid the final fever of the ball, seemed to her as the tumultuous symbol of her own life, of her self-exposures, of her surrenders.'

52. 'And the endless procession, a crowd strangely mixed and always alike, passed by with tiring regularity in the midst of the bright colours and patches of darkness, in the fairy-like confusion of the thousand leaping flames that swept like waves from the shops, lending colour to the transparencies of the windows and the kiosks, running along the pavements in fillets, letters and designs of fire, piercing the darkness with stars, gliding unceasingly along the roadway.'

Une Page d'amour: THE AMBIGUITIES OF PASSION

1. *Le Bien public*, 11 Oct. 1877; quoted by Henri Mitterand (ed.), *Les Rougon-Macquart*, II, 1620.

2. See *Oeuvres complètes*, XIV, 1396 (letter to Henry Céard, 16 July 1877); 1397 (letter to Léon Hennique, 2 Sept. 1877).

3. 'She had lived an upright and blameless life for more than thirty years. Her only passion was for justice. When she examined her own past she could not remember the briefest lapse; she seemed to have followed a straight and even path unhesitatingly. And surely as the days flowed by she would go on just as calmly, without ever stumbling. Severe in her self-confidence, she passed angry and scornful judgment on those false, romantic pictures of life that stir up the emotions. The only real way of life was her own, steady and unruffled.'

4. 'She felt, somehow, involved in their affection. And she went on day-dreaming on their behalf. . . She had lost all sense of distance, she was no longer clearly conscious of herself or of others, of where she was or of why she had come there. The copper pans were glistening on the wall, and she sat on in a sort of lethargy, a drowned expression on her face, undisturbed by the disorder of the kitchen around her. This self-abasement gave her a sense of deep delight, as though some inner need were satisfied.'

5. *The Interpretation of Dreams*, edited and translated by James Strachey (New York: Avon Books, 1967), p. 235. In discussing dream codes and dream symbolism, Freud also states that steps, ladders and staircases, and walking up and down them, signify the sexual act (ibid., p. 390). Perhaps they are associated rather with (sexual) frustration than with the sexual act in general?

6. Jean Borie has stated well the centrality of 'chambre'/'fenêtre' metaphors in *Une Page d'amour*: 'Nulle part n'est plus évident l'opposition entre contempler et sortir, nulle part plus étroite l'association du regard et de la pureté, de la sortie et de la chute' ('Nowhere is the opposition between contemplation and going out more evident, nowhere is the association between the glance and purity, going out and falling, more close'). (*Zola et les mythes, ou de la nausée au salut* [Paris: Seuil, 1971], p. 211.)

7. 'Upstairs in her room, in that familiar atmosphere of cloistered quiet, Hélène felt herself stifled. She was amazed to find the room so calm, so confined, so drowsy under its blue velvet hangings, while she herself was panting and afire with turbulent emotion. Was this really her room, this lonely, lifeless, airless place? Then violently, she threw open a window and leaned there to look out over Paris.'

8. 'she yearned, now, to fall from grace, to fall immediately and completely. This was the outcome of all her rebellious feelings, this imperious desire: to be annihilated in an embrace, to experience in one minute all that she had missed in life hitherto.'

9. Gaston Bachelard, in his elaboration of a phenomenology of the imagination, opposes the 'rationality' of the highest part of the house to the 'irrationality' of the cellar, which is associated with the unconscious: see *La Poétique de l'espace* (Paris: PUF, 1957), pp. 34–5.

10. '. . .in his drawing-room she would no doubt have retained her natural mistrustful reserve. But here they were far from the world, sharing a single chair, almost glad of the poverty and squalor that, by arousing their compassion, brought them closer together. . . And this sharing of a generous emotion shed a sort of radiance in Mère Fétu's hovel.'

11. 'A feeling of indignant protest, of angry pride mingled in her heart with a *secret*, irrepressible delight'; '. . .she pursued her quest, with nerves on edge and *secret* longings'; 'Her will was failing her; she was *secretly* tormented by thoughts she could not acknowledge'; 'But in her heart she felt a *secret*

shame, and the pressure of the child's body against her shoulder made her blush'; 'She was *dizzy* with the rapture of soaring and sinking'; '. . .the thought made her *dizzy*, set her wits reeling.'

12. 'She was hurt by the indifference with which Juliette had received her'; 'such indifference and frivolity were profoundly disheartening to Hélène, who had come there full of ardent feeling'; 'she wanted Juliette to be ruined, to see if she would still maintain the same unconcerned composure.'

13. 'Hélène slowly surveyed the room. In this respectable society, amongst these apparently decent middle-class people, were there none but faithless wives? With her strict provincial morality, she was amazed at the licensed promiscuity of Parisian life. And, bitterly, she reproached herself for having suffered so intensely when Juliette took her hand. Really, she was a fool not to have discarded her precious scruples! Adultery, here, had become smugly respectable, enlivened with a touch of stylish elegance.'

14. 'a middle-class lady who likes to entertain, give dinners, etc., and slides into adultery through boredom. Parisian adultery quite without emotion, affected and superficial.' (Notes de travail, B.N. MS. *Nouv. acq. fr.* 10318, fol. 498.)

15. 'Hitherto she had behaved more or less exactly like all the women in her set, only she had never had a love affair, and curiosity and the need to be like the rest urged her on.'

16. Notes de travail, B.N. MS. *Nouv. acq. fr.* 10318, fol. 503.

17. 'And often while she spoke his eyes met Hélène's; and neither turned away. For a moment they looked one another full in the face, deeply serious, as if they saw each other's heart; then, slowly dropping their eyes, they would smile.'

18. 'she felt shocked and startled, like a woman who feels her last garment slipping from her. . . And as he kept gazing at her, she felt he must be reading her lie on her face.'

19. 'She sat for hours with her hands hanging loose, stifling in her room, longing to go out for a breath of air and yet not moving. She felt the room was making her ill; she detested it, and resented the two years she had spent there.'

20. *The Interpretation of Dreams*, p. 430.

21. 'She felt that such a mystery was in execrable taste. . . And yet in spite of her distaste she felt a certain excitement, an irresistible attraction, and her senses were obsessed by the thought of the silence and half-light that must prevail in the pink room.'

22. Sensations fulfil a unifying role in the deliberate repetition of situations and images which mark the progression of passion. Malignon's secret apartment, with its drawn curtains, lighted candles and stifling atmosphere, recalls the Deberles' drawing-room during the children's party. During the scene in which Hélène discovers the relationship between Juliette and Malignon there is constant insistence on the growing heat and lassitude, mirroring the sleepy complacency and increasingly patent boredom: 'La chaleur grandissait, une odeur musquée s'envolait des toilettes sous le battement des éventails' ('The room was growing even warmer, and the fluttering fans wafted a musky fragrance from the dresses') (II, 981). It is the same heat, the same oppressive, sweet atmosphere, that Hélène had noted on her first visit to the Deberles' sumptuous drawing-room. The

motif of stifling heat reminds us of *La Curée*, and it anticipates the motif of claustrophobia in *Pot-Bouille*.

23. 'Around them lay a desert; there was not a sound, no human voice, nothing but a black storm-tossed sea outside. They were out of the world, a thousand leagues from any land. And this obliviousness of the bonds that connected them with men and things was so absolute that they felt as if they had been born there, that very instant, and that they would die there, presently, when they were clasped in one another's arms.'

24. See Roger Ripoll, 'Fascination et fatalité: le regard dans l'oeuvre de Zola', *Les Cahiers naturalistes*, 32 (1966), 104–16; see also John C. Lapp, 'The Watcher Betrayed and the Fatal Woman: Some Recurring Patterns in Zola', *PMLA*, LXXIV (1959), 276–84.

25. 'At last she was going to know everything; she would alight on domes and spires, and in seven or eight wafts of her wings she would see the secret things that are hidden from children.'

26. *Zola et les mythes*, p. 214.

27. This is in fact argued by Freud in *The Interpretation of Dreams*, p. 391 ff.

28. See Borie's analysis of this scene in *Zola et les mythes*, pp. 214–15.

29. The word 'laid', echoing 'le jour était trop laid' ('the weather was too unpleasant') (II, 1014) and the mention of the doll which Jeanne had buried, 'si noire et si laide' ('so black and hideous') (II, 1026), returns during the heavy description of Jeanne's alienation on her mother's return, with its sexual undertones (the missing glove, the loose belt, Hélène's moist, warm hand, the discarding of the wet clothes): 'Pourquoi donc revenait-elle si mal habillée, avec quelque chose de très *laid* et de si triste dans toutes ces affaires? Elle avait de la boue à son jupon, ses souliers étaient crevés, rien ne lui tenait sur le corps' ('Why did she come back looking so untidily dressed, with something ugly and squalid about all her things? There was mud on her petticoat, her shoes were split, and nothing seemed to fit her') (II, 1037); 'Jeanne suivait les vêtements qui tombaient un à un, comme si elle les eût interrogés, en s'attendant à voir glisser de ces linges trempés de boue les choses qu'on lui cachait' ('Jeanne watched the garments falling off one by one, as if she was questioning them, as if she expected the mud-soaked linen to disclose the secrets that were being kept from her') (II, 1039). Jeanne's fascinated contemplation and horror at the sight of the fallen clothes, 'dont la tiédeur l'importunait' ('whose warmth disturbed her'), recall Muffat's contemplation of Nana, and underlines her attachment to the series of watchers in Zola.

30. 'Whatever could that black building be? And that street, where some huge thing was hurrying along? And that whole district, which frightened her because she was sure that people were fighting there. She could not see very clearly, but honestly, there was something happening down there, it was horrid, it was something little girls oughtn't to look at... And unknown Paris, with its smoke, its continuous rumble, its mighty life, seemed to waft up to her, on this damp mild air, a smell of poverty, filth and crime that made her young head dizzy, as if she had leaned over some foul well that exhaled a choking vapour from its invisible mud... Then she was at a loss, she just felt frightened and ashamed, haunted by the persistent notion that her mother was among those horrid things, somewhere that she could not guess at, far away down there.'

31. 'She saw herself naked, and sobbed with shame as she jerked up the sheet. It seemed as if she had suddenly grown ten years older in her suffering, and that as death drew near the twelve-year-old child was mature enough to understand that this man must not touch her, must not touch her mother's body through hers.'

32. *Journal, 1889—1939* (Paris: Gallimard, Bibliothèque de la Pléiade, 1951), p. 1207 (entry dated 18 July 1934).

33. Notes de travail, B.N. MS. *Nouv. acq. fr.* 10318, fol. 503.

34. Ibid.

35. Hélène's maternal devotion is heightened by the references to her relationship with her first husband: 'Charles baisait toujours ses pieds de marbre, tandis qu'elle se montrait indulgente et maternelle pour lui' ('Charles still kissed her feet, smooth and cold as marble; and she behaved towards him like an indulgent mother') (II, 848); 'n'avait-elle pas aimé son mari, qu'elle soignait comme un enfant?' ('surely she had loved her husband, whom she cared for like a child?') (II, 849).

36. Judith Armstrong, *The Novel of Adultery* (London: Macmillan, 1976), p. 86.

37. Notes de travail, B.N. MS. *Nouv. acq. fr.* 10318, fol. 492.

38. 'I would not advise my daughter to read it, if I were a mother!!! In spite of my great age, the novel troubled and *excited* me. One feels immoderate desire for Hélène and one understands your doctor very well.' (*Correspondance*, VIII (Paris: Conard, 1930), p. 114.)

Pot-Bouille: BLACK COMEDY

1. 'Show the bourgeoisie as they really are, having already depicted the people, and show how they are more horrible in spite of their claim to represent order and decency.' (Notes de travail, B.N. MS. *Nouv. acq. fr.* 10321, fol. 1.)

2. 'To those bourgeois who say: we represent honour, morality, the family, he wished to reply: it is not true, you are the opposite of all that, your *pot-au-feu* existence merely conceals all that is rotten in family life and modern social morality.' (*Emile Zola, notes d'un ami* [Paris: Charpentier, 1882], p. 127.)

3. Notes de travail, B.N. MS. *Nouv. acq. fr.* 10321, fol. 1 (Zola's italics).

4. *Présentation des 'Rougon-Macquart'* (Paris: Gallimard, 1964), p. 188.

5. Jean Borie has demonstrated that the image of 'la maison' has multiple metaphorical meanings in Zola (*Zola et les mythes, ou de la nausée au salut* [Paris: Seuil, 1971], pp. 125–252), while Harry Levin has commented that Zola 'had that gift of institutional imagination which enabled Dickens to build his novels around such massive and pointed exaggerations as the Dust Heap and the Circumlocution Office' (*The Gates of Horn: A Study of Five French Realists* [New York: OUP, 1963], p. 323).

6. 'There was a certain gaudy splendour about the vestibule and staircase. At the foot of the stairs a gilt figure, a sort of Neapolitan woman, supported on her head a jar from which three gas-jets in ground-glass globes issued. The imitation marble panelling, white with pink edges, went right up the round stairwell at regular intervals, while the cast-iron banisters, with mahogany

handrail, were meant to look like old silver, with extravagant clusters of gold leaves. A red carpet with brass rods covered the staircase.'

7. 'Slowly he went upstairs in his turn. Only one gas-jet was alight; the staircase, in this heavy, heated atmosphere, seemed to be falling asleep. It seemed even more peaceful, with its chaste portals or rich mahogany that enclosed so many respectable hearths. Not a sound could be heard, it was like the silence of well-mannered people holding their breath. But now he heard a slight noise. Leaning over the banisters, he saw M. Gourd, in velvet cap and slippers, turning out the last gas-burner. Then the whole house was lost in solemn darkness, as if obliterated by the refinement and propriety of its slumbers.'

8. 'The staircase bore no trace of the scandals of the night; the stucco panelling preserved no reflection of a lady rushing by in her chemise, nor did the carpet retain the odour of her white body.'

9. 'In life it's only the most timid who go to the wall. Money is money, and if you haven't got any you won't get anywhere. For my part, whenever I had twenty sous I always pretended I had forty, because the great thing is to make yourself envied, not pitied. . . It's no good having a good education if you're not well dressed, for then people only look down on you. It isn't right, but that's how it is. . . I'd rather wear dirty petticoats than a cotton gown. Eat potatoes if you like, but put a chicken on the table if you have people to dinner. . . Only fools would deny that!'

10. 'from the depths of the dark, narrow courtyard only the stench of drains came up, like the smell of filth hidden by the various families and stirred up by rancorous servants.'

11. Borie sees the whole of Zola's literary enterprise as both an expression and an indictment of these forms of 'organisation culturelle': see *Zola et les mythes*, p. 8. The idea of a repressed sexuality, false puritanism and a hidden life are of course common nineteenth-century themes: see Fraser Harrison, *The Dark Angel: Aspects of Victorian Sexuality* (London: Sheldon Press, 1977) (especially 'Middle-Class Sexuality', pp. 3–154); Derek Hudson (ed.), *Munby: Man of Two Worlds* (London: John Murray, 1972); Stephen Marcus, *The Other Victorians* (London: Weidenfeld and Nicolson, 1966); (Anon.), *My Secret Life* (London, c. 1890); Ronald Pearsall, *The Worm in the Bud: The World of Victorian Sexuality* (London: Weidenfeld and Nicolson, 1969).

12. Notes de travail, B.N. MS. *Nouv. acq. fr.* 10321, fol. 1.

13. See Borie, *Zola et les mythes*, p. 14. Borie sees prostitutes and servants in Zola as fulfilling the role of 'intermédiaires infernaux' ('infernal intermediaries') who both reveal and assume 'la malédiction du corps' ('the curse of the body') (*Zola et les mythes*, p. 29).

14. 'Thus, if the workers are identified with the body, it is because they are condemned by the bourgeoisie to remain separate, to remain workers. . . We may thus formulate the following contradiction: the malady both emanates from the workers and is imposed upon them. Zola, in his 'generosity', gives them absolution, but his social vision remains at an impasse, and it will necessarily remain so as long as the body is constrained to be a kind of infernal prisoner.' (*Zola et les mythes*, pp. 26–7.)

15. 'Their affair, so carefully concealed, was now trailed through all the garbage and slops of the kitchen . . . The filthy talk of the servants defiled their

kisses, their meetings, in fact all that was still sweet and tender in their love.'

16. 'When he left her he felt dissatisfied, and he would have liked to go straight to bed and to sleep. He had gratified his passion, but it had left a disagreeable aftertaste, a touch of lechery that brought merely bitterness.'

17. 'She submitted silently and without pleasure. When she stood up, with limp wrists and her face drawn by a spasm of pain, all her contempt for the male was apparent in the black look she threw at him.'

18. *Tolstoy or Dostoevsky*, revised edition (Harmondsworth: Penguin Books, 1967), p. 33.

19. Lionel Trilling writes that *Pot-Bouille* 'is in the tradition of massive comic morality' (*A Gathering of Fugitives* [London: Secker and Warburg, 1957], p. 17) which includes Breughel, Ben Jonson, Swift, Hogarth, Heine, the later Dickens and Flaubert.

20. Notes de travail, B.N. MS. *Nouv. acq. fr.* 10321, fol. 322.

21. This drawing is reproduced in the *Oeuvres complètes*, IV, 689.

22. *Emile Zola: An Introductory Study of his Novels*, revised edition (London: Secker and Warburg, 1964), p. 119.

23. *Pot-Bouille* was immediately dramatised by William Busnach, with Zola's assistance. For a general discussion of the dramatisation of Zola's novels, see Martin Kanes, 'Zola and Busnach: The Temptation of the Stage', *PMLA*, LXXVII (1962), 109–15.

24. 'Some of the mothers clearly cherished fond dreams of marrying their daughters, as they stood with open mouths and ferocious teeth, unconsciously letting their masks slip. It was by the frenzy that pervaded the drawing room – a ravenous appetite for sons-in-law – that these middle-class ladies were possessed, as they listened to the asthmatic sounds of the piano.'

25. 'The staircase once more became as peaceful as a middle-class chapel; not a sound escaped from behind the mahogany doors, which constantly guarded the profound respectability of the several families.'

26. 'With bellies distended, they slowly and selfishly proceeded to digest, like four worthy citizens who had just been stuffing themselves, away from all family cares, . . . so they were able to unbutton and let their paunches rest on the table.'

27. 'Duveyrier, trying to understand it all, led the way, moving his limbs mechanically, like a sleepwalker, while the candle he held in his trembling hand flung the four shadows of this weird procession on the walls, like an advancing column of broken marionettes.'

28. 'It seemed as if this carpenter's garret was the cesspool of the house – a den of iniquity, the surveillance of which was revolting to all his delicate feelings and a source of trouble to him at night.'

29. 'Her belly now seemed to him to cast its shadow over the frigid cleanliness of the courtyard, and even over the imitation marble and gilded zinc decorations of the hall. Its swollen presence seemed to bring dishonour to the whole building, tainted the very walls. As it had grown, it had seemed to disturb the placid virtue of each flat.'

30. Notes de travail, B.N. MS. *Nouv. acq. fr.* 10321, fol. 391. For a detailed account of the political references in *Pot-Bouille*, see E.M. Grant, 'The Political Scene in Zola's *Pot-Bouille*', *French Studies*, VIII (1954), 342–7.

31. '. . . the bourgeoisie devoting themselves to pleasure and resisting all change. They vote in their own interests and to maintain their situation. Hatred of new ideas, fear of the people, wish to stop the Revolution with their own accession to power. When they feel threatened, they all band together.' (Notes de travail, B.N. MS. *Nouv. acq. fr.* 10321, fol. 299.)

32. 'They saw workmen, blackened with dust and soaked in blood, breaking into their houses, raping their maidservants, and drinking their wine. Doubtless, the Emperor deserved a lesson; but they began to be sorry for having given him such a severe one.'

33. 'once more flung the mantle of religion over these corrupt middle-class folk, like a master of ceremonies veiling the canker in an attempt to delay the final moment of decomposition.'

34. 'Once more he attacked the middle classes, declaring that if ever the workers took over they would soon be swept away; but the others interrupted him, loudly protesting that in the bourgeoisie lay the virtue, energy and thrift of the nation.'

35. ' "God has forsaken them", said the Abbé. "No", replied the doctor, "don't drag God into it. It's a question of bad health or a bad upbringing, that's all."

    Then, going off at a tangent, he spoilt his argument and began violently to abuse the Empire: under a republic things would surely be better. And amid the ramblings of this man of mediocre intelligence, there came the just remarks of the experienced physician thoroughly acquainted with all his patients' weaknesses. He did not spare the women, some of whom were made either corrupt or crazy by being brought up as dolls, while others had their sentiments and passions perverted by hereditary neurosis; and all of them, if they sinned, sinned vulgarly, foolishly, without desire and without pleasure. Nor was he less severe with the men – fellows who merely ruined themselves while hypocritically pretending to lead sober and virtuous lives. And in all this Jacobin frenzy one heard the inexorable death-knell of a whole class, the collapse and putrefaction of the bourgeoisie, whose rotten props were already cracking under the strain.'

36. Mitterand gives an account of this case in *Les Rougon-Macquart*, III, 1625–9.

37. 'Every page and every line of *Pot-Bouille* was written with the aim of giving the book a moral intention. It is without doubt a cruel work, but it is above all a moral work, in the true, philosophical sense of the word.' (Quoted by F. W. J. Hemmings, *Emile Zola*, second edition [Oxford: Clarendon Press, 1966], p. 145.)

38. André Gide, *Journal, 1889–1939* (Paris: Gallimard, Bibliothèque de la Pléiade, 1951), p. 1137 (entry dated 17 July 1932).

L'Argent: ENERGY AND ORDER

1. 'I would like, in this novel, not to conclude that life is disgusting (pessimism). Life as it is, but accepted in spite of everything, because of love of it for its own sake, in all its force. What I would like, in short, is that this novel should stand out from my whole Rougon Macquart series.' (Notes de travail, B.N. MS. *Nouv. acq. fr.* 10268, fol. 376.)

2. 'Link the financial theme to the political situation during the last years of the Empire, and indicate how it will all culminate in the *débâcle* of the Franco–Prussian war. In studying the state of the stock market, clearly depict the mood of the nation, its demoralisation, empty cash-boxes (?), the classes in disarray, all on the brink of collapse. The enemy has merely to enter the country and seize our lands. *So depict a decadent society throughout the whole book.* Choose the characters with this aim in mind. *Social decomposition and imminent collapse should be emphasised throughout the whole book.*' (Notes de travail, B.N. MS. *Nouv. acq. fr.* 10268, fols 427–8.)

3. 'I do not think that it will be very difficult to move the Union affair to about 1867. There had already been the collapse of the Crédit Mobilier. In fact all I need is for the public to get carried away in an outburst of speculative madness that will leave the stock market exhausted. It will be the Empire's last, spectacular gesture, its final fling, the classical dance on the volcano: the 1870 war is upon them, and they rush once more to satisfy all their sensual appetites. I need to evoke a sense of great prosperity and that this prosperity should be entirely hollow.' (Notes de travail, B.N. MS. *Nouv. acq. fr.* 10269, fols 170–1.) Zola is referring, in the first sentence of this quotation, to his desire to transpose the actual crash of the Union Générale, which occurred in 1882, to the last years of the Empire.

4. '. . . large yellow bills, placarded all over Paris, announcing the forthcoming opening of the Carmel silver mines, had ended by turning every head, kindling the first symptoms of a passionate intoxication which was destined to grow and sweep away all reason. The ground was prepared, for there, all ready, was that compost of the Empire, composed of fermenting rubbish and heated by maddened appetites, a soil extremely favourable to one of those wild growths of speculation which every ten or fifteen years choke and poison the Bourse, leaving only ruin and blood behind them. Crooked finance companies were already springing up like mushrooms; the big companies were urging people into risky speculative ventures; an intense gambling fever was breaking out amidst the uproarious prosperity of the reign, amidst a dazzling whirl of pleasure and luxury, of which the forthcoming Exhibition promised to be the final splendour, the deceptive apotheosis. And amidst the vertigo that had seized the mob, amidst the scramble for all the other bargains that were freely offered on the pavements, the Universelle was at last set in motion, like some powerful machine destined to intoxicate and crush everybody, and which violent hands were heating immoderately, to the point of explosion.'

5. 'expending his energy from morning till night in order to ensure the perfect working of this huge new machine, whose mechanism was grinding and grating and seemed likely to burst.'

6. 'What especially distressed her was the terrible pace, the continual gallop at which the Universelle was driven along, like an engine stuffed with coal and set upon diabolical rails so that it might rush on until a final shock smashed it to pieces. She was not a naïve simpleton who could be deceived; although ignorant of the technicalities of banking, she perfectly understood the reasons for this overworking, this feverishness destined to intoxicate the mob and plunge it into this mad, epidemic dance of millions.'

7. 'Was it not he who, with his unscrupulous hands, had madly overheated the enormous machine, until it had burst to atoms and injured all those whom it carried along with it?'

8. 'During the clear evenings, from the huge festive city, where everyone was seated at table in exotic restaurants, as if the city had become a colossal fair where pleasure was freely sold under the stars, there arose the supreme fit of madness, the joyous, voracious folly which overtakes great capitals threatened with destruction. And Saccard, with the flair of a cut-purse, had so clearly anticipated this paroxysm, everyone's desire to empty his pockets and throw his money to the winds, that he had just doubled the amount allowed for advertising, urging Jantrou to create the most deafening din.

9. 'And at last came the dreadful crush of the small and humble, the tramping crowd that follows large armies, passion descending from the drawing-room to the kitchen, from the bourgeois to the workman and the peasant, and sweeping along in this mad gallop of millions many poor subscribers with just a single share or three or four or ten shares apiece, concierges nearly ready to retire, old maids living with their cats, provincial pensioners with only ten sous to spend a day, country priests whom almsgiving had left almost penniless: in fact the whole haggard, hungry mass of lowly stockholders, whom a catastrophe at the Bourse sweeps away like an epidemic and at one stroke stretches in paupers' graves.'

10. 'beyond the reddish smoke on the horizon, in the distant parts of the city, it seemed as though one could hear a great cracking sound, as if a whole world were about to collapse.'

11. 'Did anyone ever see a Jew working with his hands? Were there any Jewish peasants or working men? No. Work is a dishonour, their religion almost forbids it, exalting only the exploitation of the labour of others.' Although anti-Semitism remains a minor, contingent theme in *L'Argent*, it is necessary (particularly in view of Zola's subsequent participation in the Dreyfus Affair) to distinguish Zola's view from the anti-Semitic tirades of Saccard and to establish the nature and evolution of Zola's own attitude towards the Jews: see Richard B. Grant, 'The Jewish Question in Zola's *L'Argent*', *PMLA*, LXX (1955), 955–67.

12. '. . . he had always been a man of imagination, seeing things on too grand a scale, transforming his shady deals as an adventurer into poems; and this time, with this really colossal and prosperous enterprise, he was beginning to be carried away by extravagant dreams of conquest, by so crazy, so outrageous an idea that he could not even clearly formulate it to himself.'

13. 'He was not a speculator, a soldier of fortune manoeuvring with the millions of others, dreaming, like Saccard, of heroic battles in which he should prove conqueror and win colossal booty for himself, with the aid of mercenary gold enlisted under his orders; he was, as he said good-naturedly, a simple money merchant, but the most shrewd and zealous there could be.'

14. 'Saccard, who despite his terrible appetites made due allowance for the disinterested love of money, simply for the power that it gives, felt seized with a sort of holy terror as he gazed upon that face, not that of the classical miser who hoards, but that of the blameless workman, without a fleshly instinct, who in his ailing old age had become a kind of abstract of himself, and obstinately continued to build his tower of millions . . .'

15. 'I am too passionate, that is evident. There is no other reason for my defeat; and that is why I have known defeat so often. And it must be added that, if my passion kills me, it is also my passion that gives me life. Yes, it bears me on, it lifts me up on high, and then strikes me down and suddenly destroys

all my work. To pursue passionate enjoyment is perhaps only to consume oneself . . .'

16. 'of what use was all this grandiose charity if they could not, in such spacious and salubrious surroundings, re-educate an ill-bred creature, turn a perverted child into a well-behaved man, with the upright reason of health?'

17. 'he would suddenly disappear on a spree, returning with a worn-out look and bleary eyes. It was difficult to know whether women or drink played most havoc with him.'

18. 'Perhaps she was dragged down to his level, falling lower and lower, by the very impetus of her downward course. A passion for gambling – as I have often observed – corrodes and rots everything; it turns a creature of even the highest and proudest race into a human wreck, a waste scrap swept into the gutter . . .'

19. 'So much vile wretchedness, hunger and inevitable filth on the one hand, and on the other exquisite refinement, abundance and fine living. Could money, then, acquire education, health, intelligence? And if the same human mud remained underneath, did not all civilisation consist in the superiority of smelling nice and living well?'

20. '. . . the benefits obtained through money and speculation itself. Thus a picture of railways, mines, of the country transformed and improved. Well-being. Grandiose ideas realised, great inventions brought into being, progress, life vastly improved. The idea that bad speculation is to necessary speculation what debauchery and lust are to love: without love there are no children, without speculation there are no business affairs.' (Notes de travail, B.N. MS. *Nouv. acq. fr.* 10268, fol. 430.) For an amusing demonstration of how *L'Argent* might have been read by contemporaries as a highly moral tale and as a virtual vindication of capitalism, see Gaston Cohen, '*L'Argent*', *Europe*, 83–4 (1952), 107–11.

21. See *Les Rougon-Macquart*, V, 1254.

22. '*Very important*. There is a high-minded kind of speculation, honest, useful, constructive, logical and sincere. It creates life, while the other kind of speculation – jobbery – like debauchery, leads only to death.' (Notes de travail, B.N. MS. *Nouv. acq. fr.* 10269, fol. 11.)

23. 'Since civilisation had moved from the East to the West, why should it not come back towards the East, returning to the first garden of humanity . . .? He would endow it with fresh youth; he would galvanise the earthly paradise, make it habitable again by means of steam and electricity . . .'

24. 'Not only have I set out to study the present role of money, but I also intend to show the past nature of wealth and where it will lie in the future. Hence a prominent historical element in the novel and also an important socialist element.' (*Oeuvres complètes*, XIV, 1475.)

25. See Halina Suwala, 'A propos de quelques sources de *L'Argent*', *Les Cahiers naturalistes*, 16 (1960), 651–4.

26. See especially Paul Lafargue, '*L'Argent* de Zola', in *Critiques littéraires* (Paris: Editions sociales internationales, 1936), pp. 173–211 (written in 1891–2).

27. Notes de travail, B.N. MS. *Nouv. acq. fr.* 10268, fol. 280.

28. 'Saccard made an angry gesture, for he found the answer deplorably disrespectful. He was on the point of shouting that the affair was really a

superb one, and that Maxime sadly underestimated him if he thought that he was a mere thief like the others.'

29. 'However, amidst all this waste, all these enormous estimates, she was abominably robbed; a swarm of contractors lived off her, to say nothing of the losses due to bad management; charity for the poor was being squandered. And it was Saccard who opened her eyes to this, begging her to let him set her accounts straight. And he did this in a thoroughly disinterested way, solely for the pleasure of regulating this mad dance of millions which aroused his enthusiasm.'

'. . . at the end there lay the dream of his entire life, the conquest of Paris. To be the king of charity, the adored God of the multitude of the poor, to become unique and popular, to occupy the attention of the world – it surpassed his ambition. What prodigies could he not realise if he used to good effect his business faculties, his guile, obstinacy and utter freedom from prejudice! And he would have the irresistible power which wins battles, money, coffers full of money, which often does so much harm, and which would do so much good the day it was used to satisfy his pride and pleasure.'

30. 'Now, in the mornings, in his luxurious Louis Quatorze office, Saccard was forced to bar his door when he wished to work; for there were endless assault parties, or rather a court procession, coming, as it were, to a king's *levée* – courtiers, business people, endless place-seekers and beggars clamouring adoringly for his omnipotent favours.'

31. 'in the blindness of his fever, he believed that he was still marching on to victory, with his whole nation of shareholders behind him – that intoxicated and fanaticized people of the humble and the fashionable worlds, in which pretty women of good position mingled with servant girls borne along by the same faith.'

32. 'He was made to make life, not to dress the wounds that life has made. And now he was about to find himself at work again, in the thick of the battle of interests, in the midst of that race for happiness which has brought about the very progress of humanity, from century to century, towards greater joy and greater knowledge.'

33. 'Give me good ideas and I will undertake to make them yield all desirable profit with the least possible risk. I believe that a practical man can make no better offer.'

34. 'Yes, speculation. Why does the word frighten you? . . . Speculation – why, it is the one inducement that we have to live; it is the eternal desire that compels us to live and struggle . . .

. . . Look, do you think that without – how shall I put it? – that without lust many children would be born? . . . Hardly one child is conceived for every hundred who are not conceived. It is excess that produces the necessary results, is it not?'

35. 'With the mere legitimate, moderate remuneration of labour – with nothing but well-balanced equilibrium in all transactions, life becomes just a dreary desert, a marsh in which all forces slumber and stagnate; while, if you suddenly make some dream flare up on the horizon, promise men that with one sou they will earn a hundred, propose to all these dormant people that they will join you in the quest for the impossible, and gain millions in a couple of hours, despite the most frightful risks – why then the race begins,

energies are increased tenfold, and amidst the scramble of people toiling
and sweating for their own gratification, birth is given to children, I mean
to great and beautiful living things . . . Oh! In love as in speculation there
is much filth, but without it the world would undoubtedly come to an end.'

36. 'She looked at him, and, in her love of life, of all that was strong and active,
she ended by finding him handsome, seductive in his fervour and faith.
Thus, without agreeing with his theories, which revolted the uprightness of
her clear intelligence, she pretended to be convinced.'

37. 'she did not know him yet, and was eager to believe that he was of high
intelligence, was willing and able to realise her brother's great projects,
and that he was as honest as any other man.'

38. 'I assure you that I shall feel true friendship for you if you prove the man of
action I think you are and do all the great things you say . . .'

39. 'And it was precisely this that she saw rising again – the forward,
irresistible march, the social impulse towards the greatest possible sum of
happiness, the need for action, for going ahead, without knowing exactly
where, but at all events more easily and under improved circumstances;
the globe would be turned upside down by the ant-swarm rebuilding its
abode, its work never ending, fresh sources of pleasure forever being
discovered, man's power increasing tenfold, the earth belonging to him
more and more every day. Money, aiding science, yielded progress.'

40. 'if Mme Caroline returned to that natural inherent gaiety of hers, it was
due to the courage which Saccard, with his zeal for great enterprises,
imparted.'

41. 'Mme Caroline, although she had great good sense and was not easily
influenced by feverish imaginations, yielded at last to this enthusiasm, no
longer seeing its extravagance.'

42. 'And so Mme Caroline ended by refusing to judge him, and, like a learned
woman who has read and thought too much, sought to appease her
conscience by saying that he, like all other men, was compounded of both
good and evil.'

43. 'Thus, if she was now Saccard's mistress, without having desired it,
without feeling sure that she respected him, she was buoyed up by judging
him not to be unworthy of her, attracted as she was by the qualities he
showed as a man of action, by his determination to succeed, by the belief
that he was good and useful to others.' Zola's description of Mme
Caroline's   reasoning   at   this   stage   stresses   the   vitalist   and
anti-intellectualist elements in her attitudes: 'elle était femme de clair bon
sens, elle acceptait les faits de la vie sans s'épuiser à tâcher de s'en
expliquer les mille causes complexes' ('she was a woman of clear good
sense; she accepted the facts of life without wearing herself out in trying to
explain their thousand complex causes') (V, 163; compare V, 397).

44. 'She saw Saccard as he really was, with the ravaged, complicated soul of a
financier, murky and rotting. He had no attachments or scruples, rushing
to satisfy his appetites with the unbridled instincts of a man who knows no
other limit than his own impotence.'

45. 'If her brother in the East was in such high spirits, shouting victory amidst
the yards and workshops which were being got in order, and the buildings
which were springing up, it was because in Paris the passion for gambling
was making money rain down and rot everything. Money, poisonous and

destructive, became the ferment of all social vegetation, serving as the necessary compost for great works whose execution would draw the nations together and bring peace to the earth. She had cursed money, but now she fell in awe-stricken admiration before it . . .'

46. 'It was the triumph of love – Saccard, that financial bandit, loved so absolutely by that adorable woman because she saw him, brave and active, as the creator of a world, the creator of life.'

47. Notes de travail, B.N. MS. *Nouv. acq. fr.* 10268, fol. 403.

48. 'I would need another milieu if I want to show the honesty, health and beauty associated with money. This might also give me what I want, love of life in spite of everything: despite pessimism, everything collapses, but there remains an indomitable hope in life, which never halts in its course.' (Notes de travail, B.N. MS. *Nouv. acq. fr.* 10268, fols 404–5).

49. Notes de travail, B.N. MS. *Nouv. acq. fr.* 10268, fol. 406.

50. 'I have often thought that my case is, in little, the case of humanity, which certainly lives in frightful wretchedness but is buoyed up by the youth of each succeeding generation. After each crisis that disheartens me, I experience something like a new youth, a springtime whose promise of sap warms me and uplifts my heart . . . You see, I have read far more than a woman should; I no longer know where I am going, any more than this vast world knows where it is going, for that matter. But, in spite of myself, it seems to me that I am going, that we are all going, towards something very good and thoroughly gay.'

51. 'He attacked gambling with extreme violence. The Universelle, he said, had succumbed to the mania for gambling; it had carried gambling to the point of absolute madness . . . The life-blood of a bank is its credit, so it is menaced with extinction as soon as its credit totters. But there was a question of moderation in all this.'

52. 'She could no longer remain silent; she could no longer put him aside as if he did not exist, so as to avoid judging and condemning him. He alone was guilty; this was clearly shown by each of these accumulated disasters, the frightful pile of which terrified her.'

53. 'She was profoundly disturbed, again finding in all this a proof that no man is utterly blameworthy, that there is no man who, amid all the evil he may have done, has not also done much good.'

54. 'without speculation there would be no great creative enterprises, just as no children would be conceived without lust. This excess of passion, all this energy basely expended and lost, is essential if life itself is to go on.'

55. '. . . She might have gone to live with him as his housekeeper; she might have slept with him and he might have cheated her with the courtesan. Later on, she is caught up in the disaster and it is she who concludes the book on a note of hope. This would be enough, and it would even give me a stroke of originality: the wretched Saccard is loved by someone who is fundamentally honest, and loved for his energy, his courage, and the continual hope he inspires . . . In order that she might love him, she must discover in him the speck of gold, the vein of gold which I will trace throughout the whole book.' (Notes de travail, B.N. MS. *Nouv. acq. fr.* 10268, fols 409–10.)

56. 'and it certainly amused her – she, the woman of learning, the philosopher

– to be simply a good housewife, the housekeeper of a prodigal, whom she was beginning to love *as one loves naughty children.*'

57. 'she had acquired – notably by her travels and her long residence among far-off civilisations – a broad spirit of tolerance and her well-balanced common sense.'

58. '. . . she left, still hearing the sound of those angelic voices praying for the blessings of heaven to be bestowed upon Saccard, the reckless author of catastrophes, whose mad hands had just ruined a world'; 'Mme Caroline looked at him, captivated by his very recklessness, which was becoming really grand'; 'Again she succumbed to that reckless, active power, as to some – no doubt necessary – violence in nature.'

CONCLUSION

1. See Theodore Zeldin, *France 1848–1945*, I (Oxford: Clarendon Press, 1973), pp. 18–19.
2. Micheline Tison-Braun, *La Crise de l'humanisme. Le Conflit de l'individu et de la société dans la littérature française moderne*, I: *1890–1914* (Paris: Nizet, 1958), pp. 296–7.

Bibliography

PRIMARY SOURCES

Manuscripts

Bibliothèque Nationale (Paris), *Nouvelles acquisitions françaises*, 10268–10345. Cited in the text as B.N. MS. *Nouv. acq. fr.*

Published Works

Emile Zola, *Les Rougon-Macquart*, edited by Henri Mitterand, 5 vols (Paris: Gallimard, Bibliothèque de la Pléiade, 1960–7). Page references to this edition appear in parentheses in the text.
Emile Zola, *Oeuvres complètes*, edited by Henri Mitterand, 15 vols (Paris: Cercle du Livre Précieux, 1966–70).
Martin Kanes (ed.), *L'Atelier de Zola. Textes de journaux 1865–1870* (Geneva: Droz, 1963).

SECONDARY SOURCES

(This list includes all works cited in this book and some others that I have found helpful but had no opportunity to cite directly.)

Books

Alexis, Paul, *Emile Zola, notes d'un ami* (Paris: Charpentier, 1882).
Armstrong, Judith, *The Novel of Adultery* (London: Macmillan, 1976).
Bachelard, Gaston, *La Psychanalyse du feu* (Paris: Gallimard, 1938).
——, *L'Eau et les rêves* (Paris: Corti, 1942).
——, *La Poétique de l'espace* (Paris: PUF, 1957).
Berger, Peter L. and Thomas Luckmann, *The Social Construction of Reality: A Treatise on the Sociology of Knowledge* (Harmondsworth: Penguin Books, 1971).
Bertrand-Jennings, Chantal, *L'Eros et la femme chez Zola: de la chute au paradis retrouvé* (Paris: Klincksieck, 1977).
Borie, Jean, *Zola et les mythes, ou de la nausée au salut* (Paris: Seuil, 1971).
Bottomore, T. B., *Classes in Modern Society* (London: Allen and Unwin, 1965).
Brunetière, Ferdinand, *Le Roman naturaliste* (Paris: Calmann Lévy, 1882).

Carter, A. E., *The Idea of Decadence in French Literature, 1830–1900* (University of Toronto Press, 1958), pp. 71–9.

Case, Frederick Ivor, *La Cité idéale dans 'Travail' d'Emile Zola* (University of Toronto Press, 1974).

Dupuy, Aimé, *1870–1871. La Guerre, la Commune et la presse* (Paris: Armand Colin, 1959). ('Emile Zola, chroniqueur parlementaire à Bordeaux et à Versailles', pp. 151–66).

Faguet, Emile, *Zola* (Paris: Eyméoud, 1903).

Flaubert, Gustave, *Correspondance*, VIII (Paris: Conard, 1930).

Freud, Sigmund, *The Interpretation of Dreams*, edited and translated by James Strachey (New York: Avon Books, 1967).

Gide, André, *Journal, 1889– 1939* (Paris: Gallimard, Bibliothèque de la Pléiade, 1951).

Guillemin, Henri, *Présentation des 'Rougon-Macquart'* (Paris: Gallimard, 1964).

Harrison, Fraser, *The Dark Angel: Aspects of Victorian Sexuality* (London: Sheldon Press, 1977).

Hemmings, F. W. J., *Emile Zola*, second edition (Oxford: Clarendon Press, 1966).

——, *The Life and Times of Emile Zola* (London: Paul Elek, 1977).

Hobsbawm, Eric, *The Age of Capital, 1848–1875* (London: Abacus, 1977).

Hudson, Derek (ed.), *Munby: Man of Two Worlds* (London: John Murray, 1972).

James, Henry, *The House of Fiction*, Leon Edel (ed.) (London: Hart-Davis, 1957). ('Emile Zola', pp. 220–49; 'Nana', pp. 274–80.)

Krakowski, Anna, *La Condition de la femme dans l'oeuvre d'Emile Zola* (Paris: Nizet, 1974).

Lanoux, Armand, *Bonjour, Monsieur Zola* (Paris: Le Livre de poche, 1972).

Lapp, John C., *Zola before the 'Rougon-Macquart'* (University of Toronto Press, 1964).

Levin, Harry, *The Gates of Horn: A Study of Five French Realists* (New York: OUP, 1963). ('Zola', pp. 305–71.)

Lidsky, Paul, *Les Écrivains contre la Commune* (Paris: François Maspéro, 1970).

Marcus, Steven, *The Other Victorians* (London: Weidenfeld and Nicolson, 1966).

Meakin, David, *Man and Work: Literature and Culture in Industrial Society* (London: Methuen, 1976).

Mitterand, Henri, *Zola journaliste. De l'affaire Manet à l'affaire Dreyfus* (Paris: Armand Colin, 1962).

Morazé, Charles, *La France bourgeoise XVIIIe–XXe siècles* (Paris: Armand Colin, 1947).

——, *Les Bourgeois conquérants* (Paris: Armand Colin, 1957).

(Anon.), *My Secret Life* (London, c. 1890).

Nelson, Brian, *Emile Zola: A Selective Analytical Bibliography* (London: Grant and Cutler, 1982).

Pearsall, Ronald, *The Worm in the Bud: The World of Victorian Sexuality* (London: Weidenfeld and Nicolson, 1969).

Pernoud Régine, *Histoire de la bourgeoisie en France*, 2 vols (Paris: Seuil, 1960–2).

Ridge, George Ross, *The Hero in French Decadent Literature* (Athens, Georgia: University of Georgia Press, 1961), pp. 74–80.

Robert, Guy, *'La Terre' d'Emile Zola. Etude historique et critique* (Paris: Les Belles Lettres, 1952).

Schor, Naomi, *Zola's Crowds* (Baltimore: The Johns Hopkins University Press, 1978).

Sombart, Werner, *The Quintessence of Capitalism*, translated and edited by M. Epstein (New York: Howard Fertig, 1967).

Steiner, George, *Tolstoy or Dostoevsky*, revised edition (Harmondsworth: Penguin Books, 1967).

Tison-Braun, Micheline, *La Crise de l'humanisme. Le Conflit de l'individu et de la société dans la littérature française moderne*, I: *1890–1914* (Paris: Nizet, 1958). ('Zola et l'apostolat humanitaire', pp. 292–313.)

Trilling, Lionel, *A Gathering of Fugitives* (London: Secker and Warburg, 1957). ('In defense of Zola', pp. 12–19.)

Turnell, Martin, *The Art of French Fiction* (London: Hamish Hamilton, 1959). ('Zola', pp. 93–194.)

Wilson, Angus, *Emile Zola: An Introductory Study of his Novels*, revised edition (London: Secker and Warburg, 1964).

Zeldin, Theodore, *France 1848–1945*, 2 vols (Oxford: Clarendon Press, 1973–7).

Articles

Alcorn, Clayton, '*La Curée*: les deux Renée Saccard', *Les Cahiers naturalistes*, 51 (1977), 49–55.

Baguley, David, 'Le supplice de Florent: à propos du *Ventre de Paris*', *Europe*, 468–9 (1968), 91–7.

Bertrand-Jennings, Chantal, 'Le conquérant zolien: de l'arriviste au héros mythique', *Romantisme*, 23 (1979), 43–53.

Bonnefis, Philippe, 'Le bestiaire d'Emile Zola', *Europe*, 468–9 (1968), 97–109.

——, 'Fluctuations de l'image, en régime naturaliste', *Revue des sciences humaines*, 154 (1974), 283–300.

Bourneuf, Roland, 'Retour et variation des formes dans *La Curée*', *RHLF*, LXIX (1969), 993–1008.

Bouvier, Jean, '*L'Argent*: roman et réalité', *Europe*, *468*–9 (1968), 54–64.

——, 'Le monde des affaires', in *Zola* (Coll. Génies et Réalités) (Paris: Hachette, 1969), pp. 171–91.

Bouvier-Ajam, Maurice, 'Zola et les magasins de nouveautés *(Au Bonheur des Dames)*', *Europe*, 468–9 (1968), 47–54.

Brunetière, Ferdinand, 'A propos de *Pot-Bouille*', *Revue des deux mondes* (15 May 1882).

Butor, Michel, 'Emile Zola, romancier expérimental, et la flamme bleue', *Critique*, 239 (1967), 407–37.

Chartreux, Bernard, 'Après *Germinal*', in *'Germinal'. Projet sur un roman*, Daniel Lindenberg, Jean-Pierre Vincent, Michel Deutsch and Jacques Blanc (eds) (Paris: Christian Bourgois, 1975), pp. 39–50.

Chemel, Henri, 'Zola collaborateur du *Sémaphore* de Marseille (1871–1877)', *Les Cahiers naturalistes*, 14 (1960), 555–67; 18 (1961), 71–9.

Claverie, Michel, 'La fête impériale', *Les Cahiers naturalistes*, 45 (1973), 31–49.

Cohen, Gaston, '*L'Argent*', *Europe*, 83–4 (1953), 107–11.

Delas, Daniel, 'Zola et la démocratie parlementaire 1871–1881', *Europe*, 468–9 (1968), 27–36.

Dezalay, Auguste, 'La "nouvelle *Phèdre*" de Zola ou les mésaventures d'un personnage tragique', *Travaux de linguistique et de littérature*, IX (1971), 121–34.

Duchet, Claude, Introduction to the Garnier-Flammarion edition of *La Curée* (Paris, 1970), 17–31.

Gerhardi, Gerhard C., 'Zola's Biological Vision of Politics: Revolutionary Figures in *La Fortune des Rougon* and *Le Ventre de Paris*', *Nineteenth-Century French Studies*, II (1974), 164–80.

Girard, Marcel, 'Positions politiques d'Emile Zola jusqu'à l'Affaire Dreyfus', *Revue française de science politique*, V (1955), 503–28.

Grant, E. M., 'The Political Scene in Zola's *Pot-Bouille*', *French Studies*, VIII (1954), 342–7.

Grant, Richard B., 'The Jewish Question in Zola's *L'Argent*', *PMLA*, LXX (1955), 955–67.

——, 'The Problem of Zola's Character Creation in *L'Argent*', *Kentucky Foreign Language Quarterly*, VIII (1961), 58–65.

Greaves, A. A., 'Emile Zola and the Danger of Optimism', *Pacific Coast Philology* (Northridge, California), IV (April 1969), 37–40.

Guedj, Aimé, 'Les révolutionnaires de Zola', *Les Cahiers naturalistes*, 36 (1968), 123–37.

Hamon, Philippe, 'A propos de l'impressionisme de Zola', *Les Cahiers naturalistes*, 34 (1967), 139–48.

——, 'Le personnage de l'abbé Mauduit dans *Pot-Bouille:* sources et thèmes', *Les Cahiers naturalistes*, 44 (1972), 201–11.

Hemmings, F. W. J., 'Fire in Zola's Fiction: Variations on an Elemental Theme', *Yale French Studies*, 42 (1969), 26–37.

Jaurès, Jean, '*Travail*', *La Petite République* (23 and 25 April 1901).

——, 'Conférence sur *Travail* d'Emile Zola', *L'Aurore* (16 May 1901).

Jennings, Chantal, 'Zola féministe?', *Les Cahiers naturalistes*, 44 (1972), 172–87; 45 (1973), 1–22.

Joly, Bernard, 'Le chaud et le froid dans *La Curée*', *Les Cahiers naturalistes*, 51 (1977), 56–79.

Kanes, Martin, 'Zola and Busnach: The Temptation of the Stage', *PMLA*, LXXVII (1962), 109–15.

Lafargue, Paul, '*L'Argent* de Zola', in *Critiques littéraires* (Paris: Editions sociales internationales, 1936), pp. 173–211.

Lapp, John C., 'The Watcher Betrayed and the Fatal Woman: Some Recurring Patterns in Zola', *PMLA*, LXXIV (1959), 276–84.

Leonard, Frances McNeely, '*Nana*: Symbol and Action', *Modern Fiction Studies*, IX (1963), 149–58.

Matthews, J. H., '*Things* in the Naturalist Novel', *French Studies*, XIV (1960), 212–23.

——, 'L'impressionnisme chez Zola: *Le Ventre de Paris*', *Le Français moderne*, XXIX (1961), 199–205.

Mitterand, Henri, 'L'évangile social de *Travail*: un anti-*Germinal*', *Mosaic*, V (Spring 1972), 179–87.

Nelson, Brian, 'Zola and the Ambiguities of Passion: *Une Page d'amour*', *Essays in French Literature*, 10 (1973), 1–22.

——, 'Black Comedy: Notes on Zola's *Pot-Bouille*', *Romance Notes*, XVII (Winter 1976), 156–61.

——, 'Speculation and Dissipation: A Reading of Zola's *La Curée*', *Essays in French Literature*, 14 (1977), 1–33.

——, 'Zola and the Bourgeoisie: A Reading of *Pot-Bouille*', *Nottingham French Studies*, XVII (May 1978), 58–70.

——, 'Zola's Metaphoric Language: A Paragraph from *La Curée*', *Modern Languages*, LIX (June 1978), 61–4.

——, 'Lukács, Zola, and the Aesthetics of Realism', *Studi Francesi*, 71 (1980), 251–5 (a slightly modified version of 'Lukács and Zola: Some Problems of Marxist Aesthetics', *Proceedings of the IXth Congress of the International Comparative Literature Association [Innsbruck 1979]*, vol. 4 [Institüt für Sprachwissenschaft der Universität Innsbruck, 1982], 305–9).

——, 'Energy and Order in Zola's *L'Argent*', *Australian Journal of French Studies*, XVII (1980), 275–300.

——, 'Zola and the Ideology of Messianism', *Orbis Litterarum*, XXXVII (1982), 70–82.

Newton, Joy, 'Emile Zola impressionniste' *Les Cahiers naturalistes*, 33 (1967), 39–52; 34 (1967), 124–38.

——, 'Emile Zola and the French Impressionist Novel', *L'Esprit créateur*, XIII (1973), 320–8.

Petrey, Sandy, 'Obscenity and Revolution', *Diacritics*, III (Fall 1973), 22–6.

——. 'Stylistics and Society in *La Curée*', *Modern Language Notes*, LXXXIX (1974), 626–40.

Ripoll, Roger, 'Fascination et fatalité: le regard dans l'oeuvre de Zola', *Les Cahiers naturalistes*, 32 (1966), 104–16.

——, 'Zola et les Communards', *Europe*, 468–9 (1968), 16–26.

Schor, Naomi, 'Mother's Day: Zola's Women', *Diacritics* (Winter 1975), 11–17.

——, 'Le sourire du sphinx: Zola et l'énigme de la féminité', *Romantisme*, 13–14 (1976), 183–95.

Shor, Ira N., 'The Novel in History: Lukács and Zola', *Clio*, II (1972), 19–41.

Steinmetz, Jean-Luc, 'Interscriptions (Mallarmé-Zola)', *Revue des sciences humaines*, 160 (1975), 597–617.

Suwela, Halina, 'A propos de quelques sources de *L'Argent*, *Les Cahiers naturalistes*, 16 (1960), 651–4.

——, 'Le krach de l'Union Générale dans le roman français avant *L'Argent* de Zola', *Les Cahiers naturalistes*, 27 (1964), 80–90.

Thomas, Marcel, 'Le journaliste politique', in *Zola* (Coll. Génies et Réalités) (Paris: Hachette, 1969), pp. 71–85.

Via, Sara, 'Une Phèdre décadente chez les naturalistes', *Revue des sciences humaines*, 153 (1974), 29–38.

Weinberg, Henry H., 'Ironie et idéologie: Zola à la naissance de la troisième République', *Les Cahiers naturalistes*, 42 (1971), 61–70.

Index